DISCOVER GLOUCESTERSHIRE ANCESTORS

Your Guide to the Archives

Volume 1

To

Sarah, Adam and Eleyna.

Thank you for the joy you bring to my life.

DISCOVER GLOUCESTERSHIRE ANCESTORS

Your Guide to the Archives

Volume 1

Elizabeth Jack

Hidden Heritage Publications

© Elizabeth Jack 2012
First Published 2012

All rights reserved. No part of this publication may be reproduced, stored in a retrieval system, or transmitted in any form or by any means, electronic, mechanical, photocopying, recording or otherwise, without prior permission of the author.

ISBN 978 0 9571440 0 2

Published by Hidden Heritage Publications
11 Old Cheltenham Road, Longlevens,
Gloucester, GL2 0AS, United Kingdom

www.hidden-heritage.co.uk

Printed by Severnprint: www.severnprint.co.uk

Contents

Foreword vi
Acknowledgements vi
Introduction vii

1. Gloucestershire Born and Bred 1
2. Civil Registration 17
3. The Census 31
4. Parish Registers 51
5. Nonconformist Registers 79
6. Probate 103
7. More on Births 125
8. More on Marriages 139
9. More on Death 159
10. Coroners' Records 179
11. Sessions and Assizes 193
12. Gaols and Houses of Correction 215

Notes on Volume 2 237
Bibliography 238
Index 240

Foreword

Gloucestershire Archives holds a wealth of treasures for the family historian. This very readable book provides the essential guide to starting, or progressing, your family history by mining these treasures, particularly if your ancestors came from Gloucestershire. It is packed with illustrations, maps, tables, hints and tips, and also outlines traps for the unwary and ways to avoid potential problems. Particularly welcome are the examples of virtually all the document types mentioned in the text and the very accessible introductions to each topic.

The fact that Liz Jack is an experienced, meticulous researcher who has undertaken extensive family history research at the Archives is evident throughout, especially when she examines the less familiar sources towards the end of the book. She also takes full account of key on-line sources as well as lesser known ones, and family history sources held elsewhere.

I am sure this book will appeal to a wide range of people, including those not fortunate enough to have ancestors from Gloucestershire. I thank Liz for a work of highest quality which will not easily be surpassed, and look forward to the second volume which I understand is already under way.

Heather Forbes
County & Diocesan Archivist
Gloucestershire Archives
January 2012

Acknowledgements

This book could never have been written without the help of the staff at Gloucestershire Archives; it is always a pleasure to spend time there. I thank the County Archivist, Heather Forbes, for reading the manuscript and writing the foreword, Paul Evans for his much missed evening classes, copyright advice and checking of my work and Vicky Thorpe for her ever-willingness to answer my odd and obscure questions. But thanks must also go to those behind the scenes: in particular to the cataloguing department whose work in the background over the years has enabled me to discover some unusual documents and to those who have literally walked miles fetching the archives for me from the storerooms. Unless otherwise stated, the documents included in this book have been photographed by me with the permission of Gloucestershire Archives.

During the researching and writing of this book, many friends from the family history world have helped and advised me for which I am grateful. I would mention, in particular Mike Gwilliam, Mary King, Sue Stafford, Andy and Janette Sysum, and John Williams (Registration Officer – Births, Deaths and Marriages). A special thank you goes to Bob Everett.

Finally, my love and thanks go to my daughter, Sarah, and my son, Adam, for their continuing encouragement and support. Similarly, I am grateful for the help of close family members, Trisha, Karen and Diane, whenever I have wanted to try out ideas or have needed advice with content and design problems. Thank you all!

Introduction

When I began researching my family history in Gloucestershire Archives, more than twenty years ago, I found a small book entitled *Gloucestershire Family History* written by M. E. Richards and revised by David Smith, then County Archivist, which became my guide to the collection of documents I could consult at the local record office. The book was first published over 30 years ago when genealogical research was a pastime which involved travelling to each church to look at their parish registers whilst finding someone on a census meant a trip to London to trawl through microfilms in a basement in Chancery Lane. Much has changed since then, particularly with the coming of the Internet.

Today, we can access online images and indexes for many parish registers and all censuses up to and including that for 1911. It is now possible to get a family back several generations in one session on a computer. Information is available on every aspect of life past and present, literally at our fingertips, but we need to be very wary of what genealogical information we discover on the Internet as it can sometimes be misleading and, at its worst, can be completely wrong. We should never ignore the original documents though even they are not always correct since the scribes of the past made errors just as we occasionally do.

This book is not intended to be a general guide to tracing your ancestors – there are plenty of books that do that in much more detail. Rather it attempts to give a simple background to each topic and then to provide examples of the many different types of documents available on the subject to help you fill out the details in the lives of those of your ancestors who spent time in our beautiful county of Gloucestershire. However, the documents described within are typical of the information recorded in any county in the country so the book is not necessarily limited to those researching this county.

It is extremely unlikely that you will find all these different documents relating to your own family; indeed, although I have, wherever possible, used items found during my own research into the Gwinnett family, I have also had to use examples relating to other people at times, to ensure that the topic was thoroughly covered.

When I first began researching this book, I thought I knew my way around Gloucestershire Archives pretty well but I have discovered and learned so much during the process including how much more there is to find. I was also under the erroneous impression that it would only take me a year or so to complete this work. More than two years later, I am far from the end of my work so I have decided to split it into two volumes as there is so much more that I want to include. Volume 2 is well on the way and details of what will be in it are given at the end of the book.

My intention has been to include copies of as many different documents as I could find that would tell us more about our ancestors so, to that aim, I have photographed and included as many as I can, with permission from Gloucestershire Archives and others. I am not an expert photographer but have done my best to produce photographs that allow you to see, at the very least, the type of information you will find in each item. If the writing is clear enough for you to read the names within each document, so much the better. And if you find one of your own ancestors listed therein, that is a bonus!

Cover pictures:

Left: Alfred Williams in Gloucester Gaol, 1889
Centre: Harriet Scott Sosbe (1874 – 1964)
Right: Charles Blinkhorne (1878 – 1963)

Chapter 1

Gloucestershire Born and Bred

*'And all the heart of my desire
is now to be in Gloucestershire'*

*F. W. Harvey
1888 – 1957, Gloucestershire poet*

Discover Gloucestershire Ancestors

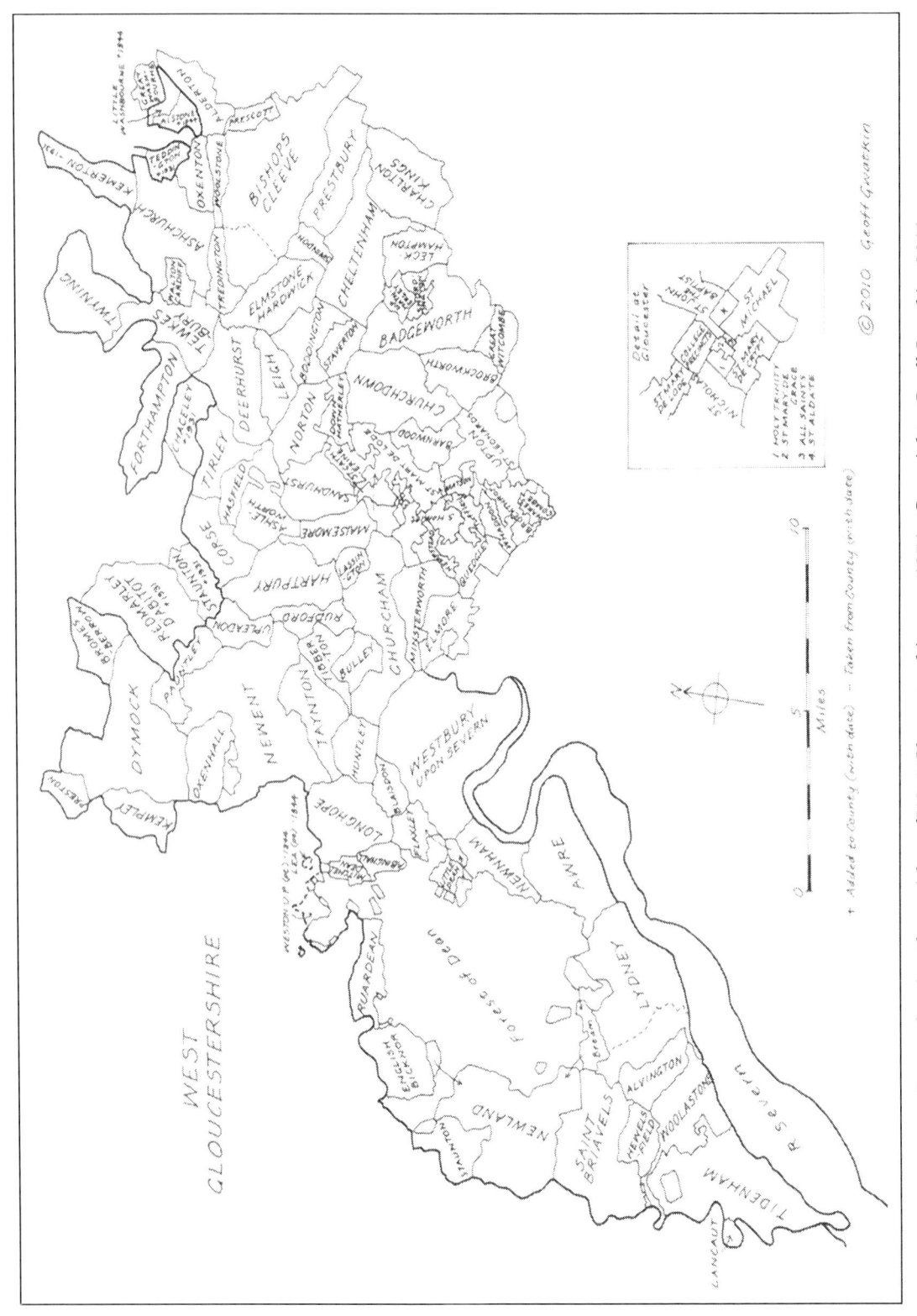

A map showing the parishes of West Gloucestershire, pre-1974. Copyright: Geoff Gwatkin, 2011.

1. Gloucestershire Born and Bred

'Begin at the beginning and go on till you come to the end: then stop.'

So said the King in Lewis Carroll's *Alice's Adventures in Wonderland*. The problem for most family historians is that you never reach the end – there is always more that you could research! Once you have looked at births, marriages, deaths and the census records from 1841 onwards, how do you develop your knowledge of the lives of the people on your family tree?

This is not intended to be a general book on how to research your family history, there are plenty of those already; rather it gives you a little background on each topic and enough information to be able to understand the types of documents that are available to assist you in finding out more about the lives of your ancestors. Whilst the types of records discussed could apply to any county in the country, those mentioned here refer specifically to events that have occurred in Gloucestershire.

Let's start with some warnings.

- ➢ Don't get involved in researching your ancestors if things such as illegitimacy, bigamy or crime will upset you. These aspects of life appeared at some time in most families in the past and, I think, add colour and interest to our family history
- ➢ There have always been different levels in society – you may discover that your ancestor was the Lord of the Manor or became a pauper in the workhouse. Whatever the level of your family, accept it for the interesting information you can find about their lives
- ➢ And most of all, do not get involved if you don't want to become addicted! If you have limited time and think you will just spend a couple of hours finding out about your family's history, this is not the pastime for you.

Begin at home with what you know already. Make a note of your full name, that of your parents and grandparents plus the dates and places of births, marriages and deaths. These are the vital records, the bare facts of their lives. Gather as much information as you can and record it accurately and fully, with the reference of where and when you found it.

Once you have recorded all you know, talk to elderly relatives, friends and neighbours to see what they can add. Most elderly people enjoy talking about their childhood and personal memories and, if not, it could be a clue to a skeleton hidden in the family closet. Frequently they can tell you something which comes as a complete surprise to you – there is usually at least a grain of truth in their tales although they might be a generation or two out.

Look around your home for additional information. This can be in the form of birth, marriage or death certificates, photographs, diaries, journals, letters and postcards, military service records, medals and badges, heirlooms, family bibles, school reports, apprenticeship indentures, medical records, examination certificates, curriculum vitae, business records, etc. Start to organise the information you have. If you use a computer, there are plenty of software packages which can help you, some of them available online for free. If you prefer not to use a computer, try drawing a tree diagram to hold your basic information.

Discover Gloucestershire Ancestors

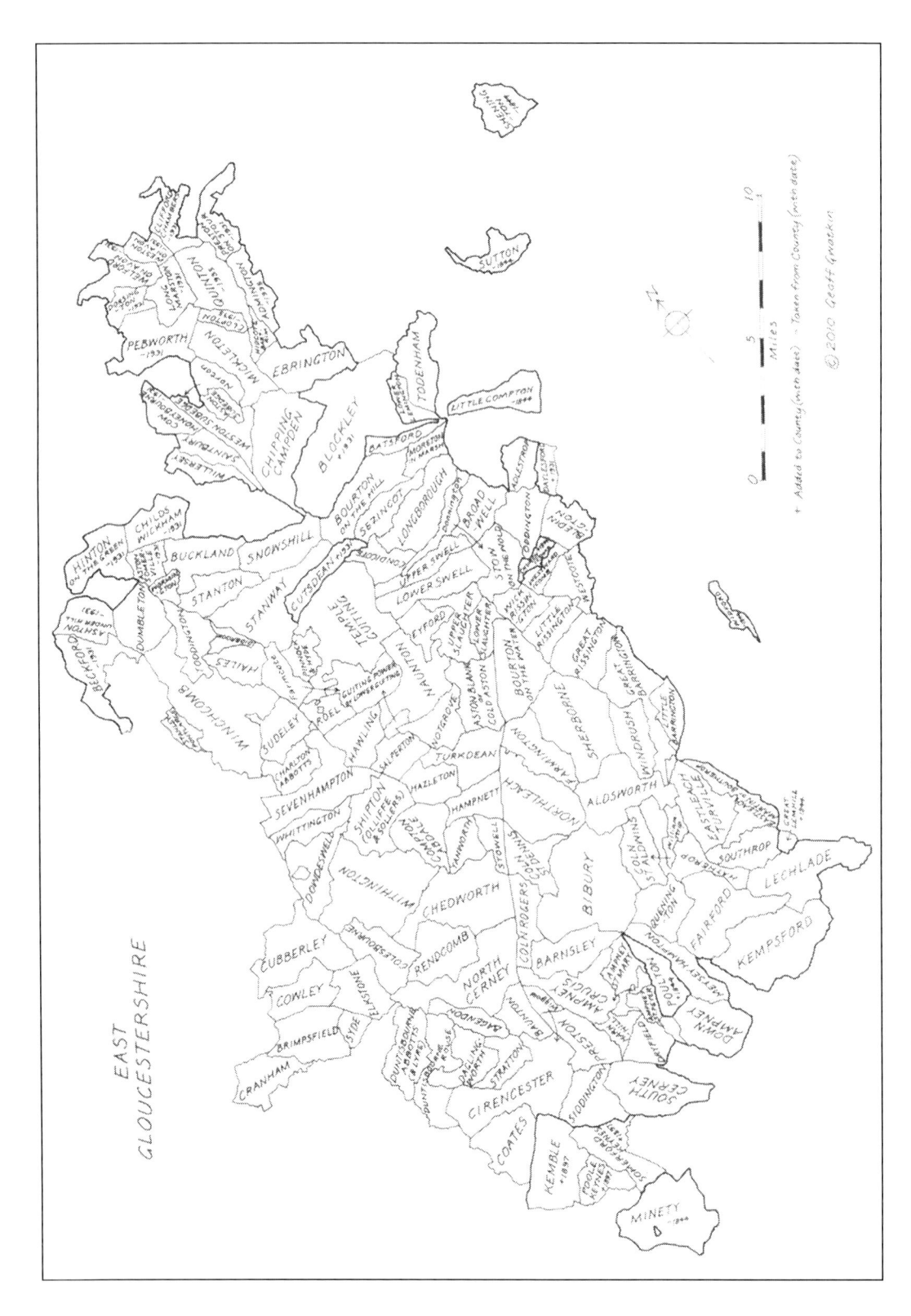

A map showing the parishes of East Gloucestershire, pre-1974. Copyright: Geoff Gwatkin, 2011.

Others prefer to use a card index or simply to record their information in note books. Whichever method you prefer to use, make sure that you are logical in your approach.

> Note: Always record the source of your information and be logical in your approach.

Collect any documentation you come across as you go along. Always record the reference number and source on the back – you never know when you will need to check it out and, several years later, you will probably have forgotten where you found it. If you discovered something of interest in a book, record its title, author, publisher and date of publication; you may need to read it again one day. In this day of the Internet, you should not forget the wealth of knowledge to be found in the books in your local library or archives.

Always start with yourself and work backwards. Follow your instinct but be methodical and logical; it is easy to be diverted. Never find someone in history with the same surname and try to work forward to link with your own family – it is not a safe way to research. For every event, you should try to locate three different records to confirm the information given. Whilst indexes are extremely useful in locating information, never rely on them. ALWAYS check the original document or a facsimile of it to be sure the transcription is accurate and complete.

Finally, before concentrating on the county of Gloucestershire, you should be aware of the rules which protect personal information from misuse. Private information is usually not available until it is 100 years old, in order to protect those people who might still be alive. So you will not be able to access the medical records of your grandparents nor the prison records of the family black sheep in the late 20th century. Also, it is commonplace these days to upload your family tree to an Internet website. You should not include details on this of anyone who is still living as it is an infringement of their privacy.

Gloucestershire is one of the most beautiful counties in England. It includes three completely different areas: the Cotswolds, with their rolling hills, shallow rivers, clumps of beech trees and pretty villages; the Severn Vale with apple and pear orchards and lush meadows towered over by the magnificent Gloucester Cathedral; and the Forest of Dean, home to the old iron and coal mines, beautiful trees and the sight of May Hill welcoming you back to the county when you have been away. It has natural boundaries with the River Wye in the west, the River Thames towards the south and the Bristol Avon in the south west, as well as the obvious boundary of the River Severn.

One of the first things of which you need to be aware when researching your ancestors is the difference between Gloucestershire (pronounced Gloss-ter-sher with emphasis on the first syllable) and Gloucester (pronounced Gloss-ter) and the confusion that it can cause. Gloucester is the *city*, the administrative capital of the *county* of Gloucestershire. However, in times past, Gloucestershire was referred to in documents as the County of Gloucester and this was often abbreviated to Gloucester so, if your 17th century ancestor, on arrival in a foreign country, said he came from Gloucester, you cannot be sure whether he was meaning

Discover Gloucestershire Ancestors

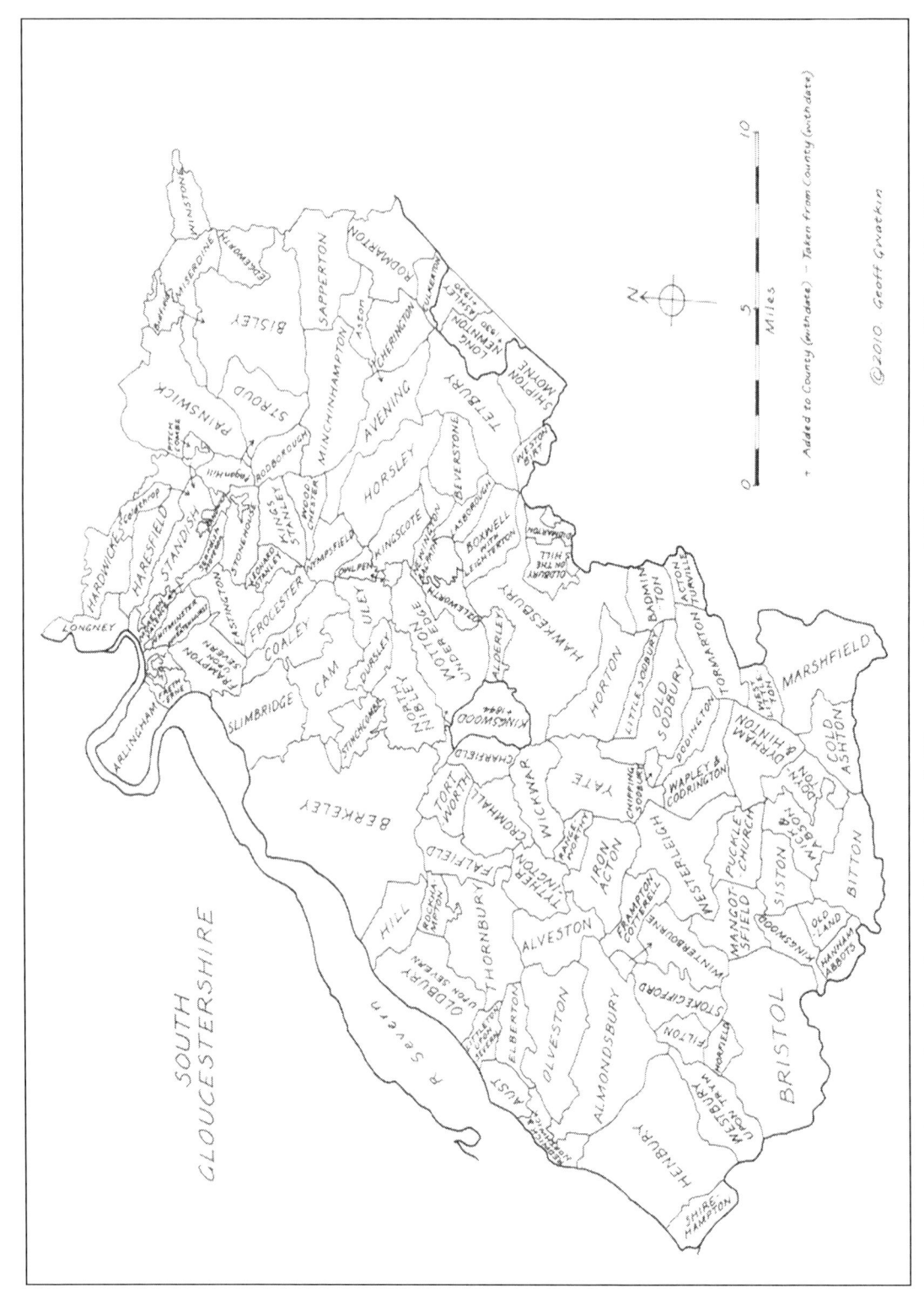

A map showing the parishes in South Gloucestershire, pre-1974. Copyright: Geoff Gwatkin, 2011.

1. Gloucestershire Born and Bred

the county or the city. He could, of course, mean both! If he meant the county, your search will be much wider and more protracted than if he meant the city.

For the purpose of understanding the archives, there have been several ways of dividing the county that need to be considered: the manor, the hundred, the borough, the diocese and the parish being the main ones. The manor was part of the feudal system, the hundreds were used for military, judicial and administrative reasons, the boroughs were granted some independence by royal charter as the population in towns grew and the diocese and its parishes were created solely for ecclesiastical administrative purposes. Over the centuries, these divisions have changed and frequently overlapped. All of them will be discussed in more detail in later chapters but, for now, a little background on the hundreds and the diocese is given.

Each hundred usually consisted of a number of parishes which lay close together but just occasionally they included more distant parishes as well. Some hundreds overlapped the current county borders and some have, since their formation, been sub-divided into smaller units, e.g. Upper and Lower Tewkesbury.

The current names for the Gloucestershire Hundreds are:

> Barton Regis, Berkeley, Bisley, Bledisloe, Botloe, Bradley, Brightwell's Barrow, Cheltenham, Cirencester, Cleeve, Crowthorne and Minety, Deerhurst and Westminster, Duchy of Lancaster, Dudstone and King's Barton, Grumbald's Ash, Henbury, Kiftsgate, Langley and Swinehead, Longtree, Pucklechurch, Rapsgate, St Briavels, Slaughter, Tewkesbury, Thornbury, Tibaldstone, Westbury, Whitstone

These names were taken from the original meeting place which was frequently distant from any one settlement, being held at a river or highway crossing, the site often marked with a stone, tree or tumulus, hence the delightfully named Grumbald's Ash and Brightwell's Barrow. The one instance where the name is still in relatively common usage in our county is the Hundred of St Briavels (sometimes abbreviated to HSB).

Hundreds were used in the Domesday Book for the purpose of tax assessment, for the Hearth Tax returns which were levied between 1662 and 1689, the 18th and early 19th century Militia Lists and the Land Tax assessments made between 1780 and 1832. More recently, the excellent Victoria County History series of reference books organises its volumes on Gloucestershire by the hundreds because 'until they ceased to exist in the 19th century, national and local records were prepared and kept on a hundred basis'.

Justices of the Peace were largely responsible for local administration from the 14th century onwards as well as undertaking their judicial roles. These unpaid justices were responsible for supervising the parish officers, the overseers of the poor and the surveyors of highways. Gradually their burden grew until, in 1888, the Local Government Act was introduced. This established County Councils which were responsible for education, highways, planning, public health and social services, among other aspects of local life.

Discover Gloucestershire Ancestors

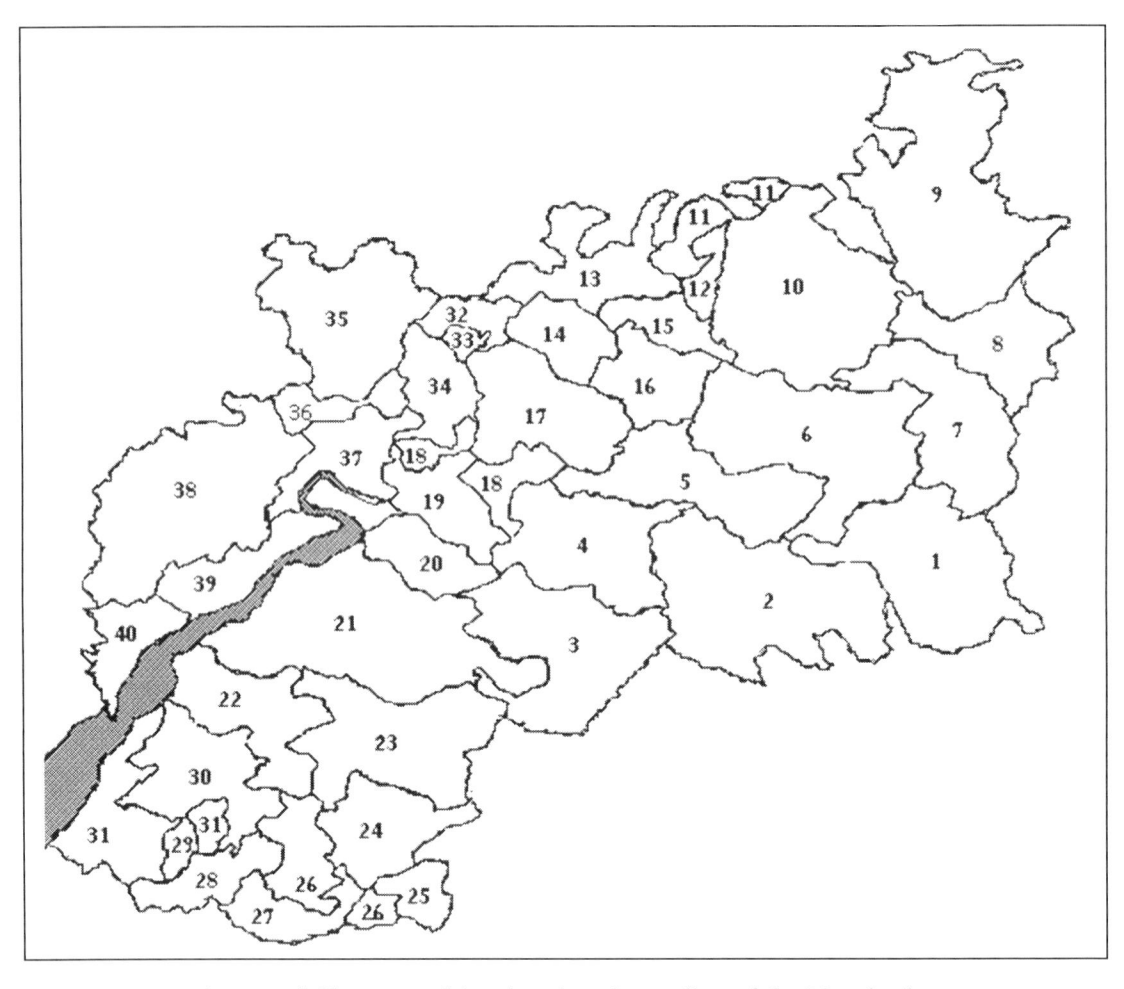

A map of Gloucestershire showing the outline of the Hundreds.

1. Brightwell's Barrow
2. Crowthorne and Minety
3. Longtree
4. Bisley
5. Rapsgate
6. Bradley
7. Lower Slaughter
8. Upper Slaughter
9. Upper Kiftsgate
10. Lower Kiftsgate
11. Tibblestone
12. Upper Tewkesbury
13. Lower Tewkesbury
14. Deerhurst
15. Cleeve
16. Cheltenham
17. Upper Dudstone and King's Barton
18. Middle Dudstone and King's Barton
19. Upper Whitstone
20. Lower Whitstone
21. Upper Berkeley
22. Lower Thornbury
23. Upper Grumbald's Ash
24. Lower Grumbald's Ash
25. Upper Thornbury
26. Pucklechurch
27. Upper Langley and Swinehead
28. Barton Regis
29. Lower Berkeley
30. Lower Langley and Swinehead

1. Gloucestershire Born and Bred

31. Henbury
32. Westminster
33. Berkeley
34. Lower Dudstone and King's Barton
35. Botloe
36. Duchy of Lancaster
37. Westbury
38. St Briavels
39. Bledisloe
40. Westbury.

By the time of the Domesday survey in 1086, the shape of the shire was fairly settled and no major changes were made until the administrative re-organisation in 1974 when the southern part of the county became Avon, which included the city of Bristol and part of northern Somerset. More recently, the southern area of the county has been renamed South Gloucestershire.

In 1541, the Diocese of Gloucester was created by Henry VIII, mainly from the ancient Diocese of Worcester and partially from the Diocese of Hereford; a year later the Diocese of Bristol was created, from the Dioceses of Worcester and Bath and Wells. The county of Gloucestershire and the Diocese of Gloucester are **not** equivalent; the Diocese of Bristol includes the southern part of the county of Gloucestershire (for more detail, see Chapter 4).

> *Note: The County of Gloucestershire and the Diocese of Gloucester are **not** equivalent. The southern part of the county is in the Diocese of Bristol.*

When it was formed in 1541, the Diocese of Gloucester was divided into ten deaneries:

> Bristol, Campden, Cirencester, Dursley, Fairford, Gloucester, Hawkesbury, Stonehouse, Stow and Winchcombe.

After the Diocese of Bristol was created, most of the rural parishes of the Bristol Deanery were transferred into it and only 10 parishes were left. This situation remained the same until 1836. Knowledge of the deaneries will have little effect on your family history research but you do need to be aware of the Peculiars.

There are four ecclesiastical Peculiars in Gloucestershire, those of Bibury, Bishop's Cleeve, Deerhurst and Withington. They were all manors belonging to the Bishop of Worcester and were not incorporated into the Diocese of Gloucester when it was founded. They remained in being until 1847. The rector of each peculiar had the right to prove wills, grant probate administrations and marriage licences. It is when seeking these in the archives that you need to be aware of the peculiars and the parishes that they covered as they may not be included in the main indexes.

Peculiar	Parishes Included
Bibury	Aldsworth, Barnsley, Bibury, Winson Chapelry
Bishop's Cleeve	Bishop's Cleeve, Stoke Orchard Chapelry
Deerhurst **	Boddington Chapelry, Corse, Deerhurst, Forthampton, Leigh, Staverton, Tirley
Withington	Dowdeswell, Withington

** Deerhurst, although a peculiar, does not appear to have claimed exemption from the jurisdiction of the Bishop or Archdeacon so marriage licences and wills from there are held with the main collections.

Gloucestershire Archives, in its capacity as the repository of the Gloucester Diocesan records, has baptism, marriage and burial registers and parish chest documents from well over 400 parishes, ranging from Weston upon Avon and Clifford Chambers in the north down to Bitton and Marshfield in the south, and from Lancaut and Tidenham in the west across to Lechlade and Todenham in the east. Three maps, produced by Geoff Gwatkin, (www.geoffgwatkinmaps.co.uk) show the county parishes divided into western, eastern and southern Gloucestershire, the East and West Gloucestershire maps being accurate for 1840, but the southern map accurate only as far as the current South Gloucestershire boundary; the rest are taken from the 1899 parishes.

> *Note: The map showing parishes in southern Gloucestershire does not equate to the current administrative area of South Gloucestershire.*

Over the years, however, some parishes have, as far as administration is concerned, moved in or out of the county, not counting those in the south of the county which belong to the Diocese of Bristol. What this means is that whilst most records are held at Gloucestershire Archives, others are held in different repositories. You should always check with a record office before going there to ensure the information you require is actually held in their archives. The parishes to watch out for are:

Parish	County / Diocese
Alstone	Worcestershire
Ashton under Hill	Worcestershire
Beckford	Worcestershire
Chaceley	Worcestershire
Childswickham	Worcestershire
Clifford Chambers	Warwickshire
Cutsdean	Worcestershire
Daylesford	Worcestershire/Diocese of Oxford
Dorsington	Warwickshire
Evenlode	Worcestershire
Hinton on the Green	Worcestershire
Honeybourne	Worcestershire
Icomb	Worcestershire
Kingswood (nr Wotton under Edge)	Wiltshire
Little Washbourne	Worcestershire
Long Marston (aka Marston Sicca)	Warwickshire
Long Newnton	Wiltshire
Pebworth	Worcestershire
Poole Keynes	Wiltshire/Diocese of Salisbury
Poulton	Wiltshire/Diocese of Salisbury

1. Gloucestershire Born and Bred

Parish	County/Diocese
Preston on Stour	Warwickshire
Quinton	Warwickshire
Redmarley D'Abitôt	Worcestershire
Shenington	Oxfordshire/Diocese of Oxford
Shorncote	Wiltshire
Somerford Keynes	Wiltshire/Diocese of Salisbury
Staunton (nr Ledbury)	Diocese of Worcester
Sutton under Brailes	Diocese of Coventry
Welford	Warwickshire
Weston upon Avon	Warwickshire
Widford	Oxfordshire/Diocese of Oxford

The last main divisions of the county which you may discover when researching your ancestors are administrative; the boroughs and the districts. The boroughs were created when a town grew in size and became self-governing. Gloucester has been a borough since before the Norman Conquest in 1066, with Tewkesbury gaining borough status in the 16th century and Cheltenham much more recently in the late 19th century. Records exist at Gloucestershire Archives for all three boroughs going back to the early days of each. Similarly, there are records from the 42 district councils that have existed, which cover a wider area than the boroughs. Mostly the records tend to be of little interest to family historians but no source should be ignored when seeking background information on your ancestor.

When researching the county of Gloucestershire, you need to be aware of duplicate and alternative place names. There are always duplicates of some names within a county (e.g. Newport or Newtown are very common names throughout the whole country) so you should take extra care to ensure that you are studying your ancestor's correct location. Some duplicate names to look out for, particularly, are:

- Bourton (Bourton on the Water or Bourton on the Hill?)
- Eastington (a parish near Stonehouse or a small village near Northleach?)
- Frampton (is it Frampton on Severn, Frampton Cotterell or Frampton Mansell?)
- Kingswood (is it near Wotton under Edge or on the outskirts of Bristol?)
- Littleworth (in Gloucester city, near Amberley, Winchcombe or Chipping Campden?)
- Oldbury (Oldbury on the Hill, Oldbury on Severn or an area of Tewkesbury?)
- Preston (near Ledbury or Cirencester or could it be Preston on Stour?)
- Staunton (is it near Coleford or Hartpury?)
- Westbury (is it Westbury on Severn or Westbury-on-Trym?).

Names which are very similar and can be wrongly transcribed are:

- Alderley and Alderton
- Alveston and Olveston
- Chalford and Charfield
- Dodington and Donnington
- Salperton and Sapperton
- Stanton and Staunton
- Tidenham and Todenham
- Whittington and Withington
- Winson and Winstone.

Discover Gloucestershire Ancestors

The parish of Cold Aston, near Northleach, is also known as Aston Blank and should not be confused with Cold Ashton, in the south of the county, near Bath. The former is in the east of the county, the latter in the far south. And, finally, the ancient parish of Wheatenhurst was officially renamed as Whitminster in 1945.

So, armed with all the information you have gathered from family and friends, from books and the Internet, you are ready to check out the original records. If you can visit the county itself but have limited time to research, always visit the parish of your ancestors; there is nothing to beat spirit of place. You can get someone else to research the records but you cannot absorb the atmosphere second-hand. Visit the church where they worshipped, find the local school they attended, go into the pub and talk to the locals; there is always someone who remembers what life was like in the village in times past. Walk the highways and byways that your forefathers trod and visit the local museums to see what their working life entailed.

Once you have absorbed that spirit of place, you are ready to look at the local archives. The main source for these will be at Gloucestershire Archives or, if your ancestors are from the south of the county, at Bristol Record Office. For both repositories, you should check the opening hours and visiting requirements online before arriving as neither offer a full six-day week opening period.

Before your visit, check out the online catalogues to see if there is something of particular interest to you; if you find something, consider ordering it in advance so that it is waiting for you on your arrival. When you locate a document in the online catalogue of Gloucestershire Archives, you will be presented with a reference for it. The first few letters of the code give you a clue to the collection to which it belongs. The codes and their corresponding collection details are given on the following page.

Several years ago, following re-organisation within the county, the Gloucestershire Collection, which had been housed at Gloucester Reference Library, was transferred to Gloucestershire Archives where details of its documents have been added to the online catalogue. This added over 15,000 documents to the Archives collection. Most of this collection now has a reference beginning with D9125. Similarly, the Bingham collection which was held at Cirencester Library and the South Gloucestershire collection of documents have both been transferred to Gloucestershire Archives in recent years and added to their online catalogue.

Other sources of information in the county are held in local studies libraries. These can be found in Cheltenham, Cinderford, Cirencester, Stow on the Wold, Stroud and Tewkesbury. These libraries have collections specific to their region including books, newspapers, periodicals, pamphlets, photographs, prints, maps, plans and directories. In the case of Tewkesbury library, there is also the Woodard database with an index pointing to a collection of local and family history sources. To check out the location and opening times of each local studies library, go to www.gloucestershire.gov.uk/libraries In South Gloucestershire, there are no specific local studies libraries but each of its libraries has its own collection of local books. To find out which books they hold about your ancestor's parish, access their online library catalogue on www.librarieswest.org.uk

1. Gloucestershire Born and Bred

Reference Code	Collection
AC	Pamphlets – archives
AG	Pamphlets – agriculture
CC	County Council (pre-1974)
CBR	Cheltenham Borough
CMS	Pamphlets – County Miscellaneous
D	Main series of deposited records
DA	District Councils (pre-1974)
DC	District Councils (post-1974)
EN	Enquiry Letters
GAL	Gloucestershire Archives Library
GBR	Gloucester Borough
GDR	Gloucester Diocesan Records
GMS	Pamphlets – Gloucester Miscellaneous
GPS	Photographs
K	County Council (post-1974)
L	Lord Lieutenant
ME	Pamphlets – Medical
MF	Microfilm
MI	Pamphlets – Military
NA	Pamphlets – National
NS	Pamphlets – Newspapers
P	Anglican Parishes
P(no.)a	Parish Councils
Pcopy	Photocopies
PS	Petty Sessions
Q	Quarter Sessions
QT	Tewkesbury Borough Sessions
S	Schools
SA	Pamphlets – Sale Particulars
TBR	Tewkesbury Borough
TC	Temporary Committees (housed at Shire Hall)
TRS	Transcripts
AR, CG, CI, FD, GE, MS, PA, PE, SM	Miscellaneous pamphlets

The codes used by Gloucestershire Archives.

No book on Gloucestershire research would be complete without a mention of *A History of the County of Gloucester* in The Victoria History of the Counties of England series of books, known affectionately as the big red books. This is the definitive reference book for information on the places in our county. The series is not yet complete but the ten volumes covered to date include:

Discover Gloucestershire Ancestors

Volume	Topic
2	Ecclesiastical, social, economic and industrial history
4	The City of Gloucester
5	The Forest of Dean
6	Stow on the Wold area
7	Fairford and Bibury area
8	Tewkesbury and the Northern Vale
9	The Northleach area of the Cotswolds
10	Upper Severnside
11	The Stroud Valleys
12	Newent and May Hill area

To see which parish has been researched so far and which volume it is in, see Appendix 1.1. Some of the information about the parishes is now online and can be accessed at:

http://www.victoriacountyhistory.ac.uk/counties/gloucestershire

So, armed with some background knowledge of the county and your own family information, you are now ready to begin tracing your ancestors in glorious Gloucestershire, using the national and local records.

Appendix 1.1
Parishes covered in *A History of the County of Gloucester* series

Parish	Volume
Abenhall	5
Adlestrop	6
Alderton	6
Aldsworth	7
Alvington	5
Ashchurch	8
Ashton under Hill	8
Aston Blank/Cold Aston	9
Avening	11
Awre	5
Aylburton	5
Barnsley	7
Barnwood	4
Beckford	8
Bibury	7
Bishop's Cleeve	8
Bisley	11

Parish	Volume
Blaisdon	10
Bledington	6
Boddington	8
Bourton on the Hill	6
Bourton on the Water	6
Brimpsfield	7
Broadwell	6
Brockweir	5
Bromsberrow	12
Chedworth	7
Cherington	11
Churcham	10
Cinderford	5
Clapton	6
Clifford Chambers	6
Coberley	7
Cold Aston/Aston Blank	9

1. Gloucestershire Born and Bred

Parish	Volume
Coleford	5
Colesbourne	7
Coln St Aldwyn	7
Coln Denis	8
Coln Rogers	9
Compton Abdale	9
Condicote	6
Corse	8
Cowley	7
Cranham	7
Deerhurst	8
Dixton	6
Dowdeswell	9
Drybrook	5
Dymock	12
Eastington (nr Stonehouse)	10
Eastleach Martin	7
Eastleach Turville	7
Edgeworth	11
Elkstone	7
Elmstone Hardwicke	8
English Bicknor	5
Eyford	6
Fairford	7
Farmington	9
Flaxley	5
Forest of Dean	5
Forthampton	8
Frampton on Severn	10
Fretherne	10
Frocester	10
Gloucester City	4
Great Barrington	6
Great Rissington	6
Great Washbourne	6
Hampnett	9
Hardwick	10
Haresfield	10
Hasfield	8
Hatherop	7
Hazleton	9
Hempsted	4
Hewelsfield	5
Highnam	10

Parish	Volume
Hinton on the Green	8
Horsley	11
Hucclecote	4
Huntley	12
Kemerton	8
Kempley	12
Kempsford	7
King's Stanley	10
Lancaut	10
Lasborough	11
Lechlade	7
Leigh	8
Leonard Stanley	10
Little Barrington	6
Little Rissington	6
Littledean	5
Longford	4
Longhope	12
Longney	10
Lower Lemington	6
Lower Slaughter	6
Lower Swell	6
Lydbrook	5
Lydney	5
Matson	4
Minchinhampton	11
Miserden	11
Mitcheldean	5
Moreton in Marsh	6
Moreton Valence	10
Nailsworth	11
Naunton	6
Newent	12
Newland	5
Newnham	10
North Cerney	7
Northleach	9
Notgrove	9
Oddington	6
Oxenhall	12
Oxenton	8
Painswick	11
Pauntley	12
Prescott	6

Parish	Volume
Prestbury	8
Preston	12
Preston on Stour	8
Quedgeley	10
Quenington	7
Randwick	10
Rendcomb	7
Rodborough	7
Rodmarton	11
Ruardean	5
Salperton	9
Sapperton	11
Saul	10
Sevenhampton	9
Sherborne	6
Shipton Moyne	11
Shipton Oliffe	9
Shipton Sollars	9
Southrop	6
St Briavels	5
Standish	10
Stanway	6
Staunton	5
Staverton	8
Stonehouse	10
Stow on the Wold	6
Stowell	9
Stroud	11

Parish	Volume
Syde	7
Taynton	12
Tetbury	11
Tewkesbury	8
Tidenham	`10
Tirley	8
Todenham	6
Tredington	8
Tuffley	4
Twigworth	4
Turkdean	9
Upper Slaughter	6
Walton Cardiff	8
Westbury on Severn	10
Westcote	6
Westonbirt	11
Wheatenhurst	10
Whitminster	10
Whittington	9
Wick Rissington	6
Windrush	6
Winson	7
Winstone	11
Withington	9
Woodchester	11
Woolaston	10
Woolstone	7

Chapter 2

Civil Registration

'Life is like a cash register, in that every account, every thought, every deed like every sale, is registered and recorded.'

Fulton John Shee
1895-1979, American clergyman and broadcaster.

Once you have gathered all the information that you can from your family and home, you are ready to start looking at the official records that relate to your ancestors. Start with the information you have on the earliest known member of your direct line. The place to begin is with **Civil Registration,** looking either for the birth of that person or the marriage of his or her parents.

Since the 1st July 1837, all births, marriages and deaths in England and Wales have, by law, to be registered. Scotland and Ireland have similar systems but different starting points; civil registration began on 1st January 1855 in Scotland, and, in Ireland, from 1st January 1864 although non-Catholic marriages were registered from 1st April 1845.

> *Note: Since the 1st July 1837, all births, marriages and deaths in England and Wales have, by law, to be registered.*

Registration was compulsory from the very beginning but, until 1875, it was the responsibility of the registrar to find and record details of births or deaths rather than the parent or next of kin and thus many events were not registered; some suggest as many as 15% went unrecorded. In particular, many births were not registered, especially during the early period. Marriages were more likely to be recorded then because these were notified directly to the Registrar General each quarter by the minister who performed the ceremony.

From 1875 onwards, it became the responsibility of the individuals concerned to register the event, with the penalty of a fine if the event was not recorded within a given time limit. There was no method of ensuring the accuracy of the information provided.

The counties of England and Wales were divided into **Registration Districts**. Some of these areas have remained unchanged but others have been adjusted several times during the intervening years. The Registration Districts did not necessarily correspond exactly to the county boundaries but were originally based instead upon the existing Poor Law Unions. Registration of a birth, marriage or death can only take place in the district in which the event occurs.

> *Note: Registration of a birth, marriage or death can ONLY take place in the district in which the event occurred.*

Suggestions are made in the following table as to which parishes were covered by which registration districts, working in a clockwise direction from north-west of the River Severn. However, life is not always that simple! In some instances, the parishes have changed since civil registration first began, sometimes more than once, from one registration district to another so it is always worth checking with the neighbouring register offices if you cannot find what you are seeking. Some help can be found on this on the Genuki website (www.genuki.org.uk) under the headings of Gloucestershire and then Civil Registration but you may find it is necessary to contact the register office itself to be absolutely sure.

2. Civil Registration

Registration District	Parishes
Chepstow, Monmouthshire	Alvington, Aylburton, Hewelsfield, Lancaut, Lydney, Saint Briavels, Tidenham, Woolaston. All were transferred to the Forest of Dean district on 1st April 1937.
Monmouth, Monmouthshire	Coleford, English Bicknor, Newland, Staunton, West Dean. All were transferred to the Forest of Dean district on 1st April 1937.
Ross, Herefordshire	Blaisdon, Lea Bailey, Ruardean. All were transferred to the Forest of Dean district on 1st October 1935.
Evesham, Worcestershire	Ashton under Hill, Aston Somerville, Aston sub Edge*, Childswickham, Cow Honeybourne, Hinton on the Green, Pebworth, Saintbury*, Weston sub Edge*, Willersley*. Those marked * were transferred to the Stow on the Wold district on 1st April 1932.
Shipston on Stour, Warwickshire	Admington, Batsford, Bourton on the Hill, Chipping Campden, Clopton, Ebrington, Hidcote Bartrim, Ilmington, Lower Lemington, Mickleton, Moreton in Marsh, Quinton, Todenham. All were transferred to the Stow on the Wold district on 1st April 1932.
Stratford upon Avon, Warwickshire	Clifford Chambers, Dorsington, Marston Sicca, Preston on Stour, Welford, Weston on Avon.
Faringdon, Berkshire	Lechlade.
Keynsham	Bitton, Hanham, Hanham Abbots, Kingswood, Mangotsfield, Oldland, Siston

From **1837 to 1851,** the registration district had volume number XI and contained offices at:

> Bristol, Cheltenham, Chipping Sodbury, Cirencester, Clifton, Dursley, Gloucester, Newent, Northleach, Stow on the Wold, Stroud, Tetbury, Tewkesbury, Thornbury, Westbury on Severn, Wheatenhurst and Winchcombe.

From **1852 to 1946,** the Gloucestershire volumes were numbered 6A and the only difference in the centres for registering births, marriages and deaths was the change of name from Clifton to Barton Regis, covering an area to the north of Bristol.

Between **1946 and 1974,** with the volume number again changed, this time to 7B, there was a more radical change reducing the number of centres to:

> Bristol, Cheltenham, Cirencester, Forest of Dean, Gloucester City, Gloucester Rural, Kingswood, North Cotswold, Sodbury, Stroud, Thornbury.

From **1974 to 2006**, the registration district volume was numbered 22. The centres at that time were:

> Bristol, Cheltenham, Cirencester, Forest of Dean, Gloucester, North Cotswold, Sodbury, Stroud, Thornbury.

Finally, in **June 2006**, all registration districts in the county came under either the single unified authority with the name of Gloucestershire or the South Gloucestershire Registration district. The latter covers the parishes of:

> Acton Turville, Almondsbury, Alveston, Aust, Badminton, Bitton, Bradley Stoke, Charfield, Coalpit Heath, Cold Ashton, Cromhall, Dodington, Doynton, Dyrham and Hinton, Falfield, Filton, Frampton Cotterell, (Frenchay Hospital), Hanham Abbots, Hawkesbury, Hill, Horton, Iron Acton, Kingswood, Little Sodbury, Mangotsfield, Marshfield, Oldbury-on-Severn, Oldland, Olveston, Patchway, Pilning and Severn Beach, Pucklechurch, Rangeworthy, Rockhampton, Siston, Sodbury, Stoke Gifford, Thornbury, Tormarton, Tortworth, Tytherington, Westerleigh, Wick and Abson, Wickwar, Winterbourne and Yate.

At the times when the registration districts were adjusted, some Gloucestershire parishes were transferred from one district to another. For instance, Berkeley came under the auspices of Stroud until 1947, was then transferred to South Gloucestershire until 1974 when it returned to the Stroud registration district once more. Further details on registration districts can be found on the Genuki web site at www.genuki.org.uk

General Register Office Indexes
When a birth, marriage or death was registered at a local Register Office, the details were sent to the General Register Office (GRO) to be compiled into a national index. The original indexes are held at the National Archives at Kew but have been filmed and copies of these films are freely available, on fiche or via the Internet, in Gloucestershire Archives (up to 1996), GFHS Family History Centre (up to 2002), Bristol Record Office (up to 1920) and Bristol Reference Library (up to 1983). Early indexes were handwritten and can be difficult to read, particularly in the filmed versions.

There are separate indexes for births, marriages and deaths (and now also for civil partnerships which came into force on 5th December 2005). Adoption records and records of still births have been included in the indexes since 1927. Up until 1983, each year was split up into quarters with, for example, all events registered between 1 January and 31 March being held in the index labelled March; thereafter they are organised by year.

Date of Registration	Index Quarter
1st January to 31st March	March
1st April to 30th June	June
1st July to 30th September	September
1st October to 31st December	December

Remember the index is based upon when events were **registered**, which for marriages is normally when the wedding took place. However, births may be registered up to 6 weeks after they occur, so a child born on 24th November may be legitimately registered in the following January and therefore indexed in the March volume for that year. Deaths have to be registered within 5 days. Where a known event appears to be missing from the GRO

2. Civil Registration

indexes, they should be found in the local registrar's records. The GRO indexes, whilst an excellent finding aid, are not perfect.

Entries in the indexes are organised in alphabetical order of surnames and, within that, alphabetical order of forenames, for each quarter or year.

e.g. Births for the September quarter of 1879:

Surname	Forename	District	Volume	Page
GWINNETT	Arthur Percy	Wolverhampton	6b	529
....	Mary Ann	Gloucester	6a	287
....	Patience Maria	Gloucester	6a	287
....	Thomas	Walsall	6b	677
....	Thomas William	Wolverhampton	6b	580

Whenever you find a birth, marriage or death entry in the indexes, write down the details *exactly* as they are written in the index, even if you know more or suspect it is not completely correct, as you must have the exact index entry when you apply to the GRO for a certificate. Don't forget to record the date including the quarter as well. Then you are ready to order your certificate.

If you cannot find an entry, always search a few years on either side of the supposed year as well as the following quarter. The spelling of surnames was not consistent as many people could not read or write so be ready to check all possible variations. Names were often recorded by speaking the name to the person who was writing it down so regional accents and speech impediments could cause the same name to be heard and therefore spelt in many different ways. Look at as many possible variants as you can think of. If no given name had been chosen when a child's birth was registered, they could have been registered simply as a Male or Female and are recorded in the index at the end of list for their surname. Names originally omitted from the index, and there are quite a few, are usually hand written at the bottom of the nearest column so check those as well.

Obtaining Birth, Marriage and Death Certificates

English and Welsh birth, marriage and death certificates are not available online so need to be ordered from one of the following:

1. The relevant local Register Office (See Appendix 2.1 for details)
2. The General Register Office at Southport
3. Online

The current (April 2010) standard charge for a certificate is £9.25 (but only £9 at a local Register Office) although it is possible to pay a much higher fee if the need to receive the certificate is urgent.

1. Ordering from the local Register Office:

To order a certificate from the **Register Office** local to where the event occurred, you need to provide as many details of the event as you can give, such as the full name of the person, date of birth, marriage or death and the location where the event occurred – the more information you provide, the more likely it is that you will receive the correct certificate.

You can either attend the local register office in person or write to them sending your cheque, made payable to the Superintendent Registrar; the certificate should be sent to you within five working days. I have always found the Gloucestershire Register Offices to be very quick and efficient when providing certificates.

Local Register Offices do *not* use the General Register Office (GRO) Index references; instead they have their own system. Volunteers, mainly from Gloucestershire Family History Society, have been indexing the Gloucestershire birth, marriage and death registers that are held in the local Register Offices. The information is gradually being put online at:

http://ww3.gloucestershire.gov.uk/bmd

The indexes are not yet complete but generally include more information than can be found on the GRO indexes. Where register entries were not clear, a second entry has been included in the index with a best guess for the name. Exact dates are not given, only the year. The results of any search can be sorted on any column by clicking on the heading. This makes it easier to link entries together.

Births:
The birth index includes almost 600,000 entries so far from all round the county of Gloucestershire but there are, as yet, very few from the Cinderford district registration office as indexing has only just begun there. The birth index contains the full name of the child, the surname of the father and mother and the former surname of the mother, together with the year of registration, the district and office where the birth was registered, the register number and the entry number. The difference between this index and the GRO Birth Index is that the mother's former name is given for all births, back to 1837 as opposed to 1911 with the national index.

Marriages:
The marriage index, containing over half a million entries, is complete for all marriages registered in Gloucestershire between 1837 and 1948 but also includes many after that time and some as recently as 2008. The marriage index contains the full names of the bride and groom, the district of registration, the parish and the building where the marriage took place, plus the register number and entry number. If the bride has been married before, then two entries are made in the index, one of them giving her previous married name, the other giving her maiden name. This can be a very useful feature.

Marriages solemnized in churches with no authorised registrar (e.g. some nonconformist churches) are included in the Gloucestershire Registration Services registers. Since the 1st April 1995, marriages could be solemnized in approved premises other than register offices, details of which are recorded in the GRS registers. However, these locations are not recorded in the marriage index. The difference between this index and the GRO index is that it contains both grooms and brides names, back to 1837, so you can check if you have the right marriage and generally gives the church in which the wedding was held.

2. Civil Registration

Deaths:
The death index is the most recent index to be started but even that has nearly 100,000 entries. Only Stroud and Cheltenham districts are being indexed at the moment. This index provides the full name of the deceased, the year of death, his or her age at death, the district and sub-district where the death was registered and the register number and entry number. The difference between this death index and the GRO death index is that the age of death is given right back to 1837, not just from 1866 so you are able to distinguish between the death of a child and that of an adult with the same name.

> *Note: Local Register Offices do **NOT** use the General Register Office (GRO) Index references.*

2. Ordering from the General Register Office in Southport:
To order a certificate from the **General Register Office** at Southport, you need to either write a letter containing the full details of what you require, i.e. the GRO Reference sending your cheque made payable to I.P.S (Identity and Passport Services), or, preferably, use an order form which can be collected from Gloucestershire Archives or Gloucestershire Family History Society Family History Centre. Complete the details and send with your cheque to GRO, PO Box 2, Southport, Merseyside, PR8 2JD. Currently, certificates are sent out about a week after the request has been received but at times of high demand, the wait can be somewhat longer.

> *Note: When ordering a certificate from Southport or online, you need to provide: Forenames, Surname, District, Volume, Page Number, Year and Quarter.*

3. To order a certificate online:
To order your certificate online, which can be done from anywhere in the world with Internet access, visit

    www.gro.gov.uk/gro/content/certificates/

The information required online is the same as needed for a certificate from Southport. For either method 2 or 3, you need the full GRO reference details, so where do you find them?

GRO Index to Births
To begin with, in 1837, this index contained only surname, forenames, district, volume number and page number. From September 1911, birth indexes included the mother's maiden name as well making it easier to be sure that you have found the correct entry. But be careful not to become confused if the mother was actually a widow on her second marriage and giving birth to a child from that marriage – her first married name is unlikely to be included.

Nowadays, the indexes also include the month of registration and a district as well as a register and entry number. You are also required to provide more information (full details of the child's name, date and place of birth, father's full name and mother's full name, including maiden name) when requesting a certificate for a birth in the last 50 years due to Data Protection requirements to prevent identity theft and fraud.

Discover Gloucestershire Ancestors

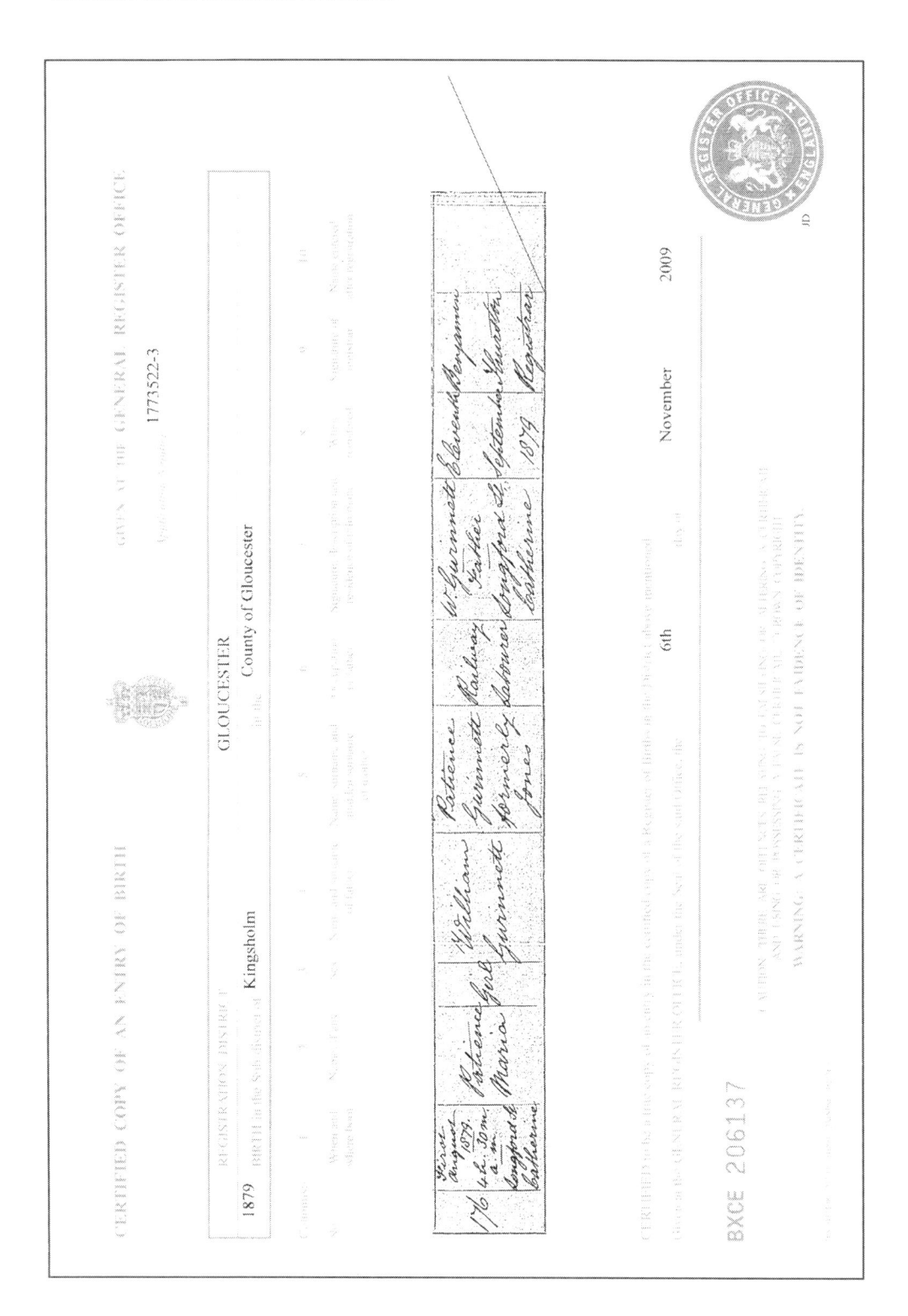

Birth Certificate of Patience Maria Gwinnett, born in 1879, one of twins.

2. Civil Registration

> *Note: From 1st July 1911, the GRO Birth Indexes have included the mother's maiden name.*

A birth certificate will contain:

- District and sub-district where birth was registered
- The place of birth. This could be either a street in a town or just the name of the village
- Day, month, year of birth. If a time is given as well, it indicates a multiple birth
- Name and sex of the child, or just the sex if no name had been chosen at that time
- The name of the father and his occupation. The name field is normally blank for an illegitimate child, unless both parents were present at registration
- The name of the mother and either her maiden name, former name or name now known by
- The name and address of the informant and either their signature or their mark
- The date of registration
- The name of the registrar
- Any name given at baptism and entered after then being reported to the registrar.

There is a final column which allows an entry for a change of name, should, for instance, a different name be used at a Christening. This is usually done within the first year but can occur within five years if there is sufficient evidence to support the claim.

Since the Fertilisation and Embryology Act of 2008, if a woman in a civil partnership gives birth to a child following artificial insemination, both women are named on the birth certificate, one as the mother, the other as the 'parent'.

Details about the parents should give you sufficient information to allow you to locate the quarter and registration district of the marriage from the GRO Marriage Index so that you can order a certificate and go back another step in your search for your ancestors. If the child was the first one born in a marriage, then checking back from the birth of the child should quickly give you the parents' marriage details. However, if the child was the tenth one born to a couple, you will have a much longer search. On average, a couple had a child every two years but this was not always the case so be prepared to find a marriage any time during the preceding thirty years or even after the birth of several children. My own grandparents married only after having had three children, all of whom died in infancy. After their marriage, they had two more children both of whom survived.

GRO Index to Marriages
Each marriage in the GRO Index should have two entries, one for the groom and one for the bride, both following the usual format including surname, forenames, district, volume and page number. To ensure that you have found the correct couple, the district, volume and page numbers for the bride and the groom should match but do be aware that these indexes are not foolproof and errors and omissions occur – as well as the usual transcription and

spelling errors there are many unmatched pairs in the index. However, it is possible to order a certificate by giving only the name of the bride or of the groom if the partner's name is unknown.

From the March quarter of 1912, the surname of the spouse also appears in each marriage entry in the index which helps you to locate the partner if previously unknown. Be aware that a widow will probably be using her previous married name rather than her maiden name. Not everyone knew or gave their exact age on their marriage certificate and many are just recorded as 'Of Full Age' meaning over 21 until the age of majority changed to 18 in 1969. Until 1929, boys could marry at the age of 14 and girls at the age of 12 as long as they had parental consent. After 1929, the age was raised to 16 for both sexes, again as long as they had the consent of their parents.

> *Note: From the 1st January 1912, the surname of the spouse was also given in the GRO Marriage Indexes.*

A marriage certificate will include:

- District and sub-district where the marriage took place
- The place of marriage
- Day, month, year of the marriage
- Full name of the groom
- Groom's age, status, occupation and residence
- Full name of the bride
- Bride's age, status, occupation and residence
- The name and occupations of the groom's father
- The name and occupation of the bride's father
- The signatures or marks of the bride and groom
- The signatures or marks of the witnesses to the wedding
- The signature of the authorised person conducting the ceremony and/or the registrar(s).

The place of marriage can be the name of the parish church where the wedding took place, the nonconformist chapel (including the religion practised there) or the local Register Office. Nonconformist churches are registered buildings but not all of them have persons authorised to perform a marriage ceremony. Since the 1990s, weddings could take place in many different 'approved premises' (such as Prestbury House Hotel, Clearwell Castle, The Great Tithe Barn at Long Newton, Hidcote Manor Garden, etc.), where the Registrar attends and records the nuptials.

If the certificate gives accurate ages for the couple (current certificates give dates of birth rather than ages) you should then be able to locate the entries for their births in the indexes. You should be able to confirm that you have the correct certificate by comparing the names of the fathers on the birth and marriage certificates. Of course, if you have common names, this is not always so easy.

2. Civil Registration

Marriage Certificate of William Gwinnett and Patience Jones, 1874.

GRO Index to Deaths

Until June 1866, the death index gave the same details as the birth index but from then on, the age of death was also included, with infants under the age of one year being recorded as 0 years. Ages at death are frequently inaccurate – the person most likely to know is no longer around to say and he or she may well not have known anyway as many people were innumerate. From 1969 onwards, the date of birth of the deceased, if known, is included in the index making it much easier to recognise your ancestor amongst several of the same name.

> *Note: From 1st July 1866, the age at death was included in the GRO Death Indexes.*

A death certificate will include:

- District, sub-district and administrative area where the death was registered
- The place of death. This could be either a street in a town or just the name of the village
- Day, month, year of death
- Name, sex and age of the deceased
- Maiden surname of a woman who had been married
- Date and place of birth
- The occupation of the deceased, or the parents for a child
- The cause of death
- The name, address and relationship/qualification of the informant with their signature or their mark.
- The date of registration.
- The name of the registrar.

The amount of information recorded on the certificates has increased over the years so not all of the items listed above will appear on early certificates.

Since the Civil Partnership Act, there have been some minor changes in the terms used on certificates. The words 'bachelor' and 'spinster' are no longer in use; the alternative word 'single' is used to describe a previously unmarried bride or groom. On death certificates, where it used to give a female's occupation including the phrase 'wife of …' it now also uses the parallel descriptions of 'husband of …' when recording a man's death, assuming that the couple have not been divorced previously, or 'surviving civil partner' in a civil partnership.

Civil registration indexes are now available on the Internet providing images of the original indexes with facilities to search for your references on a subscription or pay per view basis for individuals. Free access to these online indexes at http://www.ancestry.co.uk can be gained at Gloucestershire Archives, some local libraries in the county and the GFHS Family History Centre. A free, searchable but as yet incomplete, online index is being compiled by volunteers covering 1837 to 1983, which can be accessed at

http://www.freebmd.org.uk

2. Civil Registration

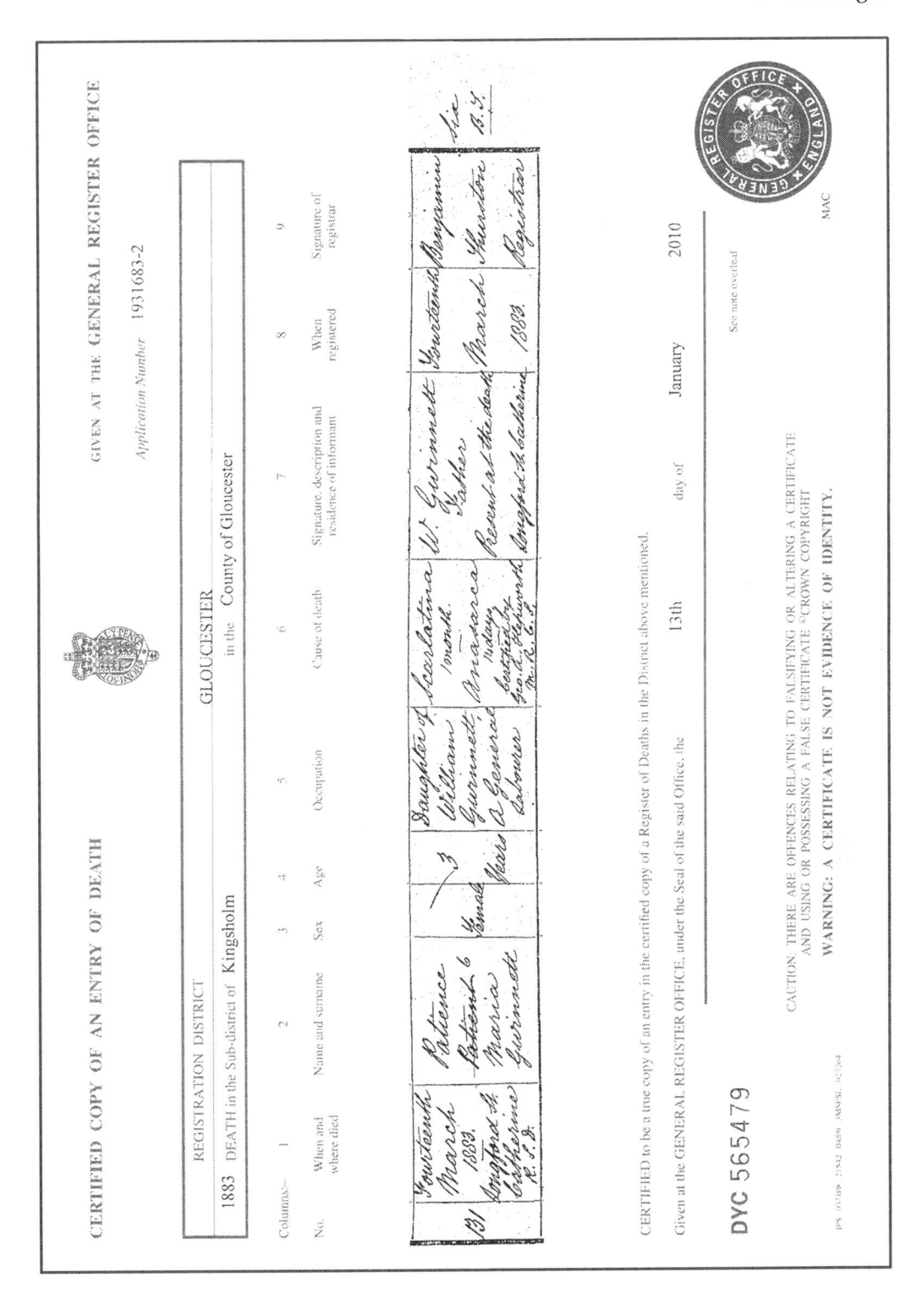

The Death Certificate of Patience Maria Gwinnett, who died in 1883, aged 3 years.

Appendix 2.1
Gloucestershire Register Offices

Cheltenham Register Office
St George's Road, Cheltenham, Gloucestershire, GL50 3EW
T:	+44 01242 532 455
E:	cheltenham.ro@gloucestershire.gov.uk

Cirencester Register Office
Cirencester Library, The Waterloo, Cirencester, Gloucestershire, GL7 2PZ
E:	cirencester.ro@gloucestershire.gov.uk

Forest of Dean Register Office
Belle Vue Centre, 6 Belle Vue Road, Cinderford, Gloucestershire, GL14 2AB
E:	forestofdean.ro@gloucestershire.gov.uk

Gloucester Register Office
Shire Hall, Westgate Street, Gloucester, Gloucestershire, GL1 2TG
E:	gloucester.ro@gloucestershire.gov.uk

North Cotswold Register Office
The Council Offices, High Street, Moreton in Marsh, Gloucestershire, GL56 0AZ
E:	northcotswold.ro@gloucestershire.gov.uk

Stroud Register Office
The Old Victorian School, Parliament Street, Stroud, Gloucestershire, GL5 1DY
E:	stroud.ro@gloucestershire.gov.uk

Certificates: All completed registers for Gloucestershire are now held at Gloucestershire Archives, Clarence Row, Alvin Street, Gloucester, GL1 3DW. To obtain copy certificates, use telephone number 01242 532455 for details to be taken and certificates despatched by post. At the time of going to print, the Registration Service is undergoing changes. For the latest information on obtaining certificates, go to:

www.gloucestershire.gov.uk/index.cfm?articleid=105401

South Gloucestershire Register Office
Poole Court, Poole Court Drive, Yate, Bristol, BS14 4PP
T:	+44 01454 863 140
E:	RegistrationService@southglos.gov.uk

Bristol Register Office
The Old Council House, Corn Street, Bristol, BS1 1JG
T:	+44 0117 903 8888
E:	register-office@bristol-city.gov.uk

Chapter 3

The Census

'Thine eyes did see my substance, yet being unperfect; and in thy book all my members were written, which in continuance were fashioned, when as yet there was none of them.'

Psalms 139, v16

This aspect of family history research is one where much change has taken place over time. Twenty years ago, if you wished to look at a census, it was necessary to look at microfilms of the area in which you were interested and work your way slowly through the film till you came to the particular entry you required. If your ancestors had moved home between one census and the next, as many of them did particularly within towns and cities, you just had to keep looking until you found them and hope that they hadn't moved far. Today, images of the censuses are online with transcriptions and indexes; they are not always perfect but are a vast improvement on previous methods.

Background

Following a request from Parliament for information on the population, the first national census of England, Wales, the Channel Islands and the Isle of Man was taken in 1801 and has been taken every ten years since except for the 1941 census which was not taken during the Second World War. The early censuses for 1801 to 1831 inclusive were merely numerical, with no names recorded and are therefore of little help to those seeking ancestral details. The national originals for these early censuses have since been destroyed.

> Note: The first national census of England, Wales, the Channel Islands and the Isle of Man was taken in 1801.

From 1801, overseers of the poor and parish clerks were requested to provide the numbers in each family in their parish and the numbers of baptisms, marriages and burials recorded in their registers. By 1821, ages were added to the collected information and, ten years later, occupations were included as well. Preliminary lists were made in the parishes, frequently listing the families by name, before extracting the statistical information required; some of these lists still exist and can be very useful to the family historian. By 1841, census enumerators had been appointed to gather the information required by Parliament. It was their job to deliver the forms to each household a few days before the census was due, to collect them afterwards and then transfer the data to the enumerators' returns.

The country had been divided into regions which reflected but weren't necessarily exactly the same as the counties of the day. In Gloucestershire, it was often the case that if a person lived near the county boundary, then their census entry might well lie with those for the neighbouring county. For instance, some Forest of Dean districts are categorised for the purpose of the census as being in Monmouthshire. So, if you do not find what you are seeking in Gloucestershire and the area you are researching is near the county boundary, always check the neighbouring county as well, before widening your area of search again. The neighbouring counties for Gloucestershire are, working clockwise from north of the Severn Estuary:

Monmouthshire, Herefordshire, Worcestershire, Warwickshire, Oxfordshire, Wiltshire, Somerset.

The dates and references for each census are:

3. The Census

Year	Date	Reference
1841	Jun 6	HO107
1851	Mar 30	HO107
1861	Apr 7	RG9
1871	Apr 2	RG10

Year	Date	Reference
1881	Apr 3	RG11
1891	Apr 5	RG12
1901	Mar 31	RG13
1911	Apr 2	RG14

Each 'county' was divided into 'pieces' and given a number; each piece was then split into enumerators' districts and also given a number or code. Every property in the district was allocated a schedule number. The schedule books were then given folio numbers, one for every double page, and finally the pages themselves were numbered. So a full reference for an individual 1851 census entry might be given as: Ref: HO107/Piece 1964/Folio 256/Page 6/Schedule 22.

Over the decades, the boundaries of the enumerators' districts changed because of the rapid growth in population during Victorian times but each district was described at the start of the schedules stating the area that was covered.

>   e.g.   The whole of the Parish of Cowley comprising Stockwell, Nettleton Bottom, Cowley Village, Air Balloon Inn, and the North side of Birdlip Street

If it was a small village then that would be all that was named but in larger towns and cities, each street visited would be given in the enumeration district description.

>   e.g.   The whole of the two parishes of Saint Mary de Crypt, and Saint Mary de Grace, Saint Mary de Crypt including from No 4 on the North East side of Northgate Street to the Cross, part of the North East side of Westgate Street, part of the South West side of Westgate Street, from No 1 the South West side of Southgate Street to Commercial Road, part of the South side of Southgate Street, part of Cross Keys lane, part of Long Smith Street, Ladybelle Gate Street (both sides) Blackfriars Street (both sides) and part of Bell Lane, Saint Mary de Grace, part of the South West side of Westgate Street, part of the North East side of Westgate Street, part of St John's Lane, Fox Entry and part of Cross Keys Lane.

Each property was given a schedule number which did ***not*** relate to the house number, where that existed – many houses in the 19th century did not have numbers. Be careful – do not assume that the number at the start of the census row is the house number. The latter may, if you are lucky, be given in the second column with the street name but even then care needs to be taken since many roads and houses have been renumbered in the intervening years, so this may not relate to an existing property.

> *Note: The Schedule number does not correspond to the House number.*

In theory, everyone should be on the census even those on board boats in ports but some people were away from home and others had no homes and were sleeping rough. In some cases, those who were in institutions such as prisons, hospitals, asylums or workhouses were recorded using only initials for the inmates. At times, it appears that some people may have deliberately avoided being recorded on a census.

Censuses 1841 to 1911
From 1841 to 1901 inclusive, the census information was arranged by parishes, districts, streets and houses which meant that not only did you see your family's details but also those of their neighbours which often allowed you to see how close parents, in-laws and other members of the family were to your ancestor. With the 1911 census, however, the individual return actually completed by the head of household is to be seen, in his or her own handwriting. To find a neighbour in the 1911 census, it is necessary to do an address search.

The contents of each census have varied over the years, from very basic to very informative. The **1841 census** was the first official census to include names and contained the most basic information, giving only forenames and surnames, approximate ages, occupations and a guide to each person's birthplace. This census was written in pencil and so has not always survived in a state that is easy to read.

A transcript for one family living in Mack House, Lower Lypiatt in Stroud in 1841, is:

Name	Age	Occupation	Born in County
George Gwinnett	70	Ag. Lab.	Y
Elizabeth Gwinnett	60	Woollen Factory	Y
Thomas Gwinnett	25	Ditto	Y
William Gwinnett	20	Ditto	Y

George's age is given as 70 but, because the ages of all people over 14 years were rounded *down* to the nearest 5 years, he could have been anything from 70 to 74 inclusive. Children up to 14 years were recorded with their true age. The ages were grouped into bands to aid statistical analysis of the population. This was only done for the 1841 census; after that, true ages were recorded as accurately as possible though as many people were still illiterate and innumerate, they did not always know their actual age.

Note: The age of anyone over 15 was rounded down to the nearest 5 years in the 1841 census.

No relationships were given in the 1841 census so although this census entry would appear to be a father, mother and two sons, that fact cannot be assumed – more information is needed to support the theory. It could be that Elizabeth was George's spinster sister or widowed sister-in-law or an even more distant relation. Similarly, the two young men could have been Elizabeth's children rather than George's. So be careful not to assume that what appears to be a family, with husband, wife and two sons, actually is a family – always find corroborating evidence to back up your theory.

3. The Census

The 1851 census for James Gwinnett. Copyright of the National Archives: Ref: HO107/1964

> *Note: No relationships were included on the 1841 census.*

Precise birthplaces were not recorded in the 1841 census so locating your ancestor's place of birth from this is not always easy. The only responses allowed were:

Code	Meaning
Y	Yes, born in county
N	No, not born in county
S	Born in Scotland
I	Born in Ireland
F	Born in Foreign parts

By 1851, the census was much more informative. As well as the name and occupation previously given, an accurate age was recorded in one of two columns (for males and females), the relationship to the head of household was provided, (e.g. Head, wife, son, brother-in-law, visitor, servant, etc.) the marital condition of each adult (e.g. Married, Single, Widowed) a place and county of birth and, in the final column, a note of disability, either blind or deaf and dumb.

In 1881, information as to whether a house was occupied was included on the census return but, otherwise, personal details on the form remained unchanged until 1891 when the Disability column was enlarged to include a category for the Lunatic, Imbecile or Idiot, and three more columns were added to record whether Employer, Employed or Neither. It is possible to get an idea of how your ancestors were living as a column was included showing the number of rooms occupied in the house if less than five.

Very little was changed in the 1901 census except that it was released online for the first time. Finally, the 1911 census, which has been released online and is available to view freely in the National Archives and a few major libraries around the country but not yet available in Gloucestershire, is completely different from all previous censuses because the return seen is that completed by the individual householder rather than the collection copied out by the enumerator.

The most useful and interesting addition on the 1911 census, apart from the number of rooms in which the family lived, is information recording how long the head of household and his wife have been married, together with the number of their children born alive and the number who have died. This can indicate quite shocking numbers of infant deaths in a family that were otherwise unsuspected.

Due to the 100 year disclosure rule, only the censuses up to and including the 1911 census are available to view as yet; however, if information from the 1921 census is required for legal purposes, the next of kin or direct descendant can pay to access a copy if the name and an accurate address are available. The 1931 census was destroyed during the Second World War and no census was taken in 1941 so, after the release of the 1921 census in 2022, no more will be available until the 1951 census is due out in 2052.

The 1891 Census for William Gwinnett. Copyright of the National Archives: Ref: RG12/2011

Census of England and Wales, 1911

No.	Name and Surname	Relationship to Head of Family	Age Male	Age Female	Particulars as to Marriage	Completed years of present Marriage	Children Born Alive	Children still Living	Children who have Died	Profession or Occupation	Industry	Employer/Worker	Working at Home	Birthplace	Nationality	Infirmity
1	William Gwinnett	Head	60		Married	37	7	5	2	General Labourer	B.W. Pople Horse Dealer	Worker		Upton St Leonards	British	
2	Patience Gwinnett	Wife		64	Married	37								Pitchcomb, Glos	British	
3	John Gwinnett	Son	26		Single					Factory Engineer	Horse Box Co	Worker	At Home	Longford, Glos		
4	Elsa Florence Gwinnett	Daughter		21	Single								At Home	Longford, Glos		

Total: Males 2, Females 2, Persons 4

Signature: William Gwinnett
Postal Address: 41 St Catherine Street, Gloucester

3. The Census

Where to view the censuses

The original census records are held in the National Archives at Kew; those not yet released are with the Office of National Statistics. Gloucestershire Archives possesses filmed copies of the original returns for the county for 1841 to 1901 which can be viewed and printed out if necessary but indexes, transcripts and images of the originals are available to be accessed without payment online at Gloucestershire Archives and the GFHS Family History Centre. There is just a small charge for a printout of any page.

The 1881 census was the first to be transcribed, indexed and made available on CD and online. This was produced by the Church of Jesus Christ of Latter Day Saints (LDS) and was and still is free to use but it does not include images of the original census page; it may therefore contain transcription errors. I cannot emphasize enough that the original document or a facsimile of it should be viewed as soon as possible.

> *Note: Always check details with the original document or a facsimile of it to be sure there were no transcription errors.*

The 1901 census was the first to be released online with images, by the National Archives, followed more recently by the 1911 edition. All censuses from 1841 to 1911 are now available online through one or other of about eight different websites but although the indexes are usually free to access, payment is required to view a transcript or a copy of the original page, either by having a subscription to the particular website or by pay-per-view.

The online versions have been indexed for ease of searching but it is essential to remember that the transcripts are not always accurate, possibly due to poorly written or wrongly spelt original entries, sometimes because the original has faded beyond clarity and maybe because of the poor reading or typing skills of the transcriber. This can occasionally lead to rather extreme entries e.g. the county of birth being transcribed as Somalia instead of Somerset! Another frequent error was finding someone with the surname of Ditto!

All transcripts have errors but by far the best and most accurate 1851 Gloucestershire transcription and index is still that produced by Gloucestershire Family History Society. This is because of the thorough checking that was used during the transcription process and the fact that the volunteers who performed the tasks were very familiar with the local names and places. This transcript is available on CD from the GFHS and can be viewed at their Family History Centre in Gloucester.

Should you fail to locate your ancestor by searching by name, it is usually possible to locate them by address and, over the years, street indexes have been produced by the GFHS to aid the process. These are available for checking at the GFHS Family History Centre.

> *Note: The best and most accurate 1851 Gloucestershire transcription and index is still that produced by Gloucestershire Family History Society.*

Discover Gloucestershire Ancestors

Pre-1841 censuses
As I mentioned earlier, some data collected for the early, pre-1841 censuses remain. In some instances, it is just a case of the names of the heads of households and the number of people in the household at the time which is better than nothing if you are trying to find out if your ancestor was in a particular parish then. Other early census documents include names of all members of the family and even ages. The information varies from one parish to another.

The Gloucestershire parishes for which early census information have been found are:

Arlingham	Horsley
Aust	Kemerton
Bisley	Naunton
Great Badminton	Stratton
Hawkesbury	Stroud

Arlingham: G.A. Ref. D2685/20
This 'Census of Householders' is a simple list consisting of 5 sheets of paper, divided into columns, headed:

> Names (Husband and wife usually)
> Place of Residence
> No. of Children at home (B & G)
> No. of children Out (B & G)
> Remarks (mainly occupation and location, see below)

Sample entries are:

> e.g. Richard Sims & Eleanor Sims, Pridend
> No. Boys at home: 3
> Waterman. Freeholder
>
> Hannah Sharp widow, Pridend
> 2b & 2g at home
> Receives 5/- per week parish relief Arlingham
>
> Thomas Carter, Hopehill
> Mary Carter, 6g at home
>   - by a former wife: 1b at home, 1b 3g out
>   - by a former husband: 2b 2g out

Sample remarks from the document are:

> Ill this three years, not able to work
> Wife very ill
> Labourer 77 years of age, not capable of work.

3. The Census

At the end of the document, there is a list of the names of the children currently in the Workhouse. They are: John Jones, James Jones and Aron Golding, Hannah, James, Henry and Charles Heaven (the children of William Heaven), Maria, Eliza, Kesiah and Caroline Lane (the children of Charlotte Lane), Mary Andrews and Edward Aldridge.

Aust: G.A. Ref. D5944/2
This is obviously the preliminary list used for extracting the statistics for the 1821 census. The document is divided into columns listing the name of the head of household, the occupation category (e.g. agriculture, blacksmith, innkeeper, etc.), and the total number of people in each household. The latter is then broken down into the number of males and females in each age group.

So, for instance, we know that John Bishop, was an agricultural worker and there were 10 people living in his house, 4 males (in ages 0 - 5, 10 - 15, 15 - 20 and 50 - 60) and 6 females (5 - 10, 10 - 15, two aged 15 - 20, one aged 40 - 50 and one in the 70 – 80 category). It should not be assumed that all adults and children listed were related.

The summary tells us that there were 24 inhabited houses but 36 families in Aust at the time with a total of 192 people altogether. The document itself is too poor to reproduce here but is legible.

Bisley: G.A. Ref. PA 47/16
This picture shows part of a transcript of the original document (GA Ref: P47a MI 1) which lists the residents of Bisley in 1821. There is a similar document for 1831. The area was divided up into sections and the residents in Bisley, Bussage, Chalford, Througham, Avenis, Oakridge and Steanbridge tithings were listed. The name of the head of household was given

41

in full, together with a letter, either A or T indicating whether the family were mainly engaged in Agriculture or Trade, manufacturing or handicrafts. Also given was the total number of males and females in the family. No indication was given as to their ages.

    e.g.   Richard Faulkes   T   3   1

This tells us that Richard Faulkes worked in trade, manufacturing or handicrafts and that, including himself, there were three males and only one female in his household.

```
BISLEY  1821 Census                    Oakridge Titheing (Cont.)
                          M  F                                M  F
101 Richard Bishop     T  2  2     151 Betty Davis         A  1  3
102 William Whiting    T  4  3     152 Sarah Kerry         A     1
103 Hannah Davis       T  4  5           Lilly Horn Stable
104 John Gardner       T  1  2     153 Robert Hayden       A  1  3
105 Peter Bucknell     A  2  2     154 John Herbert        T  2  3
106 John Bucknell      T  1  1     155 Edward Wright       T  3  1
107 Ann Jeffris        T  1  3     156 William Powell      A  2  6
108 Ann Smart          T     2     157 William Davis       A  1  2
109 Thomas Gardner     T  1        158 James Hunt          T  4  4
110 John Mason         T  1  2     159 Mr John Baker       A  1  3
111 Samuel Twissell    T  5  3     160 John Baker Jun^r    T  1  1
112 Anne Twissell      A  1  5
113 Richard Davis      T  2  2
114 Absolom Cox        T  2  1
115 Richard Hill       T  1  3
116 William Davis      T  2  2
117 Sampson Wright     A  2  4
```

Great Badminton: G.A. Ref: P32a OV9/1

There are four different documents in this bundle of records. The first three contain population information and are dated 1801, 1811 and 1821. The last one is a similar document but is undated. It is, presumably, the census information for the year 1831.

The 1801 census is entitled 'An Account of the Population of Great Badminton' and contains the following items:

Section	Heading	Sample Entry 1	Sample 2
Name	Head of House	Henry Woodman	Wm. Long
Houses	Inhabited	1	1
	No. of Families in House	1	1
	Uninhabited	0	0
Persons	Males	6	3
	Females	4	6
	Total Persons	10	9
Occupations	Agriculture	2	4
	Trade, Manufacture, Craft	1	0

3. The Census

Section	Heading	Sample Entry 1	Sample 2
	All other Persons	7	5
Totals	Total Persons	10	9
	No. of Windows	4	6
	Males	6	3
	Females	5	6

Note: The numbers have not always been added up correctly.

The format remains pretty much the same for the 1811 and 1821 censuses but by the time the 1831 census came round, the Great Badminton Overseers were using a more detailed format, very similar to that described in Aust census document, where the people in each household were recorded in five year age groups.

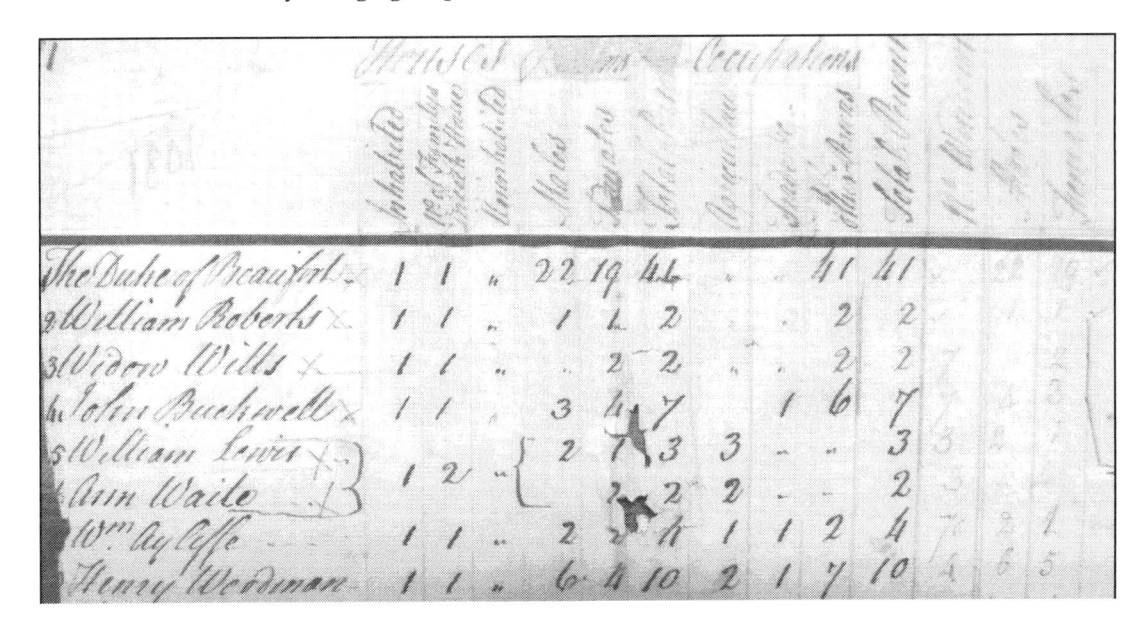

Hawkesbury: G.A. Ref: P170 OV 7/4

The population in the Hawkesbury tithings of Tresham, Kilcott and Saddlewood was recorded on 10th March 1801 and a list was drawn up naming the head of household, the number of males and females in each house and the number of inhabited and uninhabited houses.

e.g.

Names	No. of Males	No. of Females	No. of Houses inhabited	No. of houses uninhabited
Jno. Gunter	1	4	1	0
James Stinchcom	3	2	1	0
Jas. Hayward	8	2	1	0

A List of the Inhabitants of the Tything of Inesham Kilcott & Saddlewood in the Parish of Hawkesbury in the County of Glocester Mar. 15th 1801

Name	Males	Females	Inhabited	Houses Uninhabited
Fr.d Gunter	1	4	1	
James Stinchcom	3	2	1	
Giles Hiscox	3	4	1	
Mary Bartlett	2	2	1	
Nath.l Sandy	2	3	1	1
Hen.y Hayward	1		1	
Jas. Hayward	8	2	1	
Hugh Watts	3	5	1	
Wm Sandy	1		1	
Sam.l Gulley	6	1	1	
Joseph Stinchcom	3	3	1	
Ann Sandy		1	1	1
James Pincott	1	1	1	
Wm Stinchcom	2	1		

Horsley: G.A. Ref: P181 OV 7/1

To preserve it, this list has been bound in a book entitled 'Horsley: List of Householders 1811 – 1815'. The book has an index and each page contains the names of the head of each household, his or her occupation, the number of males and females in the household and whether they are tenants, owners or landlords.

Names	Occupation	No. Males	No. Females	Parish	Ownership
Walkley, Mary	Shopkeeper	1	1	Horsley	Landlady
Walkley, Rich[d]	Labourer	2	2	Horsley	Tennant
West, James	Baker	2	2	Horsley	Landlord
Wilkins, John	Carpenter	2	1	Horsley	Landlord
Window, Nath.	Weaver	5	4	Horsley	Tennant

3. The Census

Kemerton: G.A. Ref: P187 IN 4/1

This document doesn't actually mention Kemerton but presumably came from the parish chest along with other items and so is known to be of such. It consists of pre-printed pages with the name of each occupier and a series of ten questions in five groups on the left-hand page and two sets of columns on the right-hand page giving the number of males and females in each of the different age groups. The columns are headed:

Heading		Sample Entry
Name	Name of Occupier	Hy. Thornbury
Question 1	Inhabited Houses	1
Question 1	By how many families occupied	1
Question 2	Houses now Building	0
Question 3	Other Houses uninhabited	0
Question 4a	Families chiefly employed in Agriculture	0
Question 4b	Families chiefly employed in Trade, Manufacture or Handicrafts	1

Heading		Sample Entry
Question 4c	All other families not comprised in the two preceding classes	0
Question 5	Persons including children of whatever age: Males	5
Question 5	Persons including children of whatever age: Females	3
Question 5	Total of persons	8

3. The Census

Naunton: G.A. Ref: P224 CW 4/1

The 'Population of the Parish of Naunton' was recorded on 27th May 1811. Set out on a single sheet of paper, it lists, in two sets of columns, the names of the heads of household together with the number of males and females in each family and, at the bottom of the page, the totals for the village.

e.g.

Name	No. of Males	No. of Females
Josh Sadler	6	4
Wm. Yearp	5	1
Eleanor Fletcher	2	2

Discover Gloucestershire Ancestors

Stratton: G.A. Ref: P319 IN 1/7
Tucked inside the original marriage register for Stratton are four pages that have been sewn together to make a small coverless booklet. In it is written a list of all the houses in the village, numbered from 1 to 62, and for each there is a list of inhabitants together with their approximate ages. By researching the baptisms of some of the children, it is obvious that this list was created for use in completing the 1821 census.

e.g.

House No. 1
Mrs Davis	Between 60 & 70
Miss Davis	Between 20 & 30
Wm. Slatter	Between 10 & 20

House No. 2
Wm. Townsend	Between 40 and 50
Rachael Townsend	Between 40 and 50
Ann Cook	Between 20 and 30

House No. 6
Shepherd Green	Between 30 & 40
Rachael Green	Between 20 & 30
Ann Green	3 years

House No. 13
Isaac Hill	Between 40 & 50
Sarah Hill	Between 40 & 50
Fanny Hill	Between 20 & 30
James Hill	Between 15 & 20
Maria Hill	Between 10 & 15
Jacob Hill	Between 10 & 15
Isaac Hill Jn[r]	Between 5 & 10
Rich[d]. Hill	Between 5 & 10
Joseph Hill	Between 4 years
Henry Hill	2 years

House No. 62
Edward Haines	Between 40 and 50
Mrs Haines	Between 20 and 30
Miss Haines	Between 50 and 60
Miss June Haines	Between 40 and 50
The Child	1 year
Henry Russell	Between 20 and 30
Jane Washbourne	Between 15 and 20
Ann Curtis	Between 15 and 20

3. The Census

```
House No 1                Ages
Mr Davies, bet: 60 & 70
Miss Davies ——  20 & 30
Wm Slatter ——   10 & 20
House No 2
Wm Townsend      40 & 50
Rachael Townsend 40 & 50
Ann Cook ——      20 & 30
No 3
Mr Hill ——       50 & 60
Mrs Hill ——      50 - 60
No 4
Catharine Smith  60 & 70
Cath: Smith Jun  10 - 13
No 5
Cottage Town? Wm  30 & 40
Sarah Townsend    30 & 40
Mary Townsend    10 & 15
George Townsend   5 & 10
Henry Townsend    4 years
Thomas Townsend   1 Do
No 6
Shepherd Green   50 & 60
Rachael Green    20 & 30
Ann Green         3 years
```

Copy of the first page of an 1821 population list for Stratton.
G.A. Ref: P319 IN 1/7

Discover Gloucestershire Ancestors

Stroud: G.A. Ref: P320a VE 1/1
Entitled 'An Account of the Population of the Parish of Stroud in the year 1821. Lower Lypiatt Tything', this book lists 233 heads of household and for each they have recorded the name and trade of the head of household along with the number of males and females in the family, the number of families living in the house and information on other properties owned.

Heading	Sample Entry 1	Sample 2
Name	Mary Stephens	Thomas Hiles
Trade	Burler & Picker. Widow	Mustard Maker
How many in family?	8	5
Males?	2	3
Females?	6	2
By how many families is your house occupied?	1	1
Have you any Houses building?	0	0
Have you any Uninhabited	0	0

All of these pre-1841 listings are extremely useful to the family historian. Other much earlier population lists will be discussed in Volume 2.

Chapter 4

Parish Registers

'A funeral is not death, any more than baptism is birth or marriage union. All three are the clumsy devices, coming now too late, now too early, by which Society would register the quick motions of man.'

E. M. Forster
1879 – 1970, British novelist and essayist.

After you have traced your ancestors back through the civil registration records and the censuses, the next records to use for your family history research are the parish registers. By 1538, an Act of Parliament had been passed which required every baptism, marriage and burial to be recorded in the parish register, after the church service each Sunday. So, for almost three hundred years, until civil registration began in 1837, these records provide the main method of tracing your family history.

> *Note: These parish registers are records of baptisms, not births, and burials rather than deaths. Abbreviations that are commonly used for these parish register entries are CMB, that is C (Christening), M (Marriage) and B (Burial) as opposed to the BMD abbreviations of B (Birth), M (Marriage) and D (Death) used in civil registration.*

Originally, the information was recorded on paper, some of it on loose sheets, but from 1598 it was decided that parchment registers should be used and that the previous entries should be transferred to the new books. However, it was permitted for entries only from 1558 onwards to be transcribed as that was the start of the reign of Elizabeth I, hence the lack of so many very early registers. This process, as with all transcripts, was prone to error and there were many problems with registers which were damaged due to damp, mould and rats or were simply lost. So the coverage of baptisms, marriages and burials in the county in the 16th century is far from total.

Gloucestershire Archives has 28 registers for the county parishes which go back to 1538/9, six of which are supposedly the original registers rather than the copied version; included amongst these are the registers for Aston sub Edge, Eastleach Martin and Upper Slaughter. The parishes covered by the 28 very early registers are:

Adlestrop	Dymock	Taynton
Arlingham	Eastleach Martin	Upleadon
Aston sub Edge	Great Badminton	Upper Slaughter
Awre	Great Rissington	Upton St Leonards
Blockley	Naunton	Westbury on Severn
Broadwell	Oldbury on Severn	Whitminster/Wheatenhurst
Buckland	Pauntley	Whittington
Chaceley	Ruardean	Winchcombe.
Charlton Kings	Sandhurst	
Coberley	Staverton	

Many more existing Gloucestershire parish registers begin in the 1540s, 1550s and soon thereafter but it is only to be expected that, over the centuries, some registers will have been lost to such problems as fire and flood. Some complete registers are missing or so badly damaged that they are no longer produced for research, from the parishes, as shown:

4. Parish Registers

Parish	Period	Cause
Cheltenham St James	Pre 1876	Unknown
Huntley	Pre 1661	Fire at vicarage
Minsterworth	Pre 1633	Damaged by flood
Newington Bagpath	1686 – 1785	Damaged by flood in 1947
Newland	1560 – 1669, 1741 – 1784	Damaged by rats
Oldbury on Severn	1742 - 1898	Damaged by fire
Oxenhall	Pre 1664	Damaged by fire
Saul	First 3 registers, pre 1687	Damaged by flood
Snowshill	Pre 1732	Disappeared since 1941
Woolstone	Pre 1889	Destroyed in a fire

For those seeking information on their ancestors in the parish baptism, marriage and burial registers, it is worth noting that, for unknown reasons, some registers have large breaks in the entries. Those with gaps of eight years or more are recorded in Appendix 4.1.

Registers over a hundred years old should be at Gloucestershire Archives but some of the more recent registers which are not found there are still being held by the incumbent. Should you need to get access from a recent register, you should contact the incumbent of the parish who is permitted to charge you for the search.

In 1541 and 1542 respectively, the Diocese of Gloucester and the Diocese of Bristol were formed mainly from the existing Diocese of Worcester. Those parishes which are in the south of the county of Gloucestershire come under the auspices of the Diocese of Bristol, so their parish registers are normally held at Bristol Record Office. A few transcripts are held in Gloucestershire Archives. Some other parishes close to the county boundary have also changed diocese over the years, moving to or from the dioceses of Worcester, Coventry, Oxford or Salisbury. All these parishes, with their current or former diocese, are shown in Appendix 4.2.

> Note: In 1541 and 1542 respectively, the Diocese of Gloucester and the Diocese of Bristol were formed mainly from the existing Diocese of Worcester.

During the period of the Civil War and the Interregnum (or Commonwealth period), between 1641 and 1660, the recording of baptisms, marriages and burials became much more haphazard. Lay people, confusingly also called Registers, were given the responsibility to record the vital events. In some instances this would have been the parish clerk or churchwarden who had previously recorded the information, but not all Registers were reliable, conscientious or well-educated and the registration process suffered.

Many people did not have their children's birth registered during this period (births not baptisms were recorded at that time), and there was also a charge for registration, one shilling for a marriage and four pence for a birth or burial which would have discouraged many poorer people from registering their event. Once the parish register system was back in place, many children were baptised even though they were no longer infants. It is during this period that you will find the most gaps in the Gloucestershire parish registers, particularly for marriages.

Before 1754, no organised form of entry was used in the registers for each event. Some ministers separated baptisms from marriages and burials, others mixed them up. Early registers, up to 1732, were often in simple Latin.

An example from an early Badgeworth register showing a mixture of
baptisms, marriages and burials.
G.A. Ref: P31 IN 1/1

Following Hardwicke's Marriage Act, the year of 1754 saw the introduction of organised entries for marriages into a pre-printed marriage register.

An example from the Painswick marriage register of the format used
after 1754.
G.A. Ref: P244 IN 1/6

All marriages from this time had to be either by banns, as most were, or by licence. Banns registers were introduced in 1754 but most have not survived. Some banns registers allowed

4. Parish Registers

space only for the names of the bride and groom and the dates when the banns were read. Others combined this with the actual marriage details. Banns had to be read on three consecutive Sundays in the parishes of both groom and bride so that any objections to the union could be made. The marriage then had to take place in one of the two parishes. This led to some recording problems in the parish where the marriage had not taken place – the blank spaces reserved for the marriage, after the banns, were occasionally filled with the details of someone else's nuptials.

Marriage licences, bonds and allegations were recorded and many of these still exist today and are held at Gloucestershire Archives – more on these in a later chapter.

This relatively simple marriage layout lasted until 1837 when it was changed to show exactly the same information as is found on a civil marriage certificate (see Chapter 2). 1813 also saw pre-formatted registers printed specifically for baptism and for burial entries.

Under a heading stating the name of the parish, the new baptism form had room for eight entries on every page; these records included:

- the date of baptism
- the child's name
- the forenames of the parents
- the surname
- their abode
- the 'quality, trade or profession' of the father
- the name of the person performing the ceremony.

In the case of an illegitimate child, the 'quality, trade or profession' of the mother was usually entered as 'single woman'. Occasionally, the name of the reputed father was added. Some ministers included birth dates alongside the date of baptism or possibly the age at baptism but these were not specifically required.

The new 1813 burial form also had room for eight entries but contained fewer columns, the details being:

- the full name of the deceased
- the abode of the deceased
- when buried
- the age
- the name of the person performing the ceremony.

Sometimes you may be lucky enough to find additional details included about the deceased or the circumstances of the death. One or two ministers would regularly include comments on the deceased, about major epidemics or, in the case of riverside parishes, that the deceased had been found in the river.

When Baptised	Child's Christian Name	Parents Name (Christian)	Parents Name (Surname)	Abode	Quality, Trade, or Profession	By whom the Ceremony was performed
1847 April 4 No. 1601.	Enoch Whippy	Enoch & Caroline	Capner	Stroud	Wine Merchant	T. P. Little Curate
April 4 No. 1602.	Fredrick Henry	William & Ann	Davies	Stroud	Currier	T. P. Little Curate
April 4 No. 1603.	Emily Whitemarsh	Joshua & Mary	Wiltshire	Stroud	Tailor	T. P. Little Curate
April 4 No. 1604.	Emma Whitemarsh	Joshua & Mary	Wiltshire	Stroud	Tailor	T. P. Little Curate
April 4 No. 1605.	Emily Whitmarsh	John & Elizabeth	Whitemarsh	Stroud	Carrier	T. P. Little Curate
April 6th No. 1606.	Amelia	Thomas & Elizabeth	Huggins	Stroud	Nailer	George Proctor P.C.
April 15th No. 1607.	Henry	Richard & Susan	Gummett	Workhouse Painswick	Labourer	T. P. Little Curate
April 15th No. 1608.	Charles	Richard & Susan	Gummett	Workhouse Painswick	Labourer	T. P. Little Curate

An example from the Stroud registers of the baptism form used from 1813 onwards.
G.A. Ref: P320 IN 1/11

4. Parish Registers

There are no 'certificates' for baptism, marriage and burial entries in the parish registers as there are for civil registration events. However, it is usually possible to get a printout from a filmed copy of the register or a photograph of an entry in an original register to keep with your family history collection. Most of the registers have been filmed to preserve them for future generations.

There were two periods during which people had to pay to register births, marriages and deaths. From 1694 to 1706 there was a tax of 2/- per birth, 2/6d per marriage and 4/- per burial. Later, between 1698 and 1703, a stamp duty of 3d per registration was made, paupers being exempt from this. Both cases meant that some events were not recorded during these periods, as the next of kin could not or would not pay. If you are missing a baptism during either period, it is worth looking beyond the end date of either period to see if a baptism of an older child or adult can be found.

Calendar:
Before looking at the 18th century registers, it is essential to understand the changes that were made to the calendar in the middle of the century. Basically, Great Britain had not changed from the Julian Calendar (Old Style) to the Gregorian Calendar (New Style) when the rest of Europe had and it was now 11 days out of step.

With the Julian Calendar, the year began on 25th March (Lady Day) and ended on 24th March of what we would consider to be the following year. If, for example, the year was 1728 then the last three months of that year would have been recorded then as January 1728, February 1728, etc., but we today write January 1728/29 to remind us that it was what we would think of today as 1729.

This system has led many to think that a child, born, say, February 1730 was baptised before the parents were married, perhaps in April 1730, the baptism actually being 10 months after the marriage date although not apparently so to those who are unaware of the dating method.

With the Gregorian Calendar, the year began, as it does now, on 1st January and ended on 31st December. To adapt to the new system, various adjustments had to be made, as follows.

Year	Days Covered	Notes
1750	25th March 1750 to 24th March 1750/51	A full twelve months
1751	25th March 1751 to 31st December 1751	Only nine months, approx.
1752	1st January 1752 to 31st December 1752	Lacking 11 days

So, 1751 was a 'short' year. This sorted out the discrepancy with the years but did not account for our calendar being 11 days out of step so in the year 1752 the dates of 3rd September to 13th September did not exist, the calendar jumping straight from 2nd September to the 14th September.

> *Note: The year of 1751 was a very short year, starting on 25th March 1751 and ending on 31st December 1751. The year of 1752 did not have 11 days from 3rd to 13th September.*

Baptism:

In the mid-1550s, the names of sponsors (godparents) were supposed to have been entered into the baptismal registers. Few seem to have followed this order although the registers for Thornbury do contain the names of the sponsors.

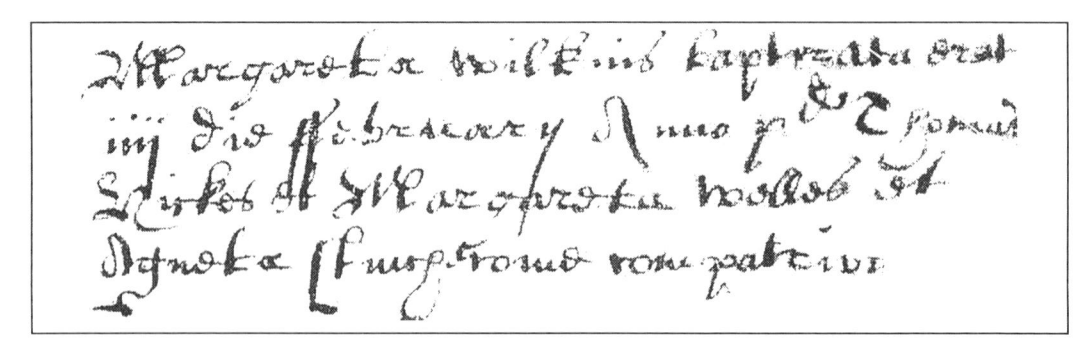

A Latin entry from the Thornbury parish registers of 1570/71. It records the baptism of Margareta Wilkins baptised on 4th February with godparents of Thomas Hickes, Margaret Welles and Agnes Stinchcome. It does not give the names of Margaret's parents.
G.A. Ref: P330 IN 1/1

Unfortunately, as these particular entries do not contain the names of the parents, it is not always possible to work out to whom the child belongs!

In fact, many early registers just gave the name of the child and the father's name, the mother being considered unimportant. An example of this can be seen on the next page in the Bisley registers where tracing your ancestor can become very difficult as there were many repeated common surnames with quite a few common forenames and no mothers' names given. Note the baptism on 23rd June 1775 of Richard to Daniel Davis, followed on 13th August 1775 of Mary to Daniel Davis and again on 24th September also 1775 with a baptism for Samuel of Daniel Davis. It is possible but very unlikely that this is the same Daniel Davis in each case but the registers give us no way of knowing for sure.

> *Note: Most early baptismal registers gave only the child's name and the father's name.*

At the opposite end of the scale, some ministers, such as the one in Stroud St. Lawrence, went to the other extreme and, as well as the names of the parents of the child, included the mother's father's name thus providing her maiden name for the researcher.

4. Parish Registers

Sometimes you may be lucky enough to find that a father's name has been suggested for an illegitimate child, e.g. reputed father being ......

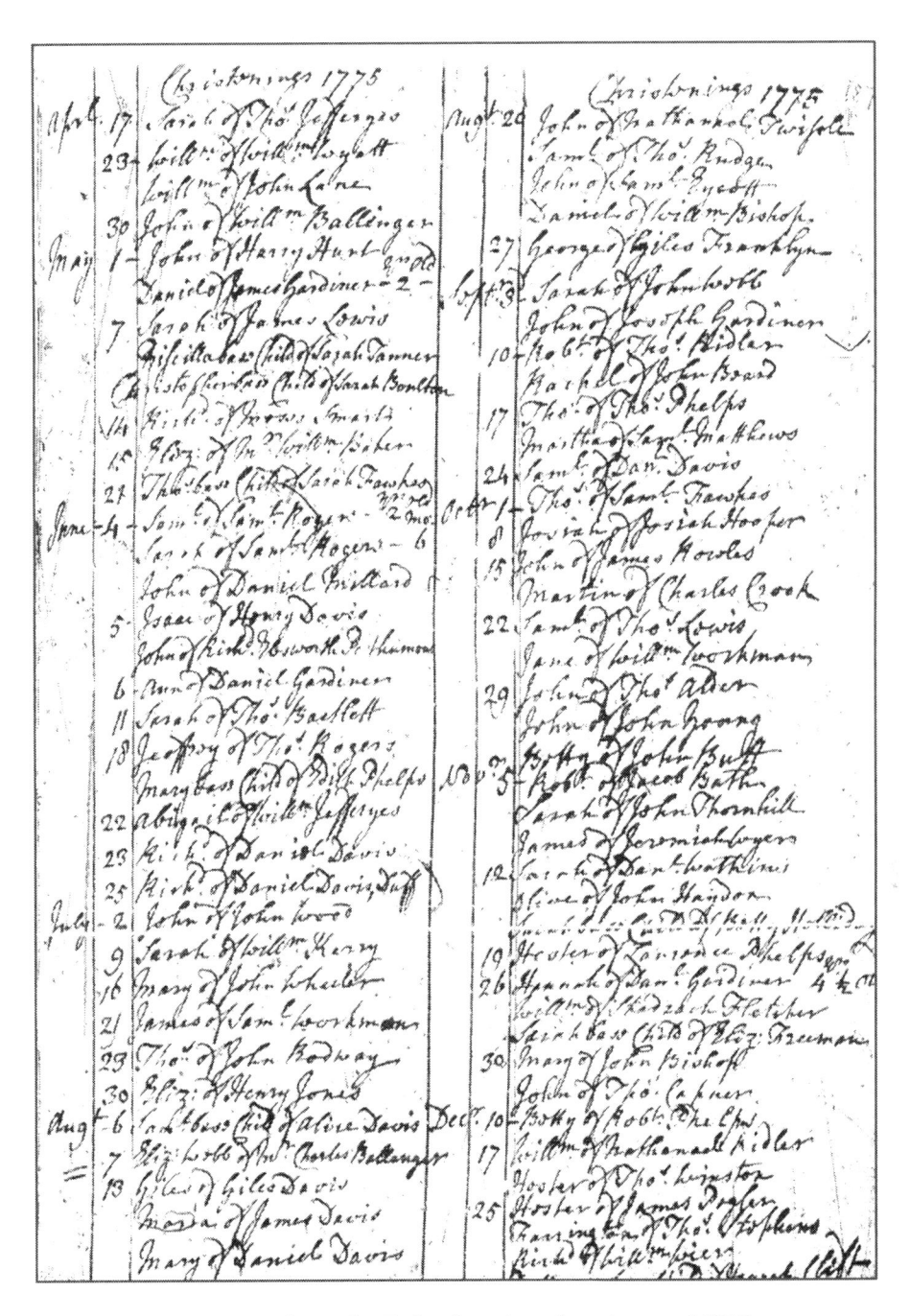

A Section from the Bisley baptismal registers of 1775.
G.A. Ref: P47 IN 1/2

A section from the Stroud baptismal register of 1794.
G.A. Ref: P320 IN 1/6

It was a common occurrence for the expectant mother to go home to her mother for the birth of her first child so look for a baptism in both the parish where she was living and the one where her parents were; the latter is possibly also where the couple married.

Most children were baptised at around one month old but, if the child was sickly when born, he or she would have had an early private baptism at home. This could lead to the appearance of two 'baptisms' in the records, one being the private baptism, the second, not strictly a baptism, being the occasion when the child, if it survived, was 'received into the church'. If the parents were nonconformists, there was a strong chance that the baby would not be baptised at all until an adult.

Note: Most but not all children were baptised around one month old but a private baptism was carried out at home if the child was not expected to survive.

4. Parish Registers

Marriage:
Before 1929, it was legal for a boy to marry at the age of 14 and a girl at the age of 12 as long as they had the consent of their parents. The age of majority, when they could marry without parental consent was 21 at that time. From 1929 until 1969, the age at which boys and girls could marry with parental consent was raised to 16 years for both sexes. The age at which they could marry without parental consent remained at 21. In 1970, the age of majority was reduced to 18 years of age.

> *Note: Before 1929, it was legal for a boy to marry at the age of 14 and a girl at the age of 12, with the consent of their parents. Without parental consent, it was 21 for both sexes.*

Early marriages had to take place in a Church of England church or chapel for all except Quakers and Jews, who were permitted to hold their own ceremonies and keep their own records. In 1837, when civil registration came in, nonconformist and Roman Catholic marriages could be held in their own buildings but had to be held in the presence of a registrar to record the information. This was the case until the 1890s when nonconformists were allowed to register their own marriages.

Entries in the marriage register were extremely basic in the early days, with just the date and the names of the bride and groom recorded. Later, when the new marriage registers were used in 1754, the parish and the marital status (bachelor, spinster, widower or widow) of each were included, as well as the signatures or marks of the couple and two witnesses.

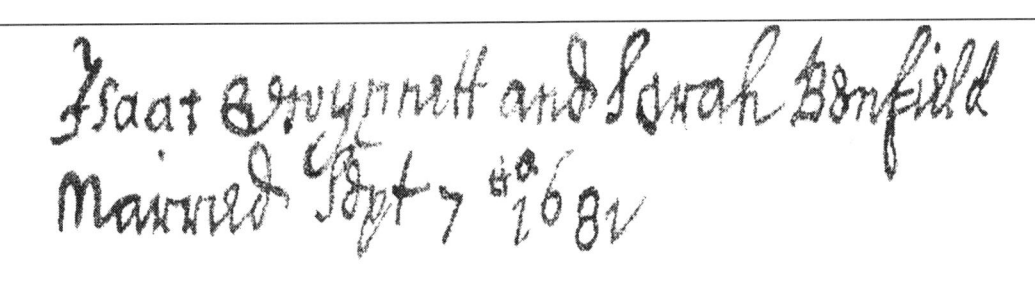

An example of an early Shurdington marriage showing minimal information.
G.A. Ref: P292 IN 1/1

By 1837, marriage records gave the same information as can be found on modern marriage certificates, namely the location (the church or register office) and the date of the marriage, whether by banns, licence or certificate, plus the names, ages, marital status, occupation, address, father's name and father's occupation for both bride and groom, together with their marks and signatures and those of their witnesses. The only difference between the marriage entry in the parish register and the marriage certificate was that the signatures in the parish registers, where they existed, were the real thing whereas on the marriage certificate, they are copies.

Burials:

People could choose where they wanted to be buried and all had the right to be buried in the parish where they died. Most, however, were buried in the churchyard of the parish where they were living at the time. The wealthier people had tombstones, many of which still exist. The less affluent had a wooden cross or nothing to indicate their burial place. From 1689 onwards, Jewish, Roman Catholic and other nonconformist graveyards were permitted.

In the second part of the 16th century, bodies had to be buried in wool to encourage the wool trade, and an affidavit was sworn to say this had been done – entries in the registers often have 'Aff' written alongside them to indicate this. This order was repealed early in the 19th century but by then few obeyed this instruction.

An entry from the Upper Slaughter burial register for 1678.
G.A. Ref: P297 IN 1/1

Burial entries tend to be very brief before 1813; in many cases they just give the name of the deceased and nothing more. If you are lucky, however, the minister may have recorded the fact that the deceased was an infant, (roughly half of all burials were for infants) and may have even given the names of the parents. As time progressed, more ministers included the age for all burials. After 1813, the age was included on the form, along with the abode, as a matter of course.

Bishop's Transcripts

In 1598, at the same time as baptisms, marriages and burials had to be recorded in parchment registers and retained at the church, the bishops decided that they, too, would like copies of the entries so churchwardens were required to transcribe the information each year until 1813, at which time it became the incumbent's task. These bishop's transcripts (BTs) were written not into books but onto individual sheets of paper so, over the centuries, many sheets have been damaged or gone missing. Do not expect to get a complete run of BTs – it could just be a single year that has survived. Just take it as a bonus if you do find new information there.

4. Parish Registers

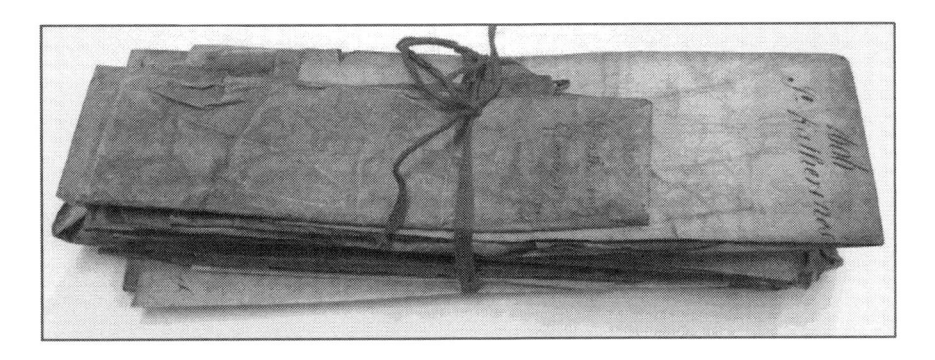

A Bundle of 17th century Bishop's Transcripts for the Parish of St. Catherine's Church, Gloucester. G.A. Ref: GDR/V1/109

The Gloucester diocese actually has some parishes with bishop's transcripts dating back before 1598, many of which also pre-date the existing parish registers. Viewing the BTs is a must for the serious researcher who wishes to confirm every piece of information gathered and you may just find that elusive item that allows you to progress to the previous generation. A table showing parishes with these early BTs and indicating those which pre-date the relevant parish register is shown in the Appendix 4.3.

The bishop's transcripts at Gloucestershire Archives are mainly on microfilm and fall into five categories.

Period	Organisation
Up to 1812	Filmed and arranged by individual parishes
1813 – 1858	Filmed by year, parishes roughly organised alphabetically
1859 – 1862	Unfilmed and unavailable due to damage
1863 – 1866	Filmed and arranged alphabetically by year
1867 – 1916	Filmed but getting patchier as the years progress

Some BTs for the city of Gloucester have survived where the parish registers have not. These are:

Parish	Period
St Aldate	1596 – 1640
St Mary de Grace	1613 – 1640
St Owen	1610 – 1638

Generally speaking, no BTs exist during the period of the Civil War and the following Interregnum, between 1640 and 1659, but there are a few Gloucestershire exceptions to this rule. They are:

Parish	Period	Notes
Bledington	1640 – 1663	
Dorsington	1640 – 1660	

Discover Gloucestershire Ancestors

Parish	Period	Notes
Dymock	1645 – 1660	Just a few for the wealthy intestates
Hill	1645 – 1660	
Shipton Sollars	1653 – 1660	
Slimbridge	1655 – 1660	

The BTs from 1813 onwards are, as I was told, creatively filed! Some parishes are out of alphabetical sequence. For instance, Gloucester parishes are sometimes grouped together under Gloucester and other times are under the heading of the individual parish, either under S for Saint or the actual letter of the saint's name. So, for St Mary de Lode, check under Gloucester, Saint and Mary until you find it. Some BTs are filed under a completely different parish and chapelries that later became parishes in their own right may be under either name.

Parish	**See BTs**
Coleford	Newland
Pinnock cum Hyde	Didbrook
Sezincote	Longborough
Sheepscombe	Painswick

Details of the bishop's transcripts which exist for each parish before 1813 can be found in *Diocese of Gloucester: A Catalogue of the Records of the Bishop and Archdeacons* by Isabel M. Kirby published by the Gloucester City Corporation in 1968. A similar book covers the parishes in the Diocese of Bristol.

Bishop's transcripts for Lea in Herefordshire and Shenington in Oxfordshire are held at Gloucestershire Archives. For other Gloucestershire parishes not in the Gloucester diocese, check the *National Index of Parish Registers: Volume V* compiled by D. J. Steel, last published by Phillimore in 1971. This will tell you the record office at which the relevant bishop's transcripts are held.

The bishop's transcripts are supposedly exact copies of parish registers but you will quite frequently find discrepancies between the two. Apart from the occasional transcription errors, you will sometimes find additional information in one that is not in the other. E.g. the reputed father of an illegitimate child may be recorded for the Bishop but not in the general register, or vice versa. The BTs are very useful for checking details that are unclear in the parish registers or that are missing from there. Where they exist, you should *always* check both parish registers and bishop's transcripts, to corroborate the information you have and to gain as much additional information as possible.

Finding Aids
As you progress in your search for knowledge about your ancestors, you may discover indexes that will help to speed up your quest. One of the best finding aids to help you is the International Genealogical Index, usually known as the IGI, which was created at the end of the 1960s by the Church of Jesus Christ of Latter Day Saints (LDS). The 100 year privacy rule was applied so few records are found beyond the 1860s but they go back to the first half of the sixteenth century when parish registers began.

4. Parish Registers

Baptismal and marriage entries from parish registers and, in some cases, from the Bishops Transcripts were recorded and entered into a vast database, which was then sorted to give the items in country / county / surname / forename and date order. All surname variants were listed together, hence the spellings of Gwynet, Gwinnett, Gwinutt, Guynet and Guinett would all be in the same group making it easier to spot unusual forms of the surname of interest.

The database originally contained mainly baptisms and marriages as these are what help researchers to get farther back through the generations; there were very few burials. But in recent years, with the increased interest in family history, individuals have been allowed to submit data to add to the IGI and this has included some birth, death and burial information, as well as baptisms and marriages.

A Section of the International Genealogical Index on microfiche showing some of the Gwinnett entries.

Sadly, this has led to more errors in the online version than appeared in the early, microfiche versions of the IGI and to the frequent inclusion of vague details where people have assumed, for instance, that a baptism or marriage has taken place without actually having any proof of that event. One such online entry reads:

> e.g. Button Gwinnett, born about 1742, of Down Hatherley, Gloucester

Button Gwinnett was actually baptised on 10th April 1735 at St Catherine's Church in Gloucester although he was, presumably, born in the vicarage of Down Hatherley where his father was minister. The date given is very inaccurate.

Another entry states:

> e.g. Paul Gwinnett married about 1800, Harnwood, Gloucester.

This IGI entry has two errors. The date is incorrect. Paul Gwinnett actually married in Bredon's Norton in Worcestershire on 23rd May 1793. Secondly, the 'of Harnwood' goes back to a misreading of the fact that Paul was baptised on 16th January 1775 in Barnwood in Gloucester. The person who provided this information has added 25 years to Paul's baptismal date to estimate a marriage date and wrongly assumed that he married in the parish of his baptism.

Incorrect records such as these are found on the Internet, read by other researchers and all too often taken as gospel. They are then entered into their own family tree and again posted on the net. They are repeated so often they gradually take on the appearance of true and accepted facts. I cannot emphasize enough that, while the IGI is an excellent finding aid, it is merely that – an aid. Be very careful to take these entries as possibilities only. You should always verify everything you find in the IGI by checking with the original document or a facsimile of it.

> *Note: The IGI is an excellent finding aid but ALWAYS check the original record or a facsimile of it in case of transcription errors.*

There is, however, another problem with the IGI - it does not cover the whole of the county of Gloucestershire. Apart from the fact that there are gaps in the original parish registers themselves, there are some Gloucestershire parishes which were not covered by the IGI at all and some 150 of them that have no entries after 1813. In particular, those parishes in South Gloucestershire that are in the Bristol Diocese were not included. A list of all the parishes omitted completely from the IGI can be seen in Appendix 4.4.

The IGI can be seen on microfiche at Gloucestershire Archives and the GFHS Family History Centre, or at the LDS Family History Centres around the world. It can also be accessed on the LDS website on www.familysearch.org on the Internet. Access to the IGI is free.

Other Finding Aids
The LDS have also produced software called the Resource File Viewer and another database, called the Vital Records Index, of births, baptisms and marriages which are not included on the IGI. It contains nearly 190,000 births and baptisms and over 93,000 marriages for the county of Gloucestershire so can fill many of the gaps found in the IGI. This is available to view at the GFHS Family History Centre. The information can also be accessed through the LDS website (see above).

4. Parish Registers

There are four other excellent databases to assist your search, produced by volunteers of the Gloucestershire Family History Society. The information on them has been thoroughly checked to try to ensure the greatest accuracy possible. The databases are:

GFHS Baptism Index	(1813 – 1837)
GFHS Marriage Index	(1754 – 1799)*
GFHS Marriage Index	(1800 – June 1837)
GFHS Burial Index	(1813 – 1851 and often more)

The information covers baptisms, marriages and burials that occurred within the Diocese of Gloucester (i.e. not South Gloucestershire) and some entries from nonconformist registers, during the mentioned period. The databases are available to view at the GFHS Family History Centre or for sale on CD from the Society (see www.gfhs.org.uk). There are several other CDs which can be purchased from the Bristol and Avon Family History Society which *do* cover the area of South Gloucestershire which is in the Diocese of Bristol (see www.bafhs.org.uk). You will also find some burials recorded on their website

Two marriage indexes which are available on the shelves at Gloucestershire Archives are Phillimore's Marriage Index and Roe's Marriage Index. Both are in book form, the latter also available on CD. Neither has complete coverage for Gloucestershire nor even for the Diocese of Gloucester.

* Recently, GFHS volunteers have produced another CD with marriages between 1754 and 1800 covering those parishes which are not already on the IGI, not included on the Forest of Dean website and not in the Phillimore Marriage Index. Therefore, all Gloucestershire marriages recorded in the registers between 1754 and 1837 which took place in the Gloucester and Bristol dioceses should now be available on CD, online or at the Archives.

Roe's Marriage Index has eight separate volumes each for Brides and for Grooms and is divided into separate periods, e.g. Up to 1600, 1601 – 1650, etc. Entries are by strict alphabetical order of surname and forename; surname variants are not put together. Each entry gives the name of the bride and groom, the parish and the year in which they married. Not all parishes were covered and the index covers fewer marriages as the 19th century commences.

1674	GWINNET	Geo & Sarah Browne (Mrs)	Tirley
1666	GWYN	Geo & Mary Williams	Bristol Mar Bonds
1672	GWYNNE	Nathaniel & Sarah Freeman	Horton
1645	GYDE	Thos & Mary Hurne	Minchinhampton

An Excerpt from Roe's Marriage Index for the late 17th Century.

Phillimore's Marriage Index is in 17 volumes and covers various parishes completely up to 1812 and, in some cases, beyond that. Entries in the volumes are in chronological order and include the names of the bride and groom and the exact date of the marriage.

> 1805]   *Dursley Marriages.*   103
>
> | | | |
> |---|---|---|
> | Joseph Bazley & Ann Steel | 11 Apr. | 1805 |
> | James Stagg, p. St. Paul, Bristol, & Mary Wilkes, this p. | 11 Apr. | ,, |
> | James Curnock, b., & Margaret Trotman, s., *lic.* | 19 Apr. | ,, |
> | Joseph Day & Ann Hancock | 1 May | ,, |
> | Richard Naish & Joanna Williams | 10 May | ,, |
> | John Hurlstone & Elizabeth Thurston | 18 May | ,, |
> | Stephen Hale & Ann Stockwell | 30 May | ,, |
> | Oneas Austin & Elizabeth Elliotts | 4 July | ,, |
> | James Webb & Elizabeth Stockwell, *lic.* | 5 July | ,, |
> | John Flight, b., p. Kingstanley, co. and dio. of Gloucester, & Charlotte Gwinnett, s., this p., *lic.*... | 7 July | ,, |

An excerpt from the Phillimore Marriage Index for Dursley.

By going online, you may find what you are seeking in Boyd's Marriage Index or Pallot's Marriage Index, both of which include some Gloucestershire parishes. However, these are normally available only on pay-to-view sites.

Over the past few years, several websites have appeared that contain transcriptions of parish registers, some specific to one village, others to a larger area. Most notable amongst them is the excellent Forest of Dean website which can be accessed on:

www.forest-of-dean.net

But more and more websites are coming along every day as villages set up their own pages, so it is always worth an Internet search to see what exists. Just don't forget that they are transcripts and few are totally error free so always check the originals.

4. Parish Registers

Appendix 4.1
Gaps in the Parish Registers

For those seeking information on their ancestors in the parish baptism, marriage and burial registers, it is worth noting that not all registers have survived in their entirety. These gaps may have occurred simply because no events happened in that parish during that period. This may well have been the case with the very small village parishes but is unlikely to be true for the larger parishes. The gaps there are more likely to be due to missing records, the illness or incompetence of the minister or a period when the church was without an incumbent at all.

Gaps of eight years or more are recorded in the table below. Smaller gaps are too numerous to list. Please note the list of parishes with damaged or missing registers earlier in the chapter – they are not included here.

Parish	Baptisms	Marriages	Burials
Acton Turville		1724 onwards	
Adlestrop		1647 – 1687	
Alderley		1737 – 1751	1737 - 1751
Ampney Crucis	1708 - 1718	1744 – 1753	
Ampney St Peter	1733 – 1742	1690 – 1753	1732 – 1742
Arlingham	1552 – 1589 1614 – 1648	1646 – 1654	1548 – 1572
Avening		1746 – 1753	
Badgeworth	1724 – 1745	1722 – 1754	1724 – 1745
Batsford		1765 – 1792	
Berkeley		1643 – 1652 1663 – 1675	
Blaisdon	1695 – 1753	1695 – 1767 1803 – 1813	1695 – 1753
Boddington		1691 – 1732	
Brimpsfield			1760 – 1786
Broadwell	1642 – 1659	1641 – 1659	1641 – 1659
Brockworth		1754 – 1812	1812 onwards
Bulley	1784 – 1805	1754 – 1797	1785 – 1805
Chaceley		1717 – 1754	1812 onwards
Cheltenham St Mary	1654 – 1675	1654 – 1675	1654 – 1675
Chipping Sodbury	1695 – 1715	1693 – 1716 1733 – 1747	1695 – 1715
Cirencester		1741 – 1750	
Clearwell			1833 – 1855
Coaley	1612 – 1625		1612 – 1625 1699 – 1736
Coln St Aldwyn	1728 0 1774	1728 – 1770	1728 – 1774
Compton Abdale		1752 – 1759	

Parish	Baptisms	Marriages	Burials
Condicote		1737 – 1751	
Corse	1767 – 1784		1767 – 1784
Daglingworth			1581 – 1608
Deerhurst		1636 – 1652	
Down Ampney	1752 – 1779		
Eastleach Turville	1759 – 1778 1864 – 1914	1749 – 1759	1749 – 1778
Ebrington		1676 – 1684	
Edgeworth	1736 – 1749		
English Bicknor	1684 – 1718	1684 – 1718	1684 – 1718
Flaxley		1638 – 1657 1755 – 1762	1646 – 1657
Frocester	1671 – 1681	1666 – 1680	1671 – 1681
Gloucester Cathedral		1755 – 1902	
Gloucester St Aldate	1642 – 1755		
Gloucester St Catherine		1738 – 1867	
Gloucester St James			1899 – 1972
Gloucester St John the Baptist		1661 – 1672 1676 – 1698	1674 – 1693
Gloucester St Mary de Crypt			1755 – 1762
Great Witcombe with Bentham		1754 – 1813	
Haresfield		1620 – 1628 1644 – 1653	
Hasfield		1640 – 1652	1636 – 1652
Hatherop		1665 – 1669 1747 – 1772 *	1665 – 1678
Hawkesbury		1891 – 1953	
Hempsted			1758 – 1796
Hill	1728 – 1764	1728 – 1764	1728 – 1764
Horsley		1667 – 1694	1667 – 1694
Icomb	1546 – 1556		
Kempley			1644 – 1669
Kempsford	1604 – 1617	1597 – 1652 1658 – 1685	1604 – 1617 1661 – 1671
Lassington		1833 – 1845 1923 – 1943	
Leigh	1639 – 1659 1665 – 1674	1639 – 1659 1665 – 1674	1644 – 1653 1664 – 1674
Little Barrington		1755 – 1805	
Longney		1743 – 1754	
Lower Lemington			1754 – 1774
Maisemore		1591 – 1654 1657 – 1678	
Mickleton		1641 – 1656	
Northleach		1728 – 1736	1726 – 1737

4. Parish Registers

Parish	Baptisms	Marriages	Burials
Old Sodbury	1687 – 1694	1687 – 1694	1687 – 1694
Owlpen			1972 – 1985
Oxenton	1737 – 1755	1735 – 1754	1738 – 1755
Painswick	1627 – 1651	1625 – 1651	1625 – 1651
			1679 – 1688
			1691 – 1705
Parkend			1856 – 1870
Pauntley		1790 – 1812	
Poole Keynes	1641 – 1652	1638 – 1661	1640 – 1662
Poulton		1782 – 1812	
Preston (nr Ledbury)		1811 – 1818	
		1833 – 1840	
Randwick	1695 – 1724	1693 – 1724	1695 – 1724
Redmarley D'Abitôt	1696 – 1702	1694 – 1702	
Rendcomb	1660 – 1679	1658 – 1687	1659 – 1679
Ruardean		1692 – 1754 **	
Saintbury		1748 – 1774	
Saul		1683 – 1701	1761 – 1769
		1748 – 1799	
Shorncote		1751 – 1761	
Shurdington	1723 – 1789	1723 – 1746	1723 – 1789
Slimbridge	1687 – 1701	1687 – 1707	1714 – 1727
	1705 – 1718		
Southrop		1745 – 1752	
Standish			1644 – 1652
Staunton (nr Coleford)		1684 – 1694	
Staverton		1667 – 1689	1670 – 1679
Stone			1793 – 1812
Stow on the Wold	1631 – 1679	1631 – 1707	1631 – 1707
Stowell	1842 – 1967		
Stratton		1640 – 1653	
Swindon (Village)		1738 – 1755	
Tewkesbury		1656 – 1663	1609 – 1633
		1666 – 1678	1638 – 1652
Tidenham	1755 – 1792	1753 – 1767	1755 – 1792
Tytherington		1844 – 1980	
Upleadon		1761 – 1790	
Upper Swell	1646 – 1656		
Upton St Leonards	1775 – 1782		1775 – 1782
Walton Cardiff ***		1856 – 1903	
Westonbirt	1697 – 1733	1697 – 1733	1697 – 1733
Whitminster/Wheatenhurst	1667 – 1684	1636 – 1698	1668 – 1684
Winstone			1649 – 1664
Withington	1621 – 1631	1621 – 1631	1621 – 1631

Discover Gloucestershire Ancestors

Parish	Baptisms	Marriages	Burials
Woodchester	1626 – 1654	1625 – 1668	1626 – 1698
Wyck Rissington		1747 – 1754	

*   Only a very few marriages are registered for this period

**   See Walford, Herefordshire, for marriages in this period

***   See Tewkesbury for marriages in this period.

Appendix 4.2
Gloucestershire Parishes not in the Diocese of Gloucester

Gloucestershire's administrative boundary and the boundary of the Diocese of Gloucester are not exactly the same. Some parishes within the county fall within a different Diocese. These are shown in the table below.

Parish	Diocese	Notes
Abson	Bristol	
Almondsbury	Bristol	
Alstone	Worcester	Before 1844
Alveston	Bristol	
Aust	Bristol	
Bitton	Bristol	
Church Honeybourne	Worcester	Before 1919
Compton Greenfield	Bristol	
Cow Honeybourne	Worcester	Before 1919
Cutsdean	Worcester	Before 1931
Dodington	Bristol	
Downend	Bristol	
Doynton	Bristol	
Dyrham and Hinton	Bristol	
Elberton	Bristol	
Evenlode	Worcester	Before 1919
Filton	Bristol	
Fishponds	Bristol	
Frampton Cotterell	Bristol	
Frenchay	Bristol	
Henbury	Bristol	
Hinton on the Green	Worcester	Before 1919
Horfield	Bristol	
Icomb	Worcester	Before 1912
Kingswood (nr Bristol)	Bristol	
Little Compton	Oxford	Since 1919
Littleton upon Severn	Bristol	
Long Newnton	Salisbury	Before 1837
Mangotsfield	Bristol	
Marshfield	Bristol	
Oldland	Bristol	
Olveston	Bristol	
Patchway	Bristol	
Pilning	Bristol	
Poole Keynes	Salisbury	Before 1837
Poulton	Salisbury	Before 1837
Preston on Stour	Coventry	Since 1918

Parish	Diocese	Notes
Pucklechurch	Bristol	
Redmarley D'Abitôt	Worcester	Before 1931
Redwick and Northwick	Bristol	
Shenington	Oxford	Since 1837
Shirehampton	Bristol	
Siston	Bristol	
Somerford Keynes	Salisbury	Before 1837
Stapleton	Bristol	
Staunton nr Ledbury	Worcester	Before 1953
Stoke Bishop	Bristol	
Stoke Gifford	Bristol	
Tormarton & West Littleton	Bristol	
Warmley	Bristol	
Westbury on Trym	Bristol	
Wick	Bristol	
Widford	Oxford	Since 1837
Winterbourne	Bristol	
Yate	Bristol	

4. Parish Registers

Appendix 4.3
Early Bishop's Transcripts at Gloucestershire Archives

The Gloucester Diocesan records housed at Gloucestershire Archives include the Bishop's Transcripts for some Gloucestershire parishes dating back before the supposed starting date of 1598. They are listed below. Many of these also pre-date the existing parish registers so are of particular interest to those seeking early ancestors. The parishes which are marked with an asterisk have Bishop's Transcripts recorded prior to the earliest existing parish registers so are definitely worth a look. But it could only be one year that has remained during that period.

Parish	Earliest BT
Adlestrop	1580
Alderley	1570
Aldsworth *	1571
Ampney Crucis	1579
Ampney St Peter *	1579
Arlingham	1573
Aston Blank / Cold Aston *	1580
Avening	1578
Awre	1586
Badgeworth	1570
Bagendon *	1577
Berkeley	1571
Beverstone	1570
Blaisdon *	1583
Bourton on the Hill	1580
Bourton on the Water *	1580
Broadwell	1580
Chedworth *	1580
Cherington	1580
Cirencester	1578
Coaley *	1580
Coberley	1578
Colesbourne *	1578
Coln St Aldwyn *	1580
Coln St Denis	1570
Cowley *	1578
Cromhall *	1571
Daglingworth *	1577
Deerhurst	1578
Down Ampney *	1572
Down Hatherley	1578
Duntisbourne Rouse	1570
Eastington nr Stonehouse	1578

Parish	Earliest BT
Eastleach Martin	1570
Eastleach Turville *	1578
Edgeworth	1579
Elkstone *	1578
Flaxley	1586
Forthampton *	1578
Frampton on Severn *	1577
Gloucester St Catherine *	1571
Gloucester St John the Baptist	1570
Gloucester St Mary de Crypt *	1570
Great Badminton	1579
Great Barrington	1580
Great Witcombe *	1570
Guiting Power	1580
Hampnett *	1571
Harescombe *	1570
Haresfield	1569
Hatherop	1578
Hawkesbury *	1578
Hewelsfield *	1586
Hill *	1571
Horsley *	1580
Horton	1578
Huntley *	1583
Kempley *	1569
Kings Stanley	1578
Kingscote *	1578
Kingswood nr Wotton *	1578
Lassington *	1570
Lea (HEF)	1583
Leonard Stanley *	1578
Little Barrington *	1581
Little Rissington	1580

Parish	Earliest BT
Longhope *	1583
Lower Lemington *	1571
Maiseyhampton	1578
Matson	1570
Mickleton *	1572
Minchinhampton	1575
Minsterworth *	1575
Mitcheldean *	1588
Moreton Valence *	1569
Newington Bagpath *	1578
Newland	1584
North Cerney	1578
North Nibley	1578
Norton *	1569
Nympsfield *	1578
Oddington *	1580
Oxenhall *	1587
Oxenton *	1578
Ozleworth *	1577
Painswick	1570
Pauntley	1586
Preston nr Cirencester *	1578
Preston nr Ledbury *	1586
Quedgeley	1570
Quenington *	1578
Rangeworthy *	1575
Rockhampton	1580
Rodmarton *	1578
Rudford *	1583
Sandhurst	1569
Sapperton *	1578
Shenington (OXF)	1578
Sherborne	1571

Parish	Earliest BT
Shipton Oliffe & Shipton Sollars *	1571
Shurdington	1578
Siddington St Peter	1578
Slimbridge *	1571
South Cerney *	1578
Standish	1569
Stanway	1580
Staunton nr Coleford *	1583
Stone *	1578
Stratton *	1578
Stroud St Lawrence *	1578
Swindon (Village) *	1570
Syde *	1578
Taynton	1583
Temple Guiting *	1580
Tetbury St Mary *	1578
Tewkesbury St Mary	1570
Thornbury	1578
Tibberton *	1586
Tidenham St Mary *	1586
Todenham *	1583
Upleadon	1585
Upper Slaughter	1580
Upton St Leonards	1569
Westbury on Severn	1586
Whitminster/Wheatenhurst	1571
Wickwar *	1578
Willersey *	1580
Woolaston *	1587
Woolstone *	1570
Wotton under Edge	1578

Appendix 4.4
Gloucestershire parishes NOT included in the IGI

These parishes were not included on the original IGI. Items from some parishes have since been added to the online version and some parishes were included on the Vital Record Index series produced on CD by the Church of Latter Day Saints.

Parish	Parish
Almondsbury	Fishponds
Alveston	Frampton Cotterell
Ampney Crucis	Gloucester – Cathedral
Aston Somerville	Gloucester – Christchurch
Aust	Gloucester – Littleworth (Extra Parochial)
Aylburton	Gloucester – St. Mary Magdalene with St. Margaret
Barnsley	Gloucester – St. Peter's Abbey
Bedminster (Bristol / Somerset)	Hailes
Bibury	Henbury
Bristol - All Saints	Honeybourne (Worcestershire)
Bristol - Cathedral	Horfield
Bristol - Christchurch	Ilmington (Warwickshire)
Bristol - Holy Trinity (St Philip)	Iron Acton
Bristol - St Ewen	Lancaut
Bristol - St James	Lasborough
Bristol - St John the Baptist (City)	Littleton on Severn
Bristol - St Leonard	Lower Slaughter
Bristol - St Mary Redcliffe	Mangotsfield
Bristol - St Michael the Archangel	Nailsworth
Bristol - St Nicholas	Olveston
Bristol - St Paul Portland Square	Parkend
Bristol - St Peter	Poulton
Bristol - St Philip and St. Jacob	Prescott (Extra Parochial)
Bristol - St Stephen (City)	Prinknash Park (Extra Parochial)
Bristol - St Thomas	Pucklechurch
Bristol - St Werburgh	Redwick and Northwick
Bristol - Temple or Holy Cross	Roel (Extra Parochial)
Christchurch	St George
Clapton	Sezincote
Clearwell	Sheepscombe
Clifton	Shirehampton
Compton Greenfield	Stanley Pontlarge
Dodington	Stapleton
Donnington	Stoke Gifford
Doynton	Sutton under Brailes
Drybrook	Wapley & Codrington
Dyrham	Westcote

Parish	Parish
East Dean (Extra Parochial)	West Dean (Extra Parochial)
Eastington (near Stonehouse)	Westerleigh
Elberton	Wick & Abson
Eyford	Winson
Falfield	Winterbourne
Filton	

The following parishes have no entries after 1813 on the original IGI. All have records up to and including 1812 except where the final date is given.

Adlestrop, Alderley, Aldsworth (1749), Alvington, Ampney St Mary, Ampney St Peter, Aston sub Edge, Avening, Badgeworth, Beverstone, Bishops Cleeve, Bisley, Bitton (1674), Boddington, Bourton on the Water, Boxwell with Leighterton, Brimpsfield, Broadwell, Brockworth, Buckland, Cam, Charfield, Cheltenham, Cherington, Chipping Sodbury, Churchdown, Cirencester, Coaley, Coates, Coberley, Coleford (1815), Compton Abdale, Condicote, Cowley, Cromhall, Daglingworth, Didbrook, Didmarton, Dorsington, Dowdeswell, Down Ampney, Down Hatherley, Driffield, Dumbleton, Duntisbourne Abbots, Duntisbourne Rous, Dursley, Eastington, Eastleach Martin, Eastleach Turville, Ebrington, Edgeworth, Elkstone, Elmstone Hardwicke, Farmington, Forthampton, Frocester, Gloucester Holy Trinity (1640), Gloucester St Aldate, Gloucester St Catherine, Gloucester St John the Baptist (1750), Gloucester St Mary de Crypt, Gloucester St Mary de Lode, Gloucester St Michael, Great Rissington, Great Washbourne, Hanham Abbots (1696), Harescombe, Haresfield, Harnhill, Hawling, Hazleton, Hempstead, Hewelsfield, Hill, Hinton on the Green, Horton, Huntley, Icomb (1701), Kingscote, Leckhampton, Lechlade, Leigh, Little Rissington, Little Sodbury, Longborough, Longhope, Lower Lemington, Maiseyhampton, Marshfield (1693), Matson, Miserden, Naunton, Newington Bagpath, Newnham, Northleach, Norton, Oddington, Oldbury on the Hill, Old Sodbury, Oxenton, Ozleworth, Pebworth, Randwick, Rangeworthy, Rockhampton, Rodmarton, Ruardean, Rudford, St Briavels, Salperton, Sandhurst, Sapperton, Saul, Shipton Moyne, Shurdington, Siddington St Mary, Siddington St Peter, Slimbridge, Snowshill, Southrop, Standish, Stanton, Stanway, Staunton, Staverton, Stinchcombe, Stone, Stow on the Wold, Stroud, Swindon, Syde, Syston (1641), Thornbury, Tidenham, Toddington, Todenham, Tortworth, Tredington, Twining, Tytherington, Upper Slaughter, Upper Swell, Upton St Leonards, Walton Cardiff, Westbury on Trym (1713), Westonbirt, Weston sub Edge, Whaddon, Whitminster, Wickwar, Willersey, Winchcombe, Winstone, Woolstone, Wormington, Wotton under Edge, Wyck Rissington, Yate.

.

Chapter 5

Nonconformist Registers

'Whoso would be a man must be a nonconformist.'

Ralph Waldo Emerson
1803 – 1882, US essayist and poet.

If you have searched the parish registers and not yet found the vital event (birth, baptism, marriage, death or burial) that you were seeking, you need to consider the possibility that your ancestor may have been a nonconformist, however fleetingly. Some people varied their religious affiliations over their lifetime, which is quite understandable given the religious upheaval that occurred during the Reformation, the Commonwealth period, the Restoration and at times thereafter.

This change could have been from or to the established Church of England, between different religions or within a particular denomination. Dissenters sometimes fell out with each other and created new splinter groups. A new minister coming into an area could introduce a difference of emphasis and people would look to find a church more suited to their beliefs. Sometimes, church or chapel attendance was merely a case of convenience, with people attending the nearest location. So, however much you think your ancestors belonged to one particular religion, be open to looking for them in any or all available registers.

A 'nonconformist', by definition, was a Christian but not an adherent of the Church of England. 'Dissenter' is another term which is used to describe such a person. You may come across the word 'recusant' meaning someone who did not attend the parish church (for which they could be fined or have goods forfeited) and which generally but not always was applied to Roman Catholics. The term 'Papist' also applied to Roman Catholics.

The treatment of nonconformists varied throughout history, sometimes being tolerant, at other times persecutory and punitive. Before 1533, during the early years of Henry VIII's reign, England was a Catholic nation but, in 1534, by an Act of Supremacy, Henry VIII declared himself Supreme Head of the Church in England. With the accession of Elizabeth I to the throne in 1559, an Act of Uniformity made the Church of England the established Church and its records became legal documents which had to be preserved, an act which all family historians should celebrate. The Act made it a legal obligation to attend church on Sundays. Those who did not agree with the principles of the Church of England started forming their own nonconformist congregations.

By the Religion Act of 1592, those who did not attend their parish church for a month, without good reason, were liable to imprisonment; if after another three months they still did not attend, the punishment was exile or death. Ministers could get life imprisonment for conducting services other than those laid down by the established church. So the records of nonconformists were not often kept as they could lead to punishment in the ecclesiastical courts.

Following the attempt by Guy Fawkes and others to blow up the Houses of Parliament in 1605, the Popish Recusants Act was introduced in 1606 during the reign of James I, stating that Roman Catholics had to be baptised, married and buried in the parish church; there were severe penalties for those who did not obey.

5. Nonconformist Registers

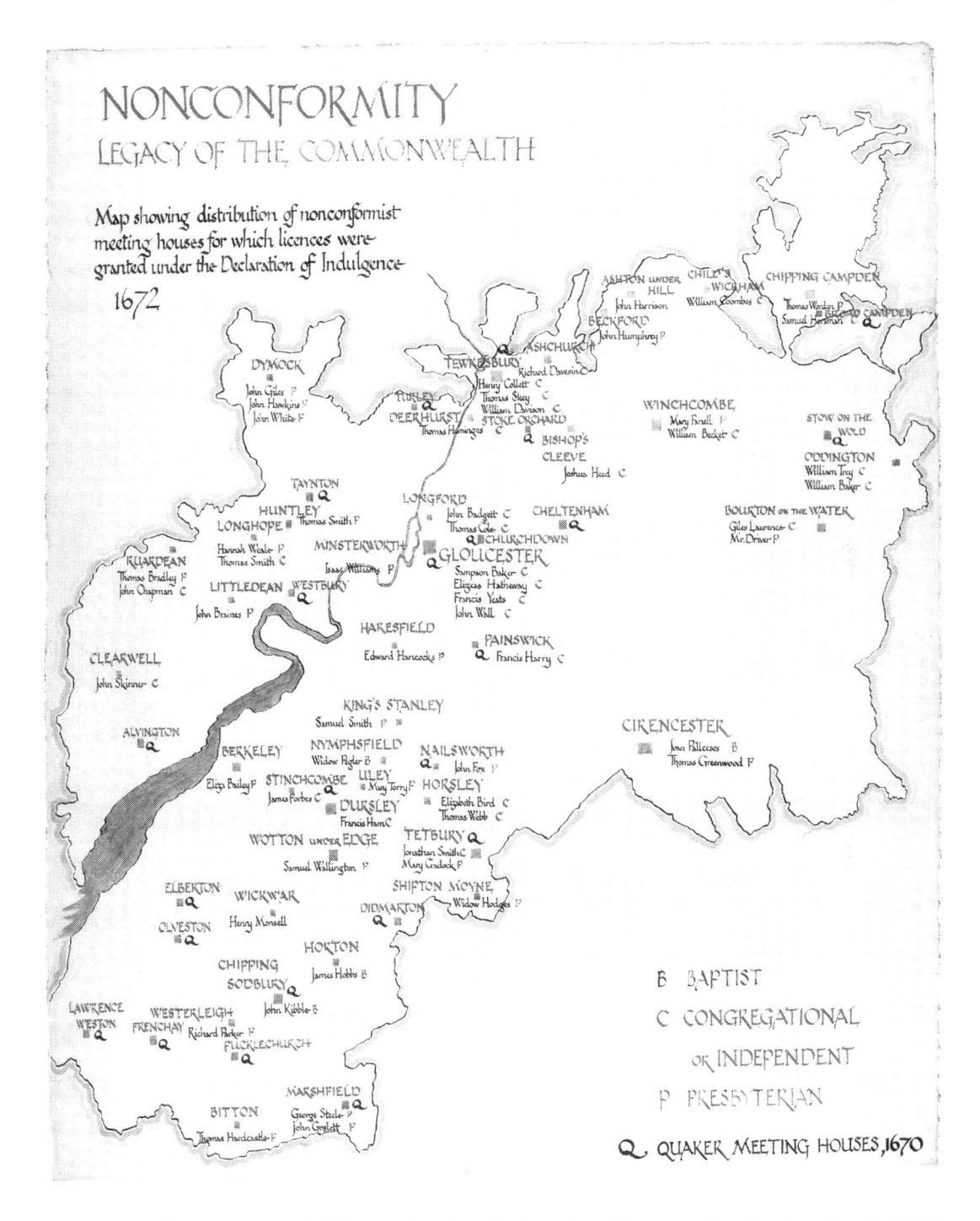

Map drawn by Miss E M Middleton showing the location of nonconformist churches in 1672.
G.A. Ref: D968/1

In the 1640s, with the coming of the Civil War, the authority of the Bishops collapsed and nonconformists were free to meet without fear. Approximately 20 years later, in 1662, with another Act of Uniformity, those ministers who did not agree with the new regulations were ejected from their livings. Over 2000 suffered in this way throughout the country, over 50 of them from Gloucestershire.

The Toleration Act of 1689 allowed Protestant dissenters to practice their own forms of religion in their own meeting houses and with their own burial grounds; this was not permitted for Roman Catholics for almost another hundred years. The nonconformist meeting houses had to be licensed by the Bishop's court or the court of the Quarter Sessions; more of these records in a later chapter.

In 1742, Dr Williams' Library in London started a nonconformist registry of births of Dissenters. Initially, this was intended to hold details of those nonconformist births that occurred within twelve miles of central London but there are many entries for those from farther afield. The registers were surrendered in 1837 and are now in the National Archives in Kew. Dr Williams' Library still exists in London today and is a source of a great many records concerning nonconformity; its catalogue can be found online at: www.dwlib.co.uk

Hardwicke's Marriage Act of 1753 made nonconformist marriages illegal except for those of the Jews and Quakers (the Society of Friends) who were permitted to keep their own records. All others had to marry in the parish church which can, therefore, give the impression that the bride and groom were really members of the Church of England when they were not necessarily so. In some cases, the couple were baptised there also before they married. Roman Catholics normally ignored this Act. Before 1753, people were permitted to contract a marriage without a church ceremony (called an irregular or clandestine marriage – more on these in a later chapter) and these events frequently went unrecorded.

> *Note: Hardwicke's Marriage Act of 1753 made nonconformist marriages illegal, except for those of Quakers and Jews.*

Soon after civil registration was introduced, a survey was made of existing nonconformist registers and it was suggested in the Non-Parochial Registers Act of 1840 that they be collected and held in the Public Record Office, now the National Archives at Kew. The majority of the early Gloucestershire registers were deposited there. Filmed copies of these registers are kept in Gloucestershire Archives and have been indexed. Many of the post-1837 registers are still held by the individual church.

When civil registration was introduced, nonconformists could marry in their own churches with their own ceremonies, but a registrar had to be present to record the information. Not until 1898 could nonconformists conduct and record their own marriage services and some still need the presence of a registrar as they do not have an authorised person to conduct the ceremony.

5. Nonconformist Registers

By 1851, almost a fifth of the population of England was nonconformist and, surprisingly, nearly half of the Welsh. So there is a good chance that, somewhere in your family tree, there are nonconformist ancestors.

Gloucestershire Nonconformist Records:
The number of nonconformist denominations that have existed throughout history is greater than those found within Gloucestershire but it is only necessary to concentrate here on the ones which have left vital records within the county. They are:

- Baptist
- Church of Christ
- Congregational / Independent
- Countess of Huntingdon's Connexion
- Jewish
- Methodist
- Moravian
- Presbyterian
- Roman Catholic
- Society of Friends / Quaker
- Unitarian
- Undenominational

Some nonconformist chapels and churches did not keep any records whilst other churches have disappeared and any records vanished with them. Some dissenting ministers kept the registers as their own property and took them when they moved on to pastures new. So far, a database of well over 600 names has been gathered for nonconformist chapels that existed or still exist in Gloucestershire but this undoubtedly includes some duplicates as buildings have changed hands and later been renamed and there are still names to add. Relatively few of these churches and chapels have deposited their records with Gloucestershire Archives.

Generally speaking, the records that you may find will be mainly births or baptisms, with a few marriages and burials. You might even come across nonconformist entries in the parish registers. One example comes from the Moreton in Marsh registers, where there is a page headed:

> "A Distinct Register of all persons Born in the Parish of Moreton in Marsh and not Baptised according to the rites and usage of the Church of England Beginning at Lammas in the year of 1705." G.A. Ref: P221 IN 1/1

The page is split into two halves, for baptisms and burials, and each has just one entry. The first states:

> Richard the Son of Richard Phipps, labourer, a reputed Papist, was born Sept. 14th.

The year for this was, presumably, 1705 but that is not obvious. The second entry is a much later burial:

John Proctor buried November (22?) 1723.

The 20th century burial register for Alvington also holds a nonconformist entry, as follows:

> The entry in the parish registers of St. Andrew's Church in Alvington for the burial of John O'Hare states, on the left, 'Papist. N.B. Notice of intention to bury is in the register' and, on the right, 'A Papist buried under Burial Law's Amendment Act 1880.' And the ceremony was performed by 'Elizabeth O'Hare (Person responsible for burial)'.
> G.A. Ref: P12 IN 1/8

Some deaths were recorded in nonconformist registers and, by the 18th century, some nonconformist churches had their own burial grounds and burial registers but most burials took place in the local parish churchyard at that time. Once their own grounds were full, nonconformists tended to use the civic cemeteries instead, many of which came into being in the mid 19th century, and where interments were carried out according to the rites of their own church.

Although most people were actually interred in the local churchyard, nonconformist burial grounds were and still are in existence in many areas of Gloucestershire. A catalogue of all known memorial sites and burial grounds, including civic cemeteries and war memorials, was produced prior to beginning a survey of the memorial inscriptions therein. It includes a list of 175 nonconformist burial grounds in the county and in Bristol. The catalogue is provided on the Memorial Inscriptions CD available on sale from the GFHS together with the inscriptions that have so far been transcribed.

5. Nonconformist Registers

From 1689, nonconformist meeting houses had to be licensed, either by the Bishop's court or by the Quarter Sessions. These records contained the names of some of the more important members of the chapel. The Personal Name Index at Gloucestershire Archives includes the names listed in the Diocesan Act Books of those dissenters applying for the licence between 1720 and 1812; unfortunately, this is a paper index available only in the searchroom. They have also been transcribed for each parish in the Hockaday Abstracts, again only available at the Archives. For a separate group of certificates, between 1784 and 1838 only a place name index exists.

You should be aware that nonconformist church members travelled much farther to worship than did the members of the Church of England who attended their local parish church. This is demonstrated by entries in the register for the Old Chapel in Stroud where it includes members from Avening, Chalford, Gloucester, Minchinhampton, Painswick, Rodborough, Tetbury, and Westonbirt within the county itself and from Brinkworth, Pinkney and Sherston in Wiltshire.

Likewise, the registers for Cam's Congregational Church includes entries for Berkeley, Bristol, Cam, Coaley, Dursley, Kings Stanley, Kingswood, North Nibley, Owlpen, Painswick, Slimbridge, Stinchcombe, Tetbury, Uley and Wotton under Edge. So, if your ancestor lived, for example, in Painswick, don't confine your search to the Painswick parish and nonconformist registers alone but throw the net much wider.

> Note: Nonconformists travelled much farther to worship than did members of the Church of England who attended their local parish church.

As there are too many individual chapels to list each one with details of the vital events that took place there, the parishes in which they are or were located will be given below for each denomination. To check the period covered by the registers, you will need to either check the Gloucestershire Archives online catalogue or visit in person. The records might include any or all of births, baptisms, adult baptisms, marriages, burials, church rolls, membership lists or monumental inscriptions.

The earliest nonconformist registers that exist within Gloucestershire Archives are those for the Gloucestershire and Wiltshire Monthly meetings of the Society of Friends. They begin with births from 1642, marriages from 1656 and burials from 1655. Almost as early are the birth registers for Coxwell Street Baptist Church in Cirencester which begin in 1651. Most, but not all, of the other registers start in the late 18th century.

If the vital records that you are seeking for a specific church are not to be found at Gloucestershire Archives, contact the Central Office for Archives for the particular denomination in which you are interested in case they are held centrally. They should be able to tell you what exists and where the records are to be found.

Discover Gloucestershire Ancestors

Baptist

The Baptists did not practice infant baptism so any reference to a baptism relates to an adult. Baptism usually but not always occurred when the person reached maturity at 21 years of age. These records can often be found in the books containing the church roll or church membership, so don't omit to check these when searching for your ancestor. Some chapels, however, did complete birth registers and about a dozen of these are held at Gloucestershire Archives.

> Note: Baptists did not practise infant baptism.

The earliest surviving register for Baptists held in Gloucestershire Archives is that from the Coxwell Street Baptist Church in Cirencester; it covers births during the period from 1651 to 1837 and burials between 1736 and 1839.

Baptists' marriages during the period between 1754 and 1837 had to take place in the Church of England parish church. Thereafter, until 1898, a registrar had to be present at the ceremony and the registers for these are held at the local Register Office. From 1898 onwards, Baptists could marry in their own church and maintain their own register. A copy register had to be forwarded to the Register Office when completed. Few early marriage registers have been deposited at Gloucestershire Archives.

Some Baptist registers exist at Gloucestershire Archives for chapels in the parishes of:

Awre	Horsley
Bibury	Kings Stanley
Bisley	Lydbrook
Blockley	Maiseyhampton
Bourton on the Water	Nailsworth
Charlton Kings	Newland
Cheltenham	Painswick
Chipping Campden	Slimbridge
Chipping Sodbury	Stow on the Wold
Cinderford	Stroud
Cirencester	Tetbury
Codrington	Tewkesbury
Cutsdean	Uley
Dymock	West Dean (Parkend)
Fairford	Woodchester
Gloucester	Wotton under Edge
Hawkesbury	Yorkley.

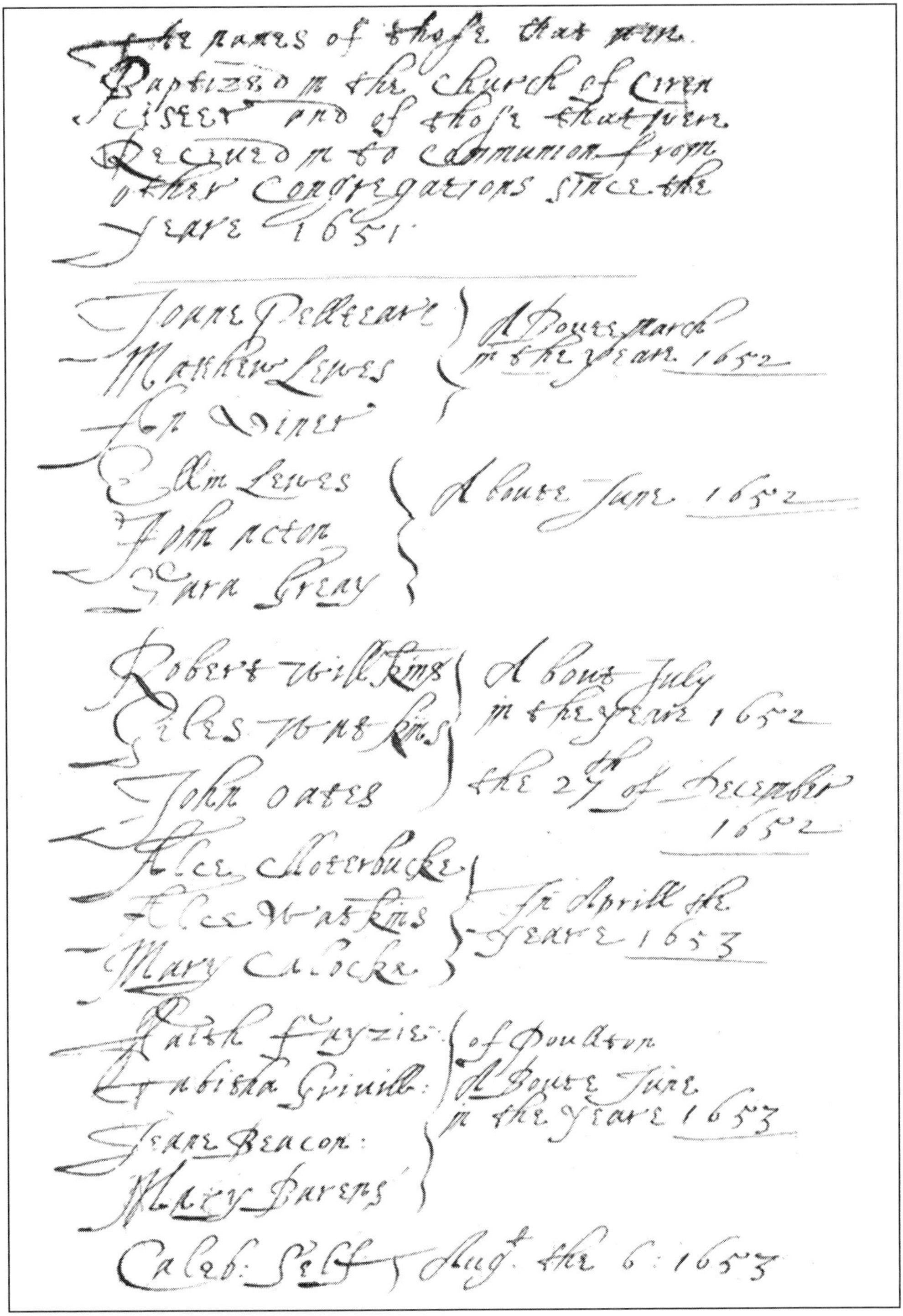

5. Nonconformist Registers

[Handwritten register entries, transcribed as legible:]

The names of those that were
Baptized in the Church of Ciren
cester and of those that were
Received into communion from
other congregations since the
yeare 1651.

Joane Pellteare ⎫ About March
Mathew Lewes ⎬ in the yeare 1652
[E]n Viner   ⎭

[A]m Lewes   ⎫
John Acton   ⎬ About June 1652
Sara Gray   ⎭

Robert Wilkins ⎫ About July
Giles Tomkins   ⎬ in the yeare 1652
                ⎭

John Oates — the 29th of December 1652

Alce Moverbucke ⎫
Elce Watkins   ⎬ in Aprill the
Mary Cocke   ⎭ yeare 1653

Faith Fryzier   ⎫ of Poulton
Tabitha Grinill ⎬ About June
Sarah Beacon   ⎬ in the yeare 1653
Mary Barens   ⎭

Caleb Self — August the 6: 1653

The first entries in the Coxwell Street Baptist Church in Cirencester dated 1651.
G.A. Ref: MF 1268

Church of Christ

This denomination developed in the 1840s from, it is believed, the Scottish and Welsh Baptists. There were two known churches of this denomination in the county:

- Church of Christ, Portland Tabernacle, Portland Street, Cheltenham
- Church of Christ, East End Tabernacle, Derby Road, Gloucester

The Cheltenham chapel was founded in 1885, the Gloucester one seven years later. Members of the church believed, like the Baptists, in adult baptism. A church roll exists for the Derby Road Tabernacle, in Gloucester, from 1892 to 1970 which includes some vital information. There are no records for the Cheltenham chapel at the Gloucestershire Archives.

> Note: The Church of Christ did not practise infant baptism.

Two consecutive pages from the Church Roll of Derby Road Tabernacle in Gloucester.
G.A. Ref: D5874/1/2

5. Nonconformist Registers

Congregational / Independent

The term 'Congregational' came into general usage in the 19th century. Before that, these churches were known as 'Independent' because they believed that each local church should be responsible for its own affairs and not be subject to a higher church authority. In the 1970s, many Congregational churches joined with Presbyterian churches to create the United Reformed Church.

The Independents believed in infant baptism but also required adults who converted to their religion to be baptised when they joined the church. The Baptist Church split from the Independents because they did not agree with infant baptism. The earliest Independent baptismal registers held in Gloucestershire Archives are for Stroud Old Chapel which begin in 1712, with burials starting from 1720.

> Note: Congregationalists / Independents practised infant baptism. They also baptised adult members when they joined the church.

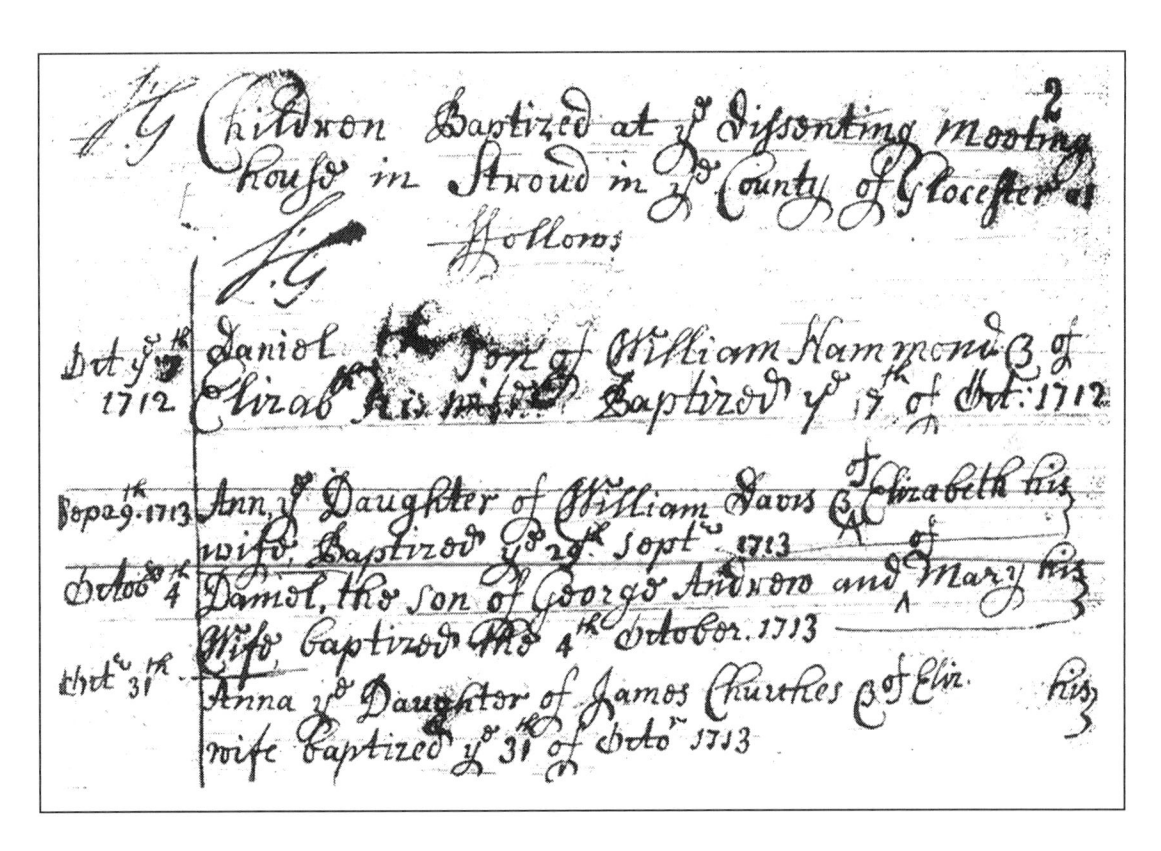

An excerpt from the Baptismal register of Stroud Old Meeting House, c.1712.
G.A. Ref: MF1270

Congregational registers exist for the parishes of:

Avening	Kingswood (nr Wotton)	Ruardean
Awre	Littledean	Saint Briavels
Berkeley	Marshfield	Slimbridge
Bisley	Minchinhampton	Stonehouse
Bristol	Mitcheldean	Stroud
Cam	Moreton in Marsh	Tetbury
Chedworth	Nailsworth	Tewkesbury
Cheltenham	Newent	Thornbury
Cirencester	Newland	Uley
Cranham	Newnham	Westbury on Severn
Fairford	North Nibley	Wickwar
Frampton Cotterell	Northleach	Winchcombe
Frampton upon Severn	Painswick	Winterbourne
Gloucester	Pitchcombe	Wotton under Edge
Kingswood (nr Bristol)	Rodborough	

Countess of Huntingdon's Connexion

This is a group of evangelical churches, founded in 1783 by Selina, Countess of Huntingdon, who split from the Church of England. At some stage it was associated with the Calvinistic Methodist movement of George Whitefield.

Connexion registers exist for the parishes of: Cheltenham, Gloucester and Coleford/Newland. These contain mainly birth and christening records with a few burial entries; the earliest baptisms date from the 1780s. The Connexion practised infant baptism.

> Note: The Countess of Huntingdon's Connexion practised infant baptism.

Hardwicke's Marriage Act meant that worshippers in the Countess of Huntingdon's Connexion had to marry, between 1754 and 1837, in the local parish church and after that, until 1898, nonconformist marriages could either be held in the local Register Office or in the nonconformist church with the registrar present; records of these, therefore, are all held by the Registrar. There is a local exception to this: two marriage registers dating from 1868 are held in the Gloucestershire Archives for St Mary's Connexion Chapel in Gloucester.

Some chapels eventually joined the Congregational denomination or the United Reformed Church. Today, there are Countess of Huntingdon's Connexion churches at Woodmancote near Cheltenham, Gotherington and Ebley. Any records relating to the Countess of Huntingdon's Connexion in Ebley will be found with the Ebley Congregational records.

5. Nonconformist Registers

> Sarah Selina Holder Daughter of James and Sarah Holder his Wife of the Parish of Stroud Water in the county of Glocester was Born May the Eight 1791 and Baptized June the thirteenth By me
>
> Thomas Watkins Minister
>
> Beatta Hillminster Daughter of William Hillminster and Mary his Wife of the Parish of Woodchester in the county of Glocester (But now living in Glocester city) was Born the 27th of May 1791 and Baptized the 19 of June
>
> By me Thomas Watkins Minister

A sample from the registers of St Mary's Chapel in Gloucester.
G.A. Ref: MF 1244

Jewish

Gloucestershire had a thriving Jewish community as far back as the Middle Ages and organised Jewish groups were in the city of Gloucester in the mid-eighteenth century but there have been only two known synagogues in the county: one in Elm Street in Cheltenham which is still active, having been built in 1837, closed in 1903 due to a lack of congregation and then re-founded in 1939, and the second one, in Gloucester, which no longer exists. The Gloucester synagogue was originally in Eastgate Street but, by 1802 had moved to Mercy Place off Southgate Street, near where the Royal Infirmary once stood.

For the Gloucester community, there is a brief handwritten document, held in Gloucestershire Archives, recording the names of the remains transferred from the Jewish burial ground 'near St. Michael's School' to the Coney Hill Cemetery in 1938. The Gloucester burials are also included on the CD 'Memorials and Citizens of Gloucester by Henry Yates Jones Taylor' produced by the Gloucestershire Family History Society.

A Transcript of some of the people buried in the Jewish Reserve at Coney Hill Cemetery, Gloucester. The remains were transferred from the old Jewish Cemetery in April 1938.
G.A. Ref: NC 66

All pre-1999 documents from the Cheltenham synagogue were recently transferred to Gloucestershire Archives (G.A. Ref: D3883). These included 'Registry of Deaths 1869-1895'.

An entry from the Registry of Deaths for members of the Cheltenham Jewish Synagogue.
Copyright of the Cheltenham Hebrew Congregation.
G.A. Ref: D3883 Box 28338

Methodist
The Methodist church began in the 1730s, originally known as Wesleyan Methodists after John Wesley. The church later split into several different movements, with a variety of names including the Methodists New Connexion, Primitive Methodists, Independent Methodists,

5. Nonconformist Registers

Calvinistic Methodists, Protestant Methodists and Bible Christians. Nowadays, almost all Methodists are united under the title of The Methodist Church.

In the beginning, the individual churches were organised into circuits with one minister who went round to the chapels. He would have one register and would complete it for all the baptisms and funerals that happened in his circuit, so the entries for each circuit cover a much wider area than you would find in a register for a single church. As the congregations grew, individual churches had their own minister and their own registers, although these still came under the auspices of the circuit. The Annual Methodist Conference oversees the circuits which meet quarterly, and they in turn oversee the individual chapels. Circuit boundaries have changed over the years so a particular church may appear in different circuits at different times.

Child baptism was practised and most of the registers now held at Gloucestershire Archives hold baptisms only. The earliest baptismal register in the archives is for Westbury-on-Trym which starts in 1793.

Marriage in a Methodist church was forbidden by the Hardwicke Marriage Act and it wasn't until 1898 that marriages were recorded by Methodist ministers. Most of these more recent marriage registers remain at the relevant church where they are still in use.

> *Note: The Methodists did practise infant baptism.*

There was a strong Methodist presence in Gloucestershire, partly due in the early years to the outdoor preaching of George Whitefield who was born at the Bell Inn in Gloucester in 1714, went to the Crypt School and from there to Pembroke College in Oxford where he met John and Charles Wesley.

Methodist Circuit registers are held in Gloucestershire Archives for the following areas:

Abenhall	Cheltenham(7)	Farmington*
Alderton	Churcham	Gloucester(5)
Aldsworth*(2)	Churchdown(2)	Great Barrington*
Andoversford	Cinderford(4)	Great Rissington*
Ashchurch	Cirencester	Hartpury
Avening	Clopton*	Hawling
Beckford	Coln Rogers	Horsley
Bibury*	Coln St Aldwyn*	Icomb*
Bishops Cleeve	Corse	Kemerton
Bisley(5)	Deerhurst	Kings Stanley
Bledington*	Didbrook	Leigh
Bourton on the Water*	East Dean(7)	Leonard Stanley
Bromsberrow	Eastington	Little Barrington*(2)
Cam	Eastleach Martin*	Longhope
Chaceley	Eastleach Turville*	Lower Swell*(2)
Charlton Kings	Fairford*	Lydbrook(2)

Lydney(3)
Minchinhampton(3)
Minsterworth
Miserden
Mitcheldean(2)
Monmouth/Forest of Dean
Moreton in Marsh*
Nailsworth
Newent(2)
Newland(4)
Newnham
Northleach*
Norton
Oddington(2)
Painswick(2)
Pauntley
Prestbury
Randwick(2)
Redmarley
Rodmarton
Ruardean(3)
Rudford
Sandhurst
Sherborne*
Shipton Oliffe
Staunton
Staverton
Stonehouse
Stow on the Wold
Stroud(2)
Tetbury
Tewkesbury(2)
Tibberton
Tirley
Toddington
Turkdean
Upton St Leonards
Upper Slaughter*(2)
Westbury on Severn(2)
Westcote*(4)
West Dean(10)
Whitminster
Winchcombe(3)
Windrush*
Withington
Woolaston(3).

*   Indicates that these were within the Oxford Methodist circuit. Transcripts are held at Gloucestershire Archives.

( )   The number in brackets is the number of different chapels with records in the circuit.

The earliest Methodist Circuit registers begin in 1829 and are all centred around the Stroud area of the county. They contain christening records. The earliest Methodist Chapel registers date from 1793 and are those for births and baptisms in Westbury-on-Trym.

There are not so many surviving registers for the individual Methodist chapels. They exist within the parishes of:

Barnwood
Berkeley
Bristol(4)
Cam
Cheltenham(4)
Churchdown
Cinderford
Cirencester
Dursley
East Dean(2)
Eastington(nr Stonehouse)
Gloucester(7)
Horsley
Leonard Stanley
Lydbrook
Lydney
Mangotsfield
Minchinhampton
Minsterworth
Monmouth/Dean Forest
Nailsworth
Newent
Newland(2)
Prestbury
Quedgeley
Rudford
Stonehouse
Stroud
Tewkesbury
Westbury on Severn
Westbury-on-Trym
West Dean(3).

If registers for both the circuit and the individual church still exist, you may find that there are duplicate entries. However, you should always check both sources, in case the event was only recorded in one register, to check for errors or the possibility of additional information.

The first entries in the baptismal register of the Royal Well Chapel on the
Cheltenham Methodist Circuit.
G.A. Ref: D3418/2/10/1

Moravian
The Moravian church, also known as the United Brethren, began in Bohemia and came to London in 1738. It was similar in doctrine to the Presbyterian church and was unusual in the fact that it was the only nonconformist church to have bishops.

There were only ever four churches of the Moravian Brethren in Gloucestershire, one in the City of Bristol in Maudlin Street, the Whitefield's Tabernacle which opened in Kingswood near Bristol in 1742, one in Apperley in the parish of Deerhurst and the last one on the border with Monmouthshire at Brockweir. The latter church is still active.

There are no known registers for the Apperley church which was eventually taken over by the Methodists, nor for the Maudlin Street church in Bristol. Any Brockweir registers are presumably still held at the church, so you will need to contact the minister for access to those. Gloucestershire Archives holds copies of the registers of baptisms and burials for the Kingswood church, the originals being held at the National Archives.

Baptisms

No.	Name	Parents	When born	Baptized	Minister	Sponsors
1	Ann	Daughter of Thomas and Sarah Jarret Kingswood	April 28th 1805		James Grundy	
2	George Ignatius	Son of George Ignatius and Esther Golding	April 6 1805	May 18. 1806	James Grundy	Departed A 6/we
3	Ephraim	Son of Charles and Susanna Golding		Feb. 22d 1807	James Grundy	

A sample of the entries in the Kingswood Moravian Church at Kingswood near Bristol.
G.A. Ref: MF 1254

Note: The Moravian Church practised child baptism.

Presbyterian

The Presbyterian Church was founded in the second half of the 16th century. Over the years, it has had strong links with the Congregational movement and in 1972, joined some of them to form the United Reformed Church. They practised infant baptism but also baptised someone when he or she joined the church so many registers include a date of birth as well as a baptismal date.

There have been several Presbyterian chapels erected in Cheltenham as well as others in Cinderford, Dursley, Gloucester, Tewkesbury, Winterbourne and Wotton under Edge.

Note: The Presbyterians practised child baptism but also baptised adults when they joined the church.

5. Nonconformist Registers

The earliest Presbyterian register for the county is from the Barton Street chapel in Gloucester. It has births and baptisms going back to 1740. A transcript is available at Gloucestershire Archives.

> *Register of Children baptized*
>
> 60. Mary, Daughter of Thomas Plight, and Mary his Wife, baptized April 20. 1740. by J. Hodge
>
> William, Son of Mr William Buchanan, and Elizabeth his Wife, baptized April 22 1740. by J. H.
>
> Stephen, Son of John Hodge, and Elizabeth his Wife baptized May 29. 1740, by the Revd Mr John Evans of Cirencester
>
> Mary, Daughter of Mr John Ashmead Junr and Hannah his Wife baptized July 13. 1740. by J. Hodge.
>
> Elizabeth, Daughter of Charles Wells and Elizabeth his Wife baptized Octobr. 5. —
>
> Richd. Son of Richd. Allen of Tewkesbury and ___ his Wife baptized there Novr. 10. by JH
>
> James, Son of William Savery and Abigail his Wife, baptized Novr. 26.

An example of the baptismal register for the Barton Street, Gloucester, Presbyterian Chapel.
G.A. Ref: MF 1267

Roman Catholic

Roman Catholics kept their own records of baptisms, marriages and burials from the 16th century but very few of the early ones have survived. Gloucestershire is included in the Roman Catholic diocese of Clifton. Only three Roman Catholic churches existed in the county before 1837; they did not surrender their registers to the National Archives in 1841. The churches were:

- ➢ St Gregory's Church in Cheltenham, which has deposited its registers from 1809 to 1964 at Gloucestershire Archives.
- ➢ St Peter's in Gloucester has registers dating from 1789. Those up to 1856 have been deposited at Gloucestershire Archives. The rest remain with the priest.
- ➢ St Joseph's Chapel, Bristol (now called the Church of St Mary on the Quay) had registers from 1777 to 1809 printed by the Catholic Record Society.

Any other Roman Catholic registers that existed for the Clifton diocese before 1780 were destroyed in the Gordon Riots. Some Roman Catholic monumental inscriptions exist in a collection by J. H. Matthews printed by Catholic Record Society.

Despite the 1606 Act which said that Roman Catholics had to be baptised, married and buried by Anglican clergy, many baptisms and marriages were carried on in secret, often in private houses, although burials appear to have taken place in the parish churchyard and are recorded in the parish registers, even as recently as the early 20th century.

> Note: Roman Catholics practised infant baptism but also baptised adults when they converted to Catholicism.

Since there were few Roman Catholic churches in the county, the congregation came from a wide area. Baptisms were performed in infancy but there were also adult baptisms when someone converted to Catholicism and baptisms of entire families at one time. Latin was usually used to record the events. From the start of the 19th century, with the influx of immigrant families, particularly those of Irish and Italian origin, there have been more Roman Catholic churches built in Gloucestershire but their registers still remain with the priest.

An example from the baptism register of St Gregory's Roman Catholic church in Cheltenham.
G.A. Ref: MF 1560

5. Nonconformist Registers

Society of Friends / Quaker

The Society of Friends, also known as the Quakers, began in the middle of the 17th century. They did not believe in baptism but did record births, marriages and burials. Births were sometimes entered retrospectively but their recording was considered important to prove legitimacy and for the inheritance of property. Standardised registers were not introduced until 1776; from 1837, the civil marriage register was adopted.

The Quakers did not have to comply with Hardwicke's Marriage Act so were permitted to hold their own marriage ceremonies. Records of these events are often much fuller than those held in the parish church, sometimes recording the names of all who attended the wedding.

Before the 18th century, many Quakers were buried in the parish churchyard but, as they had not been baptised, this was usually performed without a formal service and in unconsecrated ground without a headstone. Some Quakers were buried in their own gardens, one reportedly in Hawkesbury. Thereafter, many Meeting Houses had their own burial ground.

In Gloucestershire, the Society of Friends was particularly associated with the cloth industry so was strong in the areas around Cirencester and Nailsworth. There were also congregations established in Cheltenham, Gloucester, Painswick, Tewkesbury and in Frenchay near Bristol.

Some registers exist for all of these meetings, the earliest being for the Gloucestershire and Wiltshire Monthly Meeting which has birth records going back from 1837 to 1642, marriages from 1656 and burials from 1655. The Painswick Meeting minutes hold records of births, marriages and burials from 1647 onwards. All other records begin at a much later date.

Gloucestershire Archives holds many other Quaker records such as their Monthly Meeting Minute Books which including testimonies, records of movement to other Meeting Places across the country and sometimes overseas, intentions to marry and disownments

Dates on Quaker records should be handled with care – they used numbers for the months not names but their system corresponded to that used by the rest of the country, namely that March was the start of the year until 1751; thereafter January became the first month of the year.

The Gloucestershire Family History Society has recently produced a CD containing a transcript of and index to the Gloucestershire and Wiltshire Quaker registers held at the Archives covering the period from 1642 to 1908. This is available for purchase from the society. It covers births from 1642 to 1837, marriages from 1656 to 1908 and burials from 1655 to 1908.

> *Note: The Quakers did not believe in baptism but did keep good records of births, marriages and burials.*

A Marriage entry from the Painswick Quaker Registers of 1690.
G.A. Ref: D1340/C6/R1

Unitarian
This denomination had developed by the late 17th century mainly from the Independent or Presbyterian faiths, with influences of the Congregational and Baptist movements but the name of Unitarian was rarely used until 1813 when the Unitarian Relief Act came into force. Before that it was a crime to deny the doctrine of the Trinity, a doctrine which the Unitarians did not support. The Unitarian church was run by the individual congregations and believed in child baptism.

Some registers exist at Gloucestershire Archives for the Royal Well Chapel in Bayshill, Cheltenham which was founded in 1832 and built 12 years later. They include marriages from 1843 to 1847 and burials from 1846 to 1862 but no baptisms. The Barton Street Chapel in Gloucester was founded in 1662 but not built until 1699. It remained as a Unitarian chapel until 1967 when it became a Society of Friends meeting house. Gloucestershire Archives has a transcript of the original registers which began in 1740 and which are held at the National Archives. There are also some monumental inscription transcriptions for the latter.

5. Nonconformist Registers

The Gosditch Street chapel in Cirencester was in existence from 1672 until 1969. The only record from the Cirencester chapel, held at Gloucestershire Archives, is a transcript of some monumental inscriptions. A chapel was founded at Marshfield in 1680 and built nearly 20 years later. Any records for this church are believed to be at Bath Record Office with the Bath Trim Street Chapel records. A Stroud chapel was founded in Lansdown Road between 1876 and 1891. Again, any existing records are believed to be at Bath Record Office.

> *Note: The Unitarians practised infant baptism.*

```
           GLOUCESTER   BARTON   STREET

     REGISTER  of  CHILDREN  BAPTIZED  Since

                    March, 1740

                                    The following were
    Note: John Hodge, D.D., Minister, 1740-1749.  Registered by Dr.Hodge
       Name.       Son or daughter of       Baptized        By
                                              1740
    1. Mary        Thos and Mary Flight      20 April      J.Hodge
    2. William     Wm and Elizth Buchanan    22 April         ,,
    3. Stephen     John and Elizth Hodge     27 May        Rev.J.Evans
                                                          (of Cirencester)
    4. Mary        John and Hannah Ashmead,jr. 13 July    J. Hodge
    5. Elizabeth   Charles and Elizth Wills  8 Oct            ,,
    6. Richard     Richard and - Allen       10 Nov           ,,
                    of Tewkesbury
    7. James       William and Abigail Sawry 26 Nov           ,,
                    (? Sowery)
```

A transcript of the Barton Street Chapel baptism registers of 1740.
G.A. Ref: NC 93

Undenominational

Several of the Gloucestershire churches did not belong to any of the previously mentioned denominations but called themselves 'Undenominational'. They were sometimes called the 'Free Church' but this name can also be applied to all nonconformist denominations so it can be rather confusing at times. Many of these churches practised adult rather than infant baptism.

There were three undenominational churches with records now in Gloucestershire Archives. There are registers for the Salem Free Church of Berry Hill, Coleford, for some 20th century marriages and some monumental inscriptions for both the Cud Hill burial site in Painswick and the Common burial site in Postlip, near Winchcombe.

> Note: Many undenominational churches practised adult rather than infant baptism.

Huguenots

This chapter on nonconformists would not be complete without at least a mention of the Huguenots. They were French Protestants who arrived *en masse* in the 1680s to avoid persecution in their own country. Many of them settled in Gloucestershire, particularly in the hills south of Stroud where the cloth industry was prevalent. Some names were anglicised at the time. All registers of the Huguenot churches are held in the National Archives at Kew. All have been published by the Huguenot Society; Volume 20 of the series contains the registers of the church in Bristol. The Huguenot Library in London has a large collection of additional material relating to the Huguenots.

Indexes

The GFHS have produced three CDs containing baptisms and burials of Gloucestershire nonconformist churches and chapels (see their website for a list of chapels included) which incorporate entries from all the registers held at Gloucestershire Archives. This is additional to the Quaker CD. These CDs are available to purchase from their website.

Members of Cheltenham Local History Society have written *A Chronology of Nonconformity and Dissent in Cheltenham* which includes great detail on the history of nonconformity in the town but no record of baptisms, etc..

The Eureka Partnership has produced printed indexes to:

> Chipping Norton and Stow Primitive Circuit: Baptisms 1863-1930
> Stroud & Cirencester Wesleyan Methodist Circuit: Vol. 1 Baptisms 1811-1848; Members 1791, 1809, 1824. Vol. 2 Baptisms 1849-1928, Marriages 1849-1863

A survey of surviving nonconformist records in Gloucestershire was compiled in 1976 and the list is available in Gloucestershire Archives. It omits the area in the south of the county as that was then in Avon. A similar survey, but this time of the chapels themselves rather than the records was prepared by the Filton Historical Research Group in 1989 and lists the 'Nonconformist Chapels of Northavon', an area more or less equivalent to South Gloucestershire.

Chapter 6

Probate

'Let's choose executors, and talk of wills.'

*Richard II, Act III, Scene II by
William Shakespeare
1564 – 1616, English playwright*

Once you have drawn up the skeleton of your family tree, with as much information from vital records and censuses as you have been able to discover so far, you begin to look around for any additional records that might help to fill in the gaps and clarify some puzzling relationships. A good source of this kind of information can be found in probate records.

When someone dies, their property and personal belongings are distributed to other people, usually to members of their immediate family and friends. There are four ways of doing this:

- By means of a will, officially sanctioned by probate
- Without a valid will, officially sanctioned by letters of administration
- By a nuncupative will, officially sanctioned by letters of administration
- Unofficially without recourse to probate at all.

The official way to pass on property and personal belongings is to write a will, disposing of land, goods and money, which will eventually go to probate, the official sanction that the will has been legally accepted as valid, has conformed to the existing laws, has been properly witnessed and has not been tampered with in any way. Anyone can write a will but they are only legally binding when they have been proved (i.e. have been granted probate). A will must include at least one executor who will distribute the estate after death, must be dated and signed and then witnessed by two or more people who are not beneficiaries of the will.

The problem for genealogists is, however, that relatively few people made a will, not wanting to consider their own mortality or not expecting death to come so soon. It seems that, even today, only about one third of people make a will and, in times past, it was an even smaller proportion of the population, some suggest as little as 5%. Wills were generally made in later life although, in the past, soldiers, sailors and those travelling overseas were often persuaded to make a will before risking their lives on the wild seas and venturing to places unknown.

> Note: Fewer people made wills in the past, maybe as little as 5% of the population.

Wills were made for a variety of purposes:

- to settle affairs
- to provide for dependants
- to cover the remarriage of the widow
- to remember relatives, friends and servants
- to donate to charity.

Generally speaking, we expect those with more money and property to make a will compared to those at the lower end of the scale but this is not always the case: the Gloucestershire Archives Wills database actually lists over 500 labourers who left wills between 1541 and 1858 as opposed to less than half as many gentlemen so we should never assume that our labouring ancestors did not make provision for their family and we should always check to see if they did.

6. Probate

Comparatively few women left wills before 1882 when the Married Women's Property Act came into force; before then, a wife had no legal identity so anything belonging to a married woman was deemed to be her husband's property and would be dealt with in his will. Those who did make wills were usually widows and spinsters. Often, you will find that the will of a maiden aunt is much more informative than that of the male testator because they tended to give to a wider range of relatives, citing brothers and sisters, nephews and nieces, etc., so finding the will of a female ancestor can be very helpful in filling the gaps on your family tree.

> Note: Before 1882, a married woman rarely left a will as everything belonged to her husband; only widows and single women left wills.

You do need to be careful of the relationships mentioned in some wills; usually the relationship given is exactly as we would expect it to be today but brother or sister could, for example, mean brother-in-law or sister-in-law or step-brother or half-sister, etc.; nephew and niece could actually refer to a grandchild, and cousin may include any relation by marriage.

Sometimes, important members of the family are not mentioned at all. This does not necessarily mean they have been cut off without the proverbial penny! They may have been given money earlier, for instance to set up in business or purchase property, or have been given money as part of a marriage settlement or dowry.

A will, either in the testator's handwriting or, more usually, written by a scribe, contains some or all of the following:

- the name, occupation and residence or parish of the testator
- the date that the will was written
- a religious statement thanking God and Jesus Christ for worldly goods; if it mentions the Virgin Mary, there is a strong possibility that the testator was Roman Catholic
- a comment on the state of physical and mental health; the latter was designed to counteract challenges to the will on the basis that the testator was not in full possession of his mental faculties when the will was written
- a statement as to where the deceased wished to be buried
- an instruction to pay debts and funeral expenses
- a list of individual bequests, each one usually beginning with the word 'Item' except the first which began: 'Imprimis'. These are generally gifts to family members and relationships are normally mentioned
- the name(s) of the executor(s)
- the deceased's signature or mark
- the signatures or marks of the witnesses.

If a will was made many years before the death of the testator, he may have felt the need to change his bequests but not wished to make a completely new will. In that situation, he would add a **codicil** which again would be signed, dated and witnessed. This can often be very helpful to family historians as it could tell them of changes in the family that had occurred during the intervening period.

When probate is granted, a probate clause is added to the end of the will, which is then returned to the executor so that he can carry out the deceased person's wishes. The probate clause tells you:

- the name of the executor(s)
- when and where the will was proved.

The latter gives you an indication, using the date the will was written, of the actual date of death if it was previously unknown.

Most wills are proved within the first few months after the death of the testator but this is not always the case so check for at least five years and longer if you have reason to believe a will was definitely left. For a variety of reasons, for instance, the ill health or death of an executor, or the executor lived overseas or the will was challenged, some wills were not proved for many years and on very rare occasions, even as long as 100 years. *Bleak House* by Charles Dickens, which is based on a dispute in the Court of Chancery concerning the inheritance of the Jarndyce family, may have been fiction but was based upon the way things occasionally were. 'But Jarndyce and Jarndyce still drags its dreary length before the Court, perennially hopeless.'

> Note: Most wills are proved within a few months of the testator's death but you should always check several years thereafter if you don't find it.

The second means of distributing a person's property after death is by obtaining **letters of administration.** If a person dies intestate (without having made a will) and there is valuable property to dispose of, or there is likely to be a dispute over who gets what, the next of kin or close relative goes to the probate court and requests Letters of Administration which grant him or her the right to administer the estate and distribute the deceased person's land, goods and money, according to the fixed rules of inheritance of the time, e.g. first to the spouse, then the children, after that to the parents, and so on.

There were three different systems relating to the ancient rules of inheritance. These were:

- Primogeniture
- Gavelkind
- Borough English.

Primogeniture is the right, whether by law or by custom, of the first-born son to inherit the father's whole estate and title to the exclusion of any younger brothers and sisters. This was a Norman tradition and was the system in most common usage throughout England. Most of the early examples you find will be of this type.

The second system was that of Gavelkind whereby the tenant's inheritance was divided equally between the sons, once the widow had received her share. It was a very early system for allocating an estate found mainly in Kent, though occasionally elsewhere. It was abolished by an Act of Parliament in 1925 and is not known to have been in use in Gloucestershire

Borough English, the last of the three systems, was the ancient custom by which, if a father died intestate, his real estate went to the youngest son rather than to the eldest son. It has been suggested that the eldest son was more likely to have been provided for by his father during his lifetime and that the youngest son's needs were the greatest. Another suggestion is that, because in feudal times the landowner had the right to bed any girl who married his tenant, the legitimacy of the first-born child was suspect so the youngest son became the heir. Borough English did exist in Gloucestershire and as recently as 1914, the local council passed a resolution to maintain the ancient custom. It was finally abolished by Act of Parliament in 1924. Typing 'Borough English' into the Gloucestershire Archives online catalogue indicates six documents relating to this custom, four of them relating to locations within the City of Gloucester itself, the other two being correspondence concerning the practice.

Today, there are rules of intestacy which determine who gets what when a person has died. This depends upon the value of the deceased's estate but basically the order of inheritance goes from married or civil partner, to the children of the deceased and then to less close relatives such as parents, grandchildren, and siblings, and finally to the more distant relatives of aunts, uncles, cousins, nephews and nieces. If no relatives exist, the estate passes to the government. An alphabetical list of unclaimed estates is regularly produced of those estates for which no relative has been located. Details included on the list are the name of the deceased, date of death and a short address. e.g.

  SMITH John 5.11.1989   Cheltenham, Gloucestershire

The list, which goes back 30 years, can be found on www.bonavacantia.gov.uk

Letters of administration could also be requested if an executor couldn't or wouldn't carry out the duties required or where the guardianship of a minor is involved.

> *Note: Letters of Administration were granted to the next of kin when a person died intestate.*

The third way of disposing of someone's property after death is by way of a **nuncupative will**. This is the will produced when the deceased person managed to dictate his wishes before death but a valid will was not made and signatures witnessed. The spoken words, which had to be before at least two witnesses, were later written down by someone else.

Most nuncupative wills are easy to recognise because they begin with the word Memorandum (the example given does not) and specify that they were a spoken record of the deceased's wishes regarding his or her estate. They were declared invalid by the Wills Act of 1837 except for soldiers or sailors on active service at the time. In the event of a nuncupative will, the next of kin or another appropriate adult would apply for the Letters of Administration and then, when granted them, would carry out the deceased's wishes.

Finally, if a person died intestate and they did not have much property to distribute, this was usually done by the family or friends without official intervention. Recourse to the courts was unnecessary.

> "My will and desire is that every body should be paid every farthing I owe and if anything should remain after my debts and funeral expenses are paid my wish and desire is that my daughter Ann should have it."
>
> The above words were spoken by Elizabeth Maisey of Cheltenham in the County of Gloucester widow on the twenty sixth day of June last during her last illness and within a few hours of her death in the presence of us the undersigned who were requested by her to witness the same as witness our hands the ninth day of July one thousand eight hundred and twenty one.
>
> Elizabeth Williams
Anne Collins
Mary Maisey
Mary Giles x her mark.

The Nuncupative Will of Elizabeth Maisey of Cheltenham, 1821
G.A. Ref: GDR/B4/2/M50

Wills before 1858

Before 1858, all wills were proved in a hierarchy of ecclesiastical courts of which there were between two and three hundred. There is no centralised index covering these wills so you will probably need to check out more than one index to try to locate an ancestor's will. The church courts, which could charge to prove a will, were, in descending order of importance,

- the Prerogative Courts (of which there were two, Canterbury and York)
- the Bishops' Consistory Courts
- the Archdeaconry Courts
- the Peculiar Courts.

Which ecclesiastical court granted probate or letters of administration depended to some extent on the wealth of the deceased and where his estates were situated. If he left property in more than one diocese, then the will was usually proved in a Prerogative Court. If the deceased's estate lay within one diocese, then the will was normally proved in the Bishop's Consistory Court. For estates within one deanery, the Archdeacon's courts would be used. However, no Gloucestershire wills appear to have been dealt with by the Archdeacon's courts. Finally, if the person died in a Peculiar, then the wills were proved by the incumbent of that area.

After the Civil War and during the Commonwealth period, 1649-1660, all ecclesiastical courts were abolished so no local probate was officially carried out in the county during those years.

The system was replaced by a central Court of Civil Commission. All wills proved during this period should be found in the PCC collection at the National Archives at Kew where they have over 2000 Gloucestershire wills including, of course, those which would normally have been proved in the Prerogative Court. One such will, for Thomas Rogers of Bentham, dated 1659, has a probate clause beginning:

'The Keepers of the Liberty of England by Authority of Parliament ....' and ends ... 'Given at London under the Seale of the Court for Probate of Wills and granting Administrations the day and year aforesaid.'

However, it seems that what should have taken place did not always happen as there are over 250 wills proved during that period that are held at Gloucestershire Archives, some proved by the Bishop's Court and listed in the genealogical database. The probate clause on the will of Eleanor Brown of Beverston begins:

'This will was proved at Gloucester 2nd October 1652 before Edward Williams priest surrogate of Francis Barber Doctor of Laws, Chancellor of Godfrey Goodman, Bishop of Gloucester .....'

After 1858, when the two prerogative courts were abolished, the granting of probate or letters of administration was taken out of the hands of the religious bodies and, by the Probate Act of 1857, a national system was created under the jurisdiction of the Court of Probate.

Prerogative Court wills
The Prerogative Court of York covered the northern counties of Cheshire, Cumberland, Durham, Lancashire, Northumberland, Nottinghamshire, Westmorland and Yorkshire. The Prerogative Court of Canterbury, the more senior of the two prerogative courts, covered the rest of England and Wales.

The records of the Prerogative Court of Canterbury (abbreviated to PCC) are held at the National Archives at Kew which has an online search facility; wills found in the index there can be purchased online for a small charge and then downloaded. There are more than 30,000 Gloucestershire wills from 1541 to 1858 held there. Searches can be made using forename, surname, occupation, location, keyword or period. Use the link below to search for a PCC will for your ancestor.

http://www.nationalarchives.gov.uk/documentsonline

Although PCC wills are usually the ones of interest to Gloucestershire researchers that does not mean that a will relating to a Gloucestershire ancestor is not to be found in the Prerogative Court of York (PCY) collection so it should not be ignored. The probate documents of the PCY are held at the Borthwick Institute in York. In fact, a very brief search of the PCY index (recently added to the British Origins website), using the surnames of Smith, Jones and Brown, found two entries:

1853	Benjamin Chapman Brown of Uley
1856	Robert Edmund Mower Smith of Cheltenham.

Richard Gwinnett, although expecting to inherit his father's estate in Shurdington in Gloucestershire, was actually living and studying in Lincoln's Inn in London. The father, George Gwinnett, did not pay Elizabeth Thomas her legacy as he disapproved of her long romance with his son and she had to resort to taking him to the Court of Chancery.
This example will was proved by the Prerogative Court of Canterbury.
National Archives Ref: PROB11/561

The Prerogative Courts tended to prove wills for those people with greater wealth and with estates in more than one diocese but, once again, they do contain wills of people from the working classes. There are 67 wills for Gloucestershire labourers in the PCC collection of over 30,000 wills for county testators. The Prerogative Court of Canterbury also dealt with probate of people living and dying overseas, including soldiers and sailors.

6. Probate

Wills proved in the Consistory Court of the Bishop of Gloucester
Very early Gloucestershire wills, those proved prior to 1541, should be held at the Worcestershire or Herefordshire Record Offices because the Diocese of Gloucester did not exist until that year, when it was created from the earlier Dioceses of Worcester and Hereford. There does not appear to be an online index to these wills but books listing the wills in these two dioceses exist:

- *A Calendar of Probate and Administrative Acts in the Consistory Court of the Bishops of Hereford, 1407-1550*, edited by Michael A Faraday covers wills from many of the Forest of Dean parishes; it is organised by parish.
- *A Calendar of Wills and Administrations Registered in the Consistory Court of the Bishop of Worcester: 1451-[1652]* covers pre 1541 Gloucestershire wills for the rest of the county.

For the early wills proved in the Gloucester Diocese, there are two similar books covering later periods for Gloucestershire wills. They are:

- *A Calendar of Wills Proved in the Consistory Court of the Bishop of Gloucester, Volume 1, 1541 – 1650*. Issued by the British Record Society Ltd in 1895; Edited by W.P.W. Phillimore and L.L. Duncan.
- *A Calendar of Wills Proved in the Consistory Court of the Bishop of Gloucester, Volume 2, 1660 – 1800*. Issued by the British Record Society Ltd in 1907; Edited by W.P.W. Phillimore and E.A. Fry

A third volume, covering the period between 1801 and 1858 was intended but never reached publication. Instead, a paper index was eventually produced and this is kept in a large folder at Gloucestershire Archives.

The wills listed in these two books and the folder, covering the period from 1541 to 1858, have been entered into the online genealogical database of Gloucestershire Archives which contains a list of over 70,000 of them. As with all indexes, you should check with other sources, such as a copy of the books mentioned above, to ensure that the transcribed information is accurate. You can access the wills database at:

http://ww3.gloucestershire.gov.uk/genealogy/Search.aspx

The index can be searched on surname, forename, gender, occupation if known, year of probate, and parish. It will provide the reference that leads to the will. All the wills indexed in the database have a reference number which includes the year of probate. As the wills have all been filmed, you only need to use the year and the reference to locate a facsimile of the will on microfiche at the Archives. You can then print a copy for your records. Outsize wills have been copied onto microfilm. Should you be unable to visit the Archives in person, you can use the ordering service to get your copy, via:

http://www.gloucestershire.gov.uk/index.cfm?articleid=17203

However, the index on the genealogical database is not yet complete for the Consistory Court wills; there are some wills that still need to be included in the online database. To begin with, there are the details of nearly 600 Peculiar wills to be added, together with the information on various wills and administrations that have been deposited at Gloucestershire Archives since the Calendars were produced.

When a will was proved in the Consistory Court, the probate clause was copied into the court's Act Books and, if the will itself was subsequently lost, this could be the only place where you can find evidence that such a will once existed. Up to 1733, these clauses were in Latin. The Act Books can be found in the GDR series and are listed in the book *A Catalogue of the Record of the Bishop and Archdeacons* by Isabel M Kirby, published in 1968.

If a will was disputed, the case was taken back to the ecclesiastical court by the litigants. If the executor did not deal with the estate in the proper manner, this was also returned to the court to be examined. The surviving records for these cases are held in the GDR/B4/2 series of the Consistory Court documents of which there are over 1700. These are by far the most interesting of the probate documents you can find as they generally give more background information on the families involved.

Take, for instance, the will of George Gwinnett who died in 1734. The main section of his will, written on 2nd March 1733, stated:

> I give and bequeath unto my daughter Martha Gwinnett all my real and personal estate, all and singular of my goods, cattle and chattels of what nature and kind soever and wheresoever they be whereof I shall dye possessed, whom I also hereby nominate, make, ordain and constitute sole executrix of this my last will and testament, she paying to each of my sons and daughters within twelve months after my decease the sum of one shilling and also discharging and paying all my debts and funeral expenses.

His daughter, Martha, a spinster who was named as executrix in his will, was granted probate on 25th April 1734. She then had an inventory made of her father's 'goods, chattels, rights and creditts' which amounted in value to £165 11s 0d. During the next year, Martha paid the funeral expenses, George's rent arrears owing to the Mayor and Burgesses of the City of Gloucester as well as to other people from whom he rented property, repaid the loans and interest thereon to several people, paid the wages of Walter Jones and, amongst other oddments, paid for two hogsheads of cider that the deceased had received.

Martha was summoned to appear before the Consistory Court on 11th December 1735 to explain why she had not paid William Humphreys, maltster of Gloucester, the money that he had been owed by her father. In the court documents are the inventory that she brought to court with her and the account of all that she had spent, illustrating that she had paid out more than her father had left. The papers do not include the conclusion to which the court came. Presumably William Humphreys did not receive the money he was owed.

A copy of the will of George Gwinnett of Great Shurdington, proved at Gloucester 1723.
The probate clause, before 1773, was in Latin.
G.A. Ref: 1723/45

Will of George Gwinnett of Great Shurdington
11 March 1723

In the name of God Amen, I **George Gwinnett** of Great Shurdington in the Diocese and County of Gloucester, gent, being in reasonable good health and at present of sound judgment and good sense and memory Doe make my last Will and Testament in manner following:

Always possessing and declaring my full purpose and steadfast resolution to dye in the true faith of our Lord Jesus Christ my only Saviour and Redeemer in and through whose meritts I hope for salvation and the fitt and full pardon and foregiveness of all my great and manifold sins and offences; And my worldly estate I dispose of as followeth:

Imprimis:
All and singular all my messuages, lands, tenements, rents, reversions, hereditaments and services, closes and inclosures, meadow and pasture grounds, tythes, proffitts, …., and advantages whatsoever and wheresoever in the County of Gloucester, I do hereby give and devise to my son **George** and to his heirs and assigns forever for the payment of my just debts which I do owe or am bound for by bonds or any obligation whatsoever and for the making of full satisfaction to all such person or persons that hee shall or may find or conceive I have anyways wronged or injured.

And I do also give and bequeath to my said son **George** all my leasehold lands, goods and chattells and personall estate whatsoever for and towards the paying of my debts or to bee disposed of as he shall thinke fitt and judge reasonable.

And I do hereby make him my Executor earnestly desiring and requiring him to give to my deare friend and loving kinsman **Mr Gwinnett Freeman** and his wife Five Pounds apiece to buy them mourning.

In witness whereof. I have hereto put my hand and seale the Twentyeth day of March in the year of our Lord 1717.

- *George Gwinnett*

Sealed, signed, published and declared to be the last Will and Testament of the Testator and att his request testifyed and wittnessed by us:

- **Anth. Lucas, Joseph Longden,** *Thomas Kemp*

Transcript of the will of George Gwinnett proved in the Bishop of Gloucester's Consistory Court, 11 March 1723.

South Gloucestershire and Bristol Wills

The Gloucestershire Archives genealogical database does not include the wills and administrations proved and held in the Diocese of Bristol, that is those from parishes in the south of the county and the City of Bristol itself, but that doesn't mean there are not wills from the southern parishes held in Gloucester so you should always check the database as well as looking at what Bristol Record Office holds. The Bristol Record Office catalogue states that they hold wills up to the 1940s.

Details of indexes relating to the Diocese of Bristol wills can be found in several places. An *'Index to Bristol Wills 1572-1792'* was edited by E A Fry and published by the British Record Society in 1897. A facsimile of that book, together with *'Wills in the Great Orphan Books 1379-1674'* can be purchased on CD from ArchiveCDBooks online at:

http://www.familyhistoryresearch.org/glsparish.htm

A booklet entitled *Index to Bristol Wills 1793-1858* is available from Bristol Record Office; it lists only the surname, forename and year for each will. The same information has been produced on CD by the Bristol and Avon Family History Society and can be purchased online from:

http://www.bafhs.org.uk/index.htm

Another relevant publication is *Tudor Wills Proved in Bristol 1546 – 1603*, edited by Shelia Lang & Margaret McGregor, published by Bristol Record Society, 1993, ISBN 0 901538 14 0, which has a list of wills for people from the City of Bristol rather than the South Gloucestershire parishes giving the year of probate, full name of the testator, the occupation and parish. For each will in the index, there is a transcript or abstract giving all personal names and important details.

A Guide to the Probate Inventories of the Bristol Deanery of the Diocese of Bristol 1542 – 1804 by E & S George, published by Alan Sutton, 1988, ISBN 0 901538 09 4, does cover the South Gloucestershire parishes as well as the City of Bristol. It provides an index to the inventories and lists the year and reference, name of the testator, parish, occupation and value of the estate and indicates the inventories for which a will also exists. The authors have now produced three further books in the Bristol Record Series transcribing the inventories: *Bristol Probate Inventories 1542-1650*, *Bristol Probate Inventories 1657-1689* and *Bristol Probate Inventories 1690-1804*.

Finally, for Bristol, you can locate wills or copies of them in individual family collections by searching the online catalogue at:

http://archives.bristol.gov.uk/dserve/

> *Note: For wills from parishes in the south of the county, you should check both Gloucestershire Archives and Bristol Record Office.*

Peculiar Wills

As mentioned in Chapter 1, there were four Gloucestershire peculiars where the minister had the authority to grant probate without reference to the Bishop. These peculiars were at Bibury, Bishop's Cleeve, Deerhurst and Withington. Of these, the Deerhurst ministers appear to be the only ones not to avail themselves of this power as Deerhurst wills are to be found in the main collection. There are almost 600 wills from the other three peculiars. Each peculiar consisted of more than one parish, as listed below. You need to know the parishes covered by the peculiars as these wills are filed separately from the main probate collection. They have been indexed but the information has not yet been added to the main genealogical database. A copy can be accessed at the GFHS Family History Centre.

Peculiar	Parishes Included
Bibury	Aldsworth, Barnsley, Bibury, Winson Chapelry
Bishop's Cleeve	Bishop's Cleeve, Stoke Orchard Chapelry
Deerhurst	Boddington Chapelry, Corse, Deerhurst, Forthampton, Leigh, Staverton, Tirley
Withington	Dowdeswell, Withington

There is really little difference between a consistory court probate clause and a Peculiar court one. An example of a Peculiar probate clause is shown below.

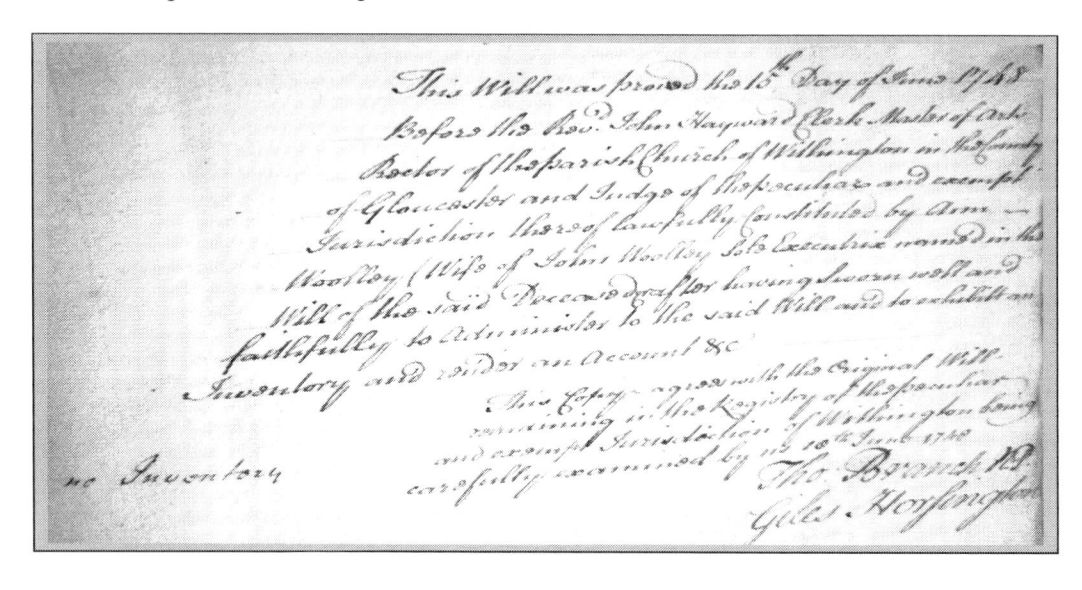

A sample probate clause from the will of John Woolley 1748,
from the Peculiar of Withington.
G.A. Ref: Withington Peculiar 94.

Wills After 1858
Following the Probate Act of 1857, the Principal Probate Registry, now called the Principal Registry of the Family Division (PRFD), was established in London along with district and sub-district registries around England and Wales; these included a district registry in Bristol and a sub-district registry in Gloucester. Thus, from 2nd January 1858, the proving of wills and the granting of letters of administration became centralised. When someone died, the executor would take the will to the local probate registry where a grant of probate was given.

The will could then be registered but only if the executor paid a fee. The registered will was copied by a clerk into a large bound volume. Assuming an accurate transcription was made (sadly this is not always the case), the copy will should differ from the original will only in the handwriting and the fact that the signatures of the testator and the witnesses will not be on the copy. All these volumes of registered wills, from 1858 to 1941, have been deposited at Gloucestershire Archives by the Gloucester Probate Registry and can be viewed there. If the executor did not pay to register the will, you will either find an entry in the indexes but no will to match it, or not find an entry at all.

Since 1858, all registered wills have been indexed in the National Probate Calendars. The original, very large and heavy books are available to search at the PRFD in High Holborn, London including the more recent volumes from 1941 to 1992. Most years needed at least four volumes to cover all entries. More recent years, from 1993 to 1995 are indexed on microfiche and since then, the details have been held on computer there. Gloucester Probate Registry, likewise, has books or microfiche covering the National Probate Calendars for most but not all years from 1941 onwards. The only complete run from 1858 to date is held at the Principal Registry of the Family Division in London.

The National Probate Calendar (NPC) indexes for the years from 1858 to 1941 are held on microfiche and can be viewed at Gloucestershire Archives, the GFHS Family History Centre or online at Ancestry. There are over six million entries. The indexes are organised first by year and then alphabetically by surname and forename, so if you are seeking a Gwinnett who died c.1891, you would find the 1891 fiche and look under G. If you don't find what you are seeking, check the following years.

For each person, the Probate Clause contains most of the following:

- the surname and forenames of the deceased
- late residence of the deceased
- date and place of death
- where and when probate took place
- the value of the deceased's estate
- the names and addresses of the executors
- the occupation and the relationship of the executors to the deceased
- the type of grant – will or administration.

Searching these indexes can sometimes provide you with information on others of the same surname who died in the same year so you can often pick up unexpected information along the way. Also, if you do not know the year of death and have to search from a particular time onwards, it is quicker to search the NPC if you think the deceased left a will as there are fewer entries but more detail on each than you will find in the GRO Death Indexes.

> Note: The National Probate Calendars cover over six million wills and administrations from 1858 to 1941.

GWINNETT, William Henry, Esq. Personal Estate: £73,851 16s 5d.	7 October. The Will with seven codicils of William Henry Gwinnett late of Gordon Cottage Cheltenham in the County of **Gloucester** Esquire who died 30 July 1891 at Gordon Cottage was proved at the **Principal Registry** by George Frederick Newmarch of Belton Uppingham in the County of Rutland Gentleman Frederick Thomas Griffiths of Cheltenham Gentleman George Clarke of the City of Worcester Gentleman Mary Elizabeth Clarke (wife of the said George Clarke) of the said City the Niece and Edward Llewellyn Griffiths of Cheltenham Gentleman the Executors

A transcript from the 1891 National Probate Calendar of the entry for the probate of William Henry Gwinnett of Cheltenham.

Gloucestershire Archives has an index to all the copy wills held there, covering the period from 1858 to 1943. The index, on individual slips of paper, can be found in the filing cabinet in the Archives.

As yet there is no online ordering service for a will made after 1858 but hopefully one will appear in the near future. To find out more about the probate service, look at:

www.hmcourts-service.gov.uk

To order a copy of an original will, you need to note down all the relevant details from the National Probate Calendars. You can then either take those details to the nearest probate registry, or to the Principal Registry of the Probate Division and order the will or administration and probate grant via them or you can write to the York Probate Sub-Registry (address at end of chapter) to order a copy by post. I have found that a quicker response is usually received from local probate offices.

The current cost of purchasing a copy of a will, whether locally or by post, is £5. This includes all the pages in the will, whether there is just one or twenty one, and the postage. Cheques should be made to the Superintendent Registrar.

Administrations
If a person died without leaving a valid will, the next of kin or other suitable person would apply to the court for a grant of administration. When granted, this gave him or her the right to administer the estate but it had to be done according to the laws of inheritance rather than to any of the deceased's previously stated preferences or the administrator's own wishes.

The administrator had to be selected according to a set order of precedence; first the surviving spouse, then one of the children if over 21, next a parent, or sibling, any next of kin such as uncle, aunt or cousin, a creditor or, finally, someone else acceptable to the court.

The administrator, promising to deal with the estate properly according to law, entered into a bond to be forfeited if this was not done. He or she would draw up an inventory of the deceased person's possessions or pay someone else to do it, pay the funeral expenses and any debts the deceased had, collect money owed, distribute the legacies and submit an account, called the probate account, of the expenditure. The inventory of personal effects had to be produced within three months of the death and the probate accounts within six months. Distribution of the estate was not permitted until one year after the grant of administration was made, to ensure all debts had been paid.

Letters of administration, often abbreviated to 'admons', were written into the court's Act Books. These give less information than is provided by most wills unless the guardianship of minors is involved, when the names of the children are mentioned. The administration bond usually identifies:

- the deceased, his place of residence, and usually his status or occupation
- the name of the next of kin or appropriate person requesting the grant of probate
- his relationship to the deceased and occupation
- the bond or amount of money the administrator had to forfeit if he did not distribute the goods as expected
- the date administration was granted.

There is no single index to PCC administrations and they are not included in the searchable index in the DocumentsOnline section on the National Archives' website, so the administrations are not available to download.

The two *Calendar of Wills* books for the Consistory Court of the Bishop of Gloucester, mentioned earlier, do not include Administrations before 1683. After that time, they are included in the Calendars but are not distinguished from the wills, so you may order a will only to discover that it is just an administration. In general, all letters of administration written before 1733 were in Latin.

There is no collection of probate accounts in Gloucestershire Archives but there are a few individual ones in the Consistory Court papers, and plenty of administration bonds and inventories.

The Administration Bond for Isaac Gwinnett, dated 1726, the first of three such bonds for three Isaac Gwinnetts, son, father and grandfather, who died, in that order in three consecutive years. Signatures helped to deduce which Isaac was which.
G.A. Ref: 1726/52

Inventories
An inventory is a detailed list of the possessions of a deceased person. It rarely included land in the early days as this did not come under the auspices of the ecclesiastical courts. The list was produced soon after death, usually by someone with an interest in the estate, often by a neighbour but occasionally by an expert, particularly where specialist trade items were involved. The inventory was then signed by witnesses and returned to the court where the executor or administrator swore that it was a 'true and accurate' valuation of the estate. The process was designed to ensure the honesty of the executor or administrator. If someone claimed that something was not on the inventory, they had to go to the court to substantiate their claim.

The inventory may include:

- The name and parish of the deceased
- The date the inventory was made
- A detailed, room-by-room list of the contents of the property including furniture, linen, kitchen utensils, etc.
- The clothes belonging to the deceased
- The money he had 'in his purse'
- Any stock or equipment owned by the deceased in his trade
- Any money owed to the deceased
- The names and signatures of the appraiser(s).

There is rarely anything in the inventory that helps with unravelling family relationships but occasionally an object is listed that can be seen on someone else's inventory or mentioned in their will so it may be possible to deduce a relationship of some kind from this. However, the list of items on the inventory often gives a fascinating insight into the daily lives of the people involved; the number of rooms they had, their furniture and furnishings, the books they read, the clothes they wore and so on; inventories should not be ignored as they help to put flesh on the bones of your ancestral skeleton.

There are over 11,000 inventories held in Gloucestershire Archives, most of them for the period after 1660 and all of them indexed in the genealogical database along with the wills. They are available on microfilm. There are only two inventories before 1587, one for Ambrose Rayson in 1557 and one for Henry Hathawaye in 1573. There are 64 of them for 1587 and, strangely, they all relate to a person with the forename of Thomas!

> Note: There are over 11,000 inventories held at Gloucestershire Archives, the earliest being dated 1557.

In the following example, relating to the death of George Gwinnett, it is interesting to note that the will was written on 29th September 1708, George was buried five days later on 4th October 1708 and the inventory was made two days after that on 6th October 1708. However, the will itself was not actually proved until nearly four years later on 26th August 1712.

> A True & perfect Inventory of all and
> singular the Goodes Chatells, rights and Creditts
> of George Gwinnett late of Lidney in the
> County of Glouc'r Gent: Deed: taken & apprized
> this sixth day of October Anno D'ni 1708 by
> us whose names are hereunto subscribed
>
> | | | £ | s | d |
> |---|---|---|---|---|
> | Imprimis | His doth wearing apparell & money in purse | 04 | 00 | 00 |
> | Item | Two feather bedds & two flock bedds with all furniture thereto belonging | 06 | 00 | 00 |
> | Item | Linen of all sorts | 03 | 00 | 00 |
> | Item | Chests Trunks boxes & Chaires | 00 | 10 | 00 |
> | Item | Brasse & pewter | 01 | 05 | 00 |
> | Item | one silver Watch | 01 | 00 | 00 |
> | Item | one hand Gunn | 00 | 10 | 00 |
> | Item | Two Iron Grates, all other Iron ware & all other Lumber Goodes | 02 | 05 | 00 |
> | | | 18 | 10 | 00 |
>
> Rich'd Williams } Apprizors
> John King

'A True and Perfect Inventory' of the 'goods, chattels, rights and credits'
of George Gwinnett of Lydney taken 6th October 1708.
G.A. Ref: 1712/147.

6. Probate

A True and perfect Inventory of all and singular the Goodes Chattells, rights and Creditts of George Gwinnett Late of Lidney in the County of Gloucester, Gent, deceased, taken and apprized this sixth day of October Anno Domini 1708 by us whose names are hereunto subscribed.

	£	s	d
Imprimis: The deceased's wearing apparel and money in purse	4	0	0
Item: two feather beds and two flock beds with all furniture thereof belonging	6	0	0
Item: Linen of all sorts	3	0	0
Item: Chests trunks boxes and chaires	0	10	0
Item: Brasse and Pewter	1	5	0
Item: One silver watch	1	0	0
Item: One hand gun	0	10	0
Item: Two iron grates. All other iron ware and all other lumber goodes	2	5	0
	18	10	0

Richard Williams and John King, Apprizers

Transcript of the Inventory of George Gwinnett of Lydney dated 1708.

If you have checked all the previous places for probate documents and still not found what you are seeking, try looking in:

- family collections – you may find copy wills or unsigned and unproven wills here
- estate papers – deeds and wills are often included to substantiate ownership claims
- solicitors' deposits – may contain original or copy wills and other probate documents
- the parish chest – these sometimes include abstracts or copies of wills where the deceased donated gifts to the church
- charity records – will include details of charitable gifts such as money for the poor
- borough records – includes abstract of wills of city benefactors.

You may not find complete wills but often the abstracts can be just as informative, since they often include names and relationships to the testator.

Lately, will transcripts and abstracts have begun appearing online, put there by volunteers. Check out:

www.genuki.org.uk/big/eng/GLS/ProbateRecords/index.html

or the Forest of Dean website where the names of beneficiaries are being linked to the wills index.

www.forest-of-dean.net/?Wills Index

Useful Addresses

If you wish to purchase a copy of a will that has been proved locally since 1858, you should contact your local Probate Registry, i.e. either Gloucester or Bristol. A copy of a will currently costs £5 and that is the same whether the will has one or 30 pages.

LONDON

Probate Department
Principal Registry of the Family Division
First Avenue House
42-49, High Holborn
Holborn, London, WC1V 6NP
Tel: 020 7947 6939
Email: londonpersonalapplicationsenquiries@hmcourts-service.gsi.gov.uk

BRISTOL
Bristol District Probate Registry
Ground Floor
The Crescent Centre
Temple Back
Bristol, BS1 6EP
Tel: 0117 927 3915
Email: bristoldprenquiries@hmcourts-service.gsi.gov.uk

GLOUCESTER
Gloucester Probate Sub-Registry
2nd Floor
Combined Court Building
Kimbrose Way
Gloucester, GL1 2DG
Tel: 01452 834966
Email: gloucesterpsrenquiries@hmcourts-service.gsi.gov.uk

YORK
Postal Searches and Copies Department
York Probate Sub-Registry
1st Floor, Castle Chambers
Clifford Street
York
YO1 9RG
Tel: 01904 666 7777
Email: YorkPSRenquiries@hmcourts-service.gsi.gov.uk

Chapter 7

More on Births

'There was a birth, certainly, and we had evidence and no doubt.'

*T. S. Eliot
1888 – 1965, playwright*

Today we consider the birth of a child to be a happy event but that is not always the case and, in times past, it was frequently less so, as mothers died much more often, with many stillbirths, infant deaths and illegitimacy. At the end of the 18th century, maternal mortality was in the region of 1 in 100 births. A century later, something like 20% of all infants died before they reached the age of one.

Stillbirths
Stillbirths were not recorded at the General Register Office until 1st July 1927. This register is not generally available to be searched; special permission has to be granted by the Registrar General before it can be accessed. Before 1927, there was no overall record kept of stillbirths but an occasional entry may be found in the local parish burial registers.

A note included in the Horton parish register, written by the midwife in 1921, before the official registration of still births, certified that a male child had been still-born to a particular mother. The minister had added "Stillborn, therefore not entered in either Birth or Burial register". G.A. Ref: P182 IN 1/12.

> *Note: Stillbirths were not recorded by the General Register Office until 1st July 1927.*

An article in the *Cheltenham Examiner* of 1859, stated that, in London at least,

> 'it is the prevailing custom to send the bodies of still-born children to the metropolis workhouses, in order that they may be interred in the coffins of adult paupers.'

During one week alone, five such bodies were received at one London workhouse. Whether a similar situation occurred in Gloucestershire is not known.

Records of early stillbirths are usually few and far between, but many are included in the *Register of Burials in the Tredworth Burial Ground in The City of Gloucester* that has been produced by GFHS. It covers the period from 1857 to 1901. The earliest stillbirth located with a simple search of the CD proved to be a burial on 23rd June 1860 of the still born child of Emily Awford in consecrated ground.

You may also find documentation relating to such an event in the Coroner's papers. One example is that of a child born to Elizabeth Price in Wickwar in August 1862. Elizabeth Price was a single schoolmistress at Wickwar Girls School, when she became pregnant. On 10th August she gave birth to a baby girl which her younger sister, Annie, the only one present at the birth, said was stillborn. Annie proceeded to take the body to the privy where it was found some days later by the village constable

Various witnesses were called to appear at the inquest which was to be held in the White House Inn in Wickwar; they made their statements, including Annie Price. Sadly, before the inquest was concluded, Elizabeth Price herself died and a second inquest had to be called.

7. More on Births

G.A. Ref: CO1/I/8/1/7   G.A. Ref:. CO1/I/8/C/8

The death of the mother in or soon after childbirth caused difficulties. In the case of the death of a married woman, the man frequently remarried quite quickly so that he had a wife to look after his other children, unless the grandparents or other family members were able to care for them. If the mother had herself been recently widowed or if the mother was unmarried, then the child became an orphan on the death of the mother and some means had to be found to care for him or her.

Foundlings and Orphans

An abandoned child was called a foundling, as opposed to an orphan whose parents had died, though they were both treated in much the same way. The abandoned baby was usually left in a place where he or she could easily be discovered such as in the church porch. The responsibility for orphans and foundlings fell to the parish from the 16th to 19th centuries so the churchwarden would organise the baptism. After that, the 1834 Poor Law Amendment Act made the Guardians of the Poor responsible for dealing with foundlings and orphans.

The names given to the child were often chosen to indicate unknown parentage, e.g. Hester Only or with regard to the place where he or she was found and the saint's name for the parish. For example, a boy might be called James Church as he was found in the entrance to St. James's Church. The baby would be put out to a wet nurse in the parish and, when old enough, sent to the workhouse and later apprenticed by the parish to a local tradesman or farmer or sent in to service. The majority of foundlings were illegitimate and it is unlikely that the names of either of the parents will be located in the records.

A baby girl, found in Clarence Street, Gloucester, in 1888 was given the name of Mary Barton; this would appear to be because she was discovered in the district of Barton St Mary. A normal registration was made but the birth certificate showed certain differences from those of children registered by a parent. In the column stating where and when born was written 'Living child, 6 weeks old, found outside front door of 30 Clarence Street, 8th November 1888'. Under the heading of surname, father's name, mother's name and father's occupation was written the word 'Unknown'. The informant was given as 'George Higgins found the child'. Sadly, there is also a death registered on 17th November 1888 under the name of Mary Barton at the Union Workhouse aged 2 months, with parents unknown, registered by the master of the workhouse.

> A CHILD ABANDONED IN GLOUCESTER. — George Higgins, of No. 4, Sherborne-street, who works for Mr. John Smith, pork butcher, 30, Clarence-street, found in the lobby of the latter house at about a quarter-past eight on Thursday night a female child, which must have been deposited there between eight and a quarter past eight. The child, who was apparently about three months old, had been well wrapped up before being left, being dressed in a long white robe, light blue hood trimmed with cream-coloured frilling, a cream-coloured woollen shawl or wrap, and over the whole was a grey woollen shawl. A white fall covered her face. There was also a quantity of underclothing, but there were no marks on any of the articles. There was also by its side a feeding bottle full of milk. The police are making inquiries into the matter. In the meantime the little stranger is being carefully attended to.

An entry from the *Gloucester Journal* dated 10th November 1888

After civil registration came into being in 1837, the foundlings were entered in the General Register Office Birth Indexes after names beginning with the letter Z. Under the surname heading is written 'Unknown'. Early foundlings were listed merely as being 'Male' or 'Female' but occasionally a forename is recorded, as in the instance below from the December quarter of 1856.

Surname	Forenames	District	Volume	Page
Unknown	Emma	Kings Norton	6c	388
Unknown	Male	Gloucester	6a	205
Unknown	Female	Kensington	1a	51
Unknown	Female	Kensington	1a	59

By December 1888, most foundlings were still being recorded with the surname of 'Unknown' but their given name appears frequently to have included their new forename.

Surname	Forenames	District	Volume	Page
Unknown	George Laybourne	Forden	11b	189
Unknown	Eveline Annie B	Pancras	1b	89
Unknown	George Hope	St Geo H. Sq	1a	407
Unknown	**Mary Barton**	**Gloucester**	**6a**	**273**
Unknown	Richard Causon	W. Derby	8a	277

7. More on Births

A Foundling Hospital was opened by Thomas Coram in 1741 in London with the aim of looking after abandoned children (see www.foundlingmuseum.org.uk). Later, four more foundling hospitals were set up around the country but none in Gloucestershire. The babies were left in a basket outside the hospital and a bell was rung to announce their presence. No names were left, either for the child or for the mother. The child was given a new name. A piece of cloth was attached to the child by the mother so that, if her circumstances were to change in the future and she could collect her offspring, the correct child could be recognised. As with the foundlings who were looked after in the parish, the foundling was sent out to a wet nurse to be cared for until old enough to be sent back to the hospital where he or she would receive an education.

In the Brimpsfield parish register of 1758, there is an entry relating to the baptism of Hester Wells, the daughter of Joseph and Elizabeth Wells of Birdlip. Hester was sent to the 'Fanlin' hospital in London. Sadly, her mother had been buried a few days earlier, on 12th April and, presumably, the father had no means of looking after the child. G.A. Ref: P58 IN 1/2.

Over the years, many other organisations and charities set up orphanages and children's homes, the most well-known of these being Dr. Barnardo's Homes, which began in 1867. (See www.barnados.org.uk). The only three Barnardo homes in Gloucestershire were started at a much later date: Badgeworth Court in Badgeworth was the first (1945–1964), followed by the Elizabeth Bishop House in Stoke Bishop, Bristol (1948–1970) and a little later, Hatherley Brake in Down Hatherley (1950–1978).

Within Gloucestershire, there were two other well-known orphanages or children's homes as well as a few that are less well known. The first two are the Müller Orphanage in Bristol, opened in 1832, which dealt with 18,500 orphans throughout the years and has its own museum and archives (see www.mullers.org), and the Gyde Home, which opened in Painswick in 1918, was later handed over to the Children's Society in 1933 and finally closed in 1985.

Less well-known Gloucestershire children's homes include:

- Cheltenham Female Refuge (later called the North Parade Home for Girls)
- Protestant Orphanage for Boys in Cheltenham
- St Lucy's Home or Children's Orphanage, Gloucester
- St. Elizabeth Orphanage of Mercy, Eastcombe near Bisley
- Bussage House of Mercy
- Dryleaze Children's Home in Wotton under Edge
- Downend Cottage Homes, Downend, Bristol
- Ebley House, Ebley, near Stroud.

Most of these were started in the 20th century and dealt with older children rather than infants.

Adoption
Before 1927, adoption was an informal and unregistered event. If a child needed looking after by a family not their own, he or she was just handed over and nothing official was recorded.

The child usually took the new family's surname although this was not always the case. From then on, he or she appeared to be an ordinary member of the new family. Any record of adoption before 1927 will therefore be very difficult to locate, particularly among the labouring classes, although an occasional record has survived to indicate that a person was adopted. You may also be fortunate enough to find a reference to an adopted child in a parish register or a will. For example, an entry on the Brimpsfield burial register of 1754 refers to the burial of 'William Chance, the adopted son of Edward and Jone Hayward of Brimpsfield'. G.A. Ref: P58 IN 1/2

From 1927 onwards, adoption became a formal, court procedure. The adopter had to be 21 years older than a child of the same sex and 30 years older for a child of the opposite sex. Once a court had agreed an adoption order for a child, the Registrar General would provide a certificate which contains:

- Name of the court
- Date of the order
- Date of birth of the child
- Name of the child as adopted (not the birth name)
- Names of adoptive parents
- Address of adoptive parents
- Occupation of adoptive parents.

The General Register Office holds an Adopted Children's Register together with an index to it which contains entries for all adoptions since 1st January 1927. It gives the adopted name of the child and the date of adoption. Another file holds a link between the adopted child and the original birth record. Access to this information is only available to the adoptee or possibly his or her children.

From 1926 some adoption cases were dealt with in the Quarter or Petty Sessions courts and details of these are held in their records. However, the 100 year disclosure rule applies to these registers so they are currently closed to the general public.

> Note: Official adoption records did not begin until 1st January 1927.

Illegitimacy
Most families have an illegitimate child somewhere in their ancestry; it is nothing to be ashamed of but does lead to difficulties in tracing one branch of your family tree. The use of an alias in records, such as John Smith alias Jones, often indicates illegitimacy, where one parent has the name Smith and the other is Jones. Frequently, the middle name of an illegitimate child is a pointer towards the father and can be used to try to identify the missing parent.

If the name of the father was known to the minister, he might be recorded in the baptismal register as the reputed or putative father.

7. More on Births

Be wary of family stories that imply that the girl was assaulted by a gentleman such as the master of the big house or one of his sons; these stories may or may not be true, although it did sometimes happen. If this were indeed the case, check the parish chest (registers, vestry minutes, churchwarden's accounts, Overseers of the Poor papers, etc.) for evidence, to see if the mother was paid off by the man concerned (did her circumstances suddenly improve?), or was she married off to another estate worker or even, just occasionally, were either mother or child mentioned in the will of the father or his family?

An entry from the Ruardean baptismal register of 1821.
G.A. Ref: P275 IN 1/7

In the Index to the Overseers of the Poor Papers relating to the Tetbury examination of Ann Howell, G.A. Ref: P328a OV/5/1/54, there is an entry which reads:

18 Dec 1828
William Richards of Dursley, gentleman, father of the child with which Ann Howell is pregnant.

In your search for your ancestors, you will notice many entries in the parish registers where a mother only is named when her child is baptised. The child may be called illegitimate, base born, bastard child, spurious or given various other names to imply that the mother was unmarried. She may have been described as a 'singlewoman', normally recorded as such in the column for the parent's occupation after 1813. On the other hand, if the mother was a widow whose husband had recently died, to indicate that the child was conceived in matrimony, the entry may well use the phrase 'posthumous child of X'.

In the early days, it was the parish's responsibility to support an unmarried woman and child if the father would not or could not marry her or her family could not take her in and provide for her. It was a sad fact that few unmarried women could support themselves and a child. Children born illegitimately in a parish would, from 1743, belong to the mother's parish of settlement. If the father was persuaded to marry the mother, the child belonged to his parish of settlement. Illegitimate children were occasionally not baptised so you may not locate a baptismal entry at all but most of them were as it gave them an official parish to which they 'belonged'.

When it became obvious that a single girl was pregnant, she would be questioned by the parish authorities and encouraged to give the name of the father so that he could be traced and made to support her and the child. This bastardy examination would be recorded. She might have been threatened with or even given a gaol sentence if she did not reveal the father's name, assuming, of course, that she knew it. This was particularly hard for the girl if the child was the result of incest. She may not wish to name the relative if it meant depriving the family of its breadwinner. In most villages, there was usually someone who knew who the father was likely to be; this was less so in towns and cities.

A declaration by Rebecca Clifford of South Cerney that she had been raped in Tewkesbury.
From the Overseers of the Poor Papers for South Cerney.
G.A. Ref: P71 OV 5/3

When it became obvious that Rebecca Clifford of South Cerney was pregnant in 1775 she was called before the parish authorities to answer questions as to the name of the father. She claimed that, on an overnight visit to Tewkesbury, she was raped by a fellow lodger in the inn. She said she had never seen him before or since the event and that she did not know his name.

Before long, Rebecca decided to tell the truth about the cause of her pregnancy ….

7. More on Births

Two months after the bastardy examination, Rebecca Clifford made a subsequent declaration that John Hemsley was really the father.
From the Overseers of the Poor Papers for South Cerney.
G.A. Ref: P71 OV 5/3

Once the name of the man was known, he would be sent for and questioned by the parish authorities, usually the Overseers of the Poor, and told of the girl's examination naming him. In the first instance, he would be encouraged to marry her to make 'an honest woman' of her, the parish occasionally paying for the licence to help persuade him, but if he was already married or not willing to do so, he would be required to pay to support her and her child, by a bastardy or affiliation order. This could involve paying for her lying-in expenses and support for the child until 14 years of age.

Thomas Stratford was summoned to appear at the Fairford Petty Sessions and ordered to pay 1s 6d per week to support the illegitimate child of Catherine Williams.
G.A. Ref: Q/CR 25/3

Many records relating to illegitimacy have been indexed from the Overseers of the Poor Papers; this index contains over 45,000 names though they do not all refer to illegitimacy. Not all records have survived. The index, contained in Gloucestershire Archives Genealogical Database, is available for searching online via their website. It gives:

- Surname
- Forenames
- Age
- Year
- Occupation
- Place
- Reference.

The place referred to in the index is not necessarily the place at which the event occurred; it may refer to the abode of the reputed father; the reference given is the clue to the location of the mother. Abstracts have been made from these papers and are available to view at Gloucestershire Archives where the originals are held. Not all Overseers Papers were included when this index was produced; for instance, there is a large collection of such papers for Dursley which were originally in the Gloucestershire Collection held at Gloucester City Library which were transferred to the Archives a few years ago. Many others are held in the parish chest collections at the Archives so always check their online parish catalogue to see what is available for the areas in which you are interested.

If the man admitted paternity and was willing to support the woman and child, he would sign a bastardy bond, but he would be pressured into admission if he denied it. In the latter case, he could well be taken to the Assize Court where, unless he was able to prove his absence from the area at the essential time, he would again be ordered to sign a bastardy bond and might have ended up with a short stay in prison.

c.1826   Elizabeth Vizard gave birth to a bastard child and Anthony Tuck the father was apprehended and committed to Horsley Gaol. Jarvis Tuck bound for his brother Anthony Tuck. G.A. Ref: P328a OV 5/9/5

Some men, when faced with the possibility of having to pay for their offspring, absconded from the area and joined the Army or Navy where they escaped prosecution. An entry relating to this might be found in the Quarter Sessions papers.

The 16th to 18th century records of the Consistory Court also include references to bastards as it was churchwarden's duty to report moral lapses or 'incontinency' to the Bishop. These included affiliation and maintenance orders and related papers. These records are not indexed and, before 1733, were in Latin. Once he had received a report, the Bishop would then require the woman to appear before him to answer to the charge. Such a case occurred in 1764 when two women, Sarah Gardiner and Love Stalks of Bisley, were summoned to appear at the Consistory Court.

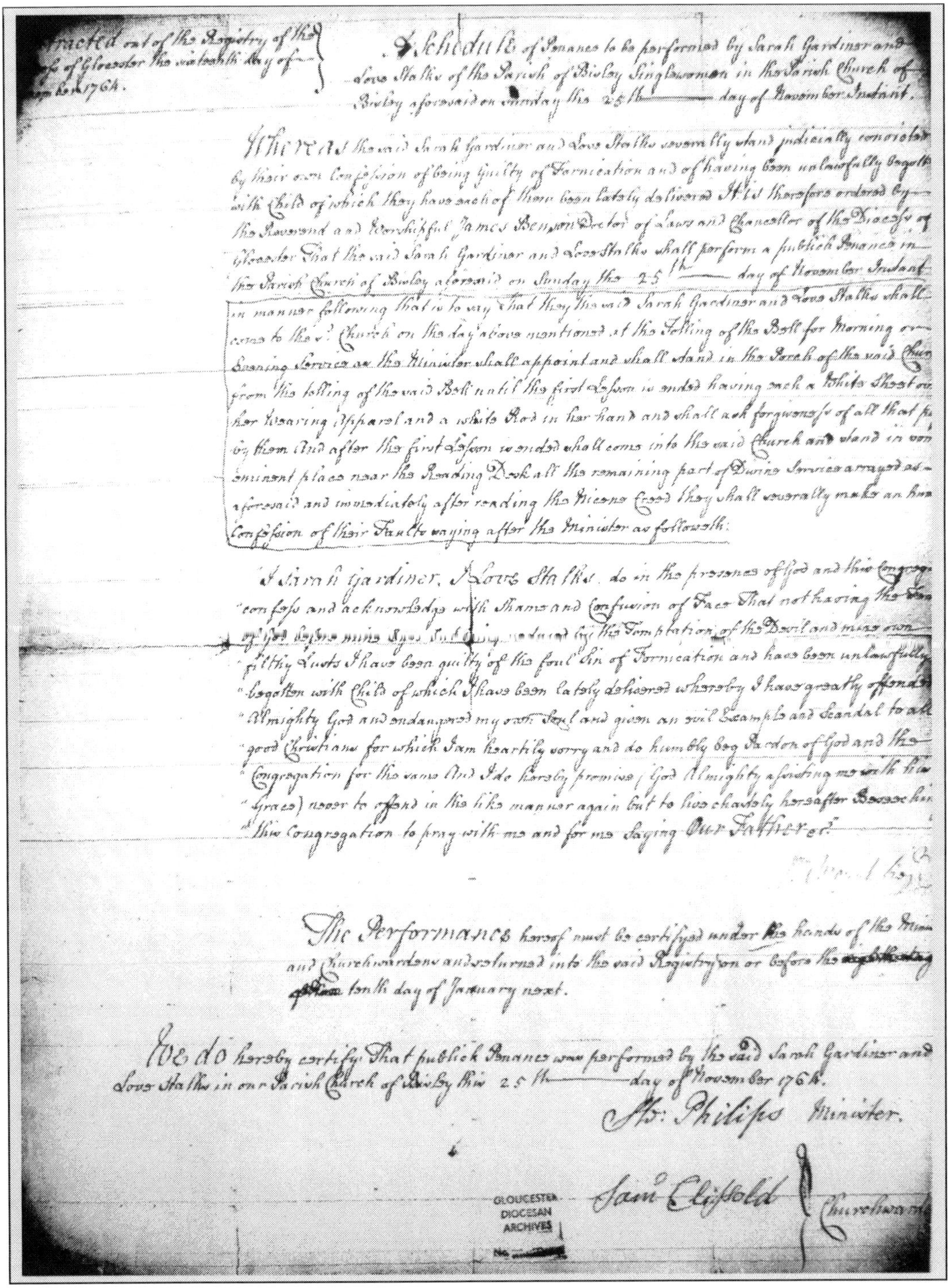

[Ext]racted out of the Registry of the [Diocese] of Gloucester the sixteenth day of [Nov]ember 1764.

A Schedule of Penance to be performed by Sarah Gardiner and Love Stalks of the Parish of Bisley Singlewomen in the Parish Church of Bisley aforesaid on Sunday the 25th day of November Instant.

Whereas the said Sarah Gardiner and Love Stalks severally stand judicially convicted by their own Confession of being Guilty of Fornication and of having been unlawfully begotten with Child of which they have each of them been lately delivered It is therefore ordered by the Reverend and Worshipful James Benson Doctor of Laws and Chancellor of the Diocese of Gloucester That the said Sarah Gardiner and Love Stalks shall perform a publick Penance in the Parish Church of Bisley aforesaid on Sunday the 25th day of November Instant in manner following that is to say That they the said Sarah Gardiner and Love Stalks shall come to the said Church on the day above mentioned at the Tolling of the Bell for Morning or Evening Service as the Minister shall appoint and shall stand in the Porch of the said Church from the tolling of the said Bell until the first Lesson is ended having each a White Sheet over her wearing Apparel and a white Rod in her hand and shall ask forgiveness of all that pa[ss] by them And after the first Lesson is ended shall come into the said Church and stand in som[e] eminent place near the Reading Desk all the remaining part of Divine Service arrayed as aforesaid and immediately after reading the Nicene Creed they shall severally make an hum[ble] Confession of their Faults saying after the Minister as followeth:

"I Sarah Gardiner, I Love Stalks do in the presence of God and this Congrega[tion] confess and acknowledge with Shame and Confusion of Face That not having the fea[r] of God before mine Eyes but being seduced by the Temptation of the Devil and mine own filthy Lusts I have been guilty of the foul Sin of Fornication and have been unlawfully begotten with Child of which I have been lately delivered whereby I have greatly offended Almighty God and endangered my own Soul and given an evil Example and Scandal to all good Christians for which I am heartily sorry and do humbly beg Pardon of God and the Congregation for the same And I do hereby promise (God Almighty assisting me with his Grace) never to offend in the like manner again but to live chastely hereafter Beseeching this Congregation to pray with me and for me saying Our Father &c."

The Performance hereof must be certified under the hands of the Mini[ster] and Churchwardens and returned into the said Registry on or before the ~~eighteenth day of~~ tenth day of January next.

We do hereby certify That publick Penance was performed by the said Sarah Gardiner and Love Stalks in our Parish Church of Bisley this 25th day of November 1764.

Ja: Philips Minister.

Saml Clissold Churchwar[den]

GLOUCESTER DIOCESAN ARCHIVES

The Penance given to Sarah Gardiner and Love Stalks of Bisley, 1764.
G.A. Ref: GDR/B4/1/274

Abstracted out of the Registry of the Diocese of Gloucester the 16th day of November 1764.

A Schedule of Penance to be performed by Sarah Gardiner and Love Stalks of the Parish of Bisley Singlewomen in the Parish Church of Bisley aforesaid on Sunday 25th day of November instant.

Whereas the said Sarah Gardiner and Love Stalks severally stand judicially convicted by their own confession of being Guilty of Fornication and of having been unlawfully begotten with child of which they have each of them been lately delivered It is therefore ordered by the Reverend and Worshipful James Benson Doctor of Laws and Chancellor of the Diocese of Gloucester That the said Sarah Gardiner and Love Stalks shall perform a publick Penance in the Parish Church of Bisley aforesaid on Sunday 25th day of November instant in manner following: that is to say that they the said Sarah Gardiner and Love Stalks shall come to the said church on the day above mentioned at the Tolling of the Bell for Morning or Evening Service as the Minister shall appoint and shall stand in the porch of the said church from the tolling of the said bell until the first lesson is ended having each a white sheet over her wearing apparel and a white rod in her hand and shall ask forgiveness of all that pass by them. And after the first lesson is ended shall come into the said church and stand in some eminent place near the Reading Desk all the remaining part of the Divine Service arrayed as aforesaid and immediately after reading the Nicene Creed they shall severally make an humble confession of their faults saying after the Minister as followeth:

"I Sarah Gardiner/Love Stalks do in the presence of God and this congregation confess and acknowledge with shame and confusion of face that not having the fear of God before mine eyes but being seduced by the Temptation of the Devil and mine own filthy Lusts I have been guilty of the foul Sin of Fornication and have been unlawfully begotten with child of which I have been lately delivered whereby I have greatly offended Almighty God and endangered my own Soul and given an evil Example and Scandal to all good Christians for which I am heartily sorry and do humbly beg Pardon of God and the Congregation for the same. And I do hereby promise (God Almighty assisting me with his Grace) never to offend in this like manner again but to lie chastely hereafter beseeching this Congregation to pray with me and for me Saying Our Father, etc."

The Performance thereof must be certified under the hands of the Minister and Churchwardens and returned into the said Registry on or before the tenth day of January next.

We do hereby certify that publick Penance was performed by the said Sarah Gardiner and Love Stalks in our Parish Church in Bisley this 25th day of November 1764.

Ste. Philips, Minister
Saml. Clissold, Churchwarden.

A Transcript of the Penance for Sarah Gardiner and Love Stalks of Bisley, 1764.

7. More on Births

Nonconformist churches, particularly the Quakers, regarded moral behaviour as very important and would counsel the couple if they felt there was likely to be a problem. Although there were fewer illegitimate nonconformist baptisms, they still occurred.

> Report being made that a servant of Thomas Taylor of Ashton Haynes being with child, charges his son Robert Taylor with being the author thereof; William Beesley and Warner Elkington are appointed to visit him thereon.

A classic case of the son of the house making a servant pregnant. Two members of the Society of Friends are dispatched to try to persuade him to marry her.
G.A. Ref: D1340 B1/M2

> The friends appointed having visited Robert Taylor, who doth not deny the crimes layed to his charge, and as he doth not appear to have any due sence of his said misconduct. This meeting concludes he is thereby gone out of the unity of friends & deems him to be no longer member of our society; and appoints Henry Wilkins & Warner Elkington a testimony to prepare against his said out goings & him therein against next meeting & acquaint him herewith.

Robert Taylor obviously refused to marry the servant and was dismissed from the Society of Friends.
G.A. Ref: D1340 B1/M2

In 1834, the Poor Law Act transferred responsibility for dealing with illegitimate children and single mothers to the Guardians of the Poor and many single mothers and children ended up in the local workhouse. The 1844 Poor Law Amendment Act gave women the right to sue for maintenance in the Petty Sessions courts so you may well find information relating to bastardy cases, including maintenance orders and defaulters, there.

When civil registration came in during 1837, births of illegitimate children were registered leaving a blank space where the father's name would normally have been. If you cannot find a birth registration in the index under the supposed father's name, try looking under the mother's maiden name. Before 1875 the mother could supply the father's name, but since then he had to be present at the registration or supply an affidavit stating that he was the father for his name to be included on the birth certificate. Before 1926 an illegitimate child was given the mother's surname when the birth was registered. After that time, if the mother subsequently married the father, the child's surname could be changed to reflect his father's name.

> *Note: An illegitimate child was almost always given the mother's surname.*

You may find that a child is brought up using the name of the father, if the parents were living together as man and wife, but that, when the child grew up, he or she would revert to their official name, i.e. their mother's maiden name, and would then be married under her name. Illegitimate children were sometimes told of their origin as they matured, in order to prevent them falling for and wishing to marry an unsuspected half-sibling. On marriage, be aware that an illegitimate person may have invented a fictitious name to be entered on the certificate for his or her father or may have used a grandfather's name to hide their shame when the marriage register is completed.

> *Note: An illegitimate person often invented a father's name when getting married to cover his or her embarrassment.*

So, depending on when the birth occurred, to look for the father of an illegitimate child, you should check:

- Parish registers
- Bishops' transcripts
- Vestry minutes
- Churchwarden's accounts
- Overseers of the Poor accounts
- Overseers of the Poor papers
- Quarter Sessions records
- Petty Sessions records.

Chapter 8

More on Marriages

'Marriage is popular because it combines the maximum of temptation with the maximum of opportunity.'

George Bernard Shaw
1856 – 1950, Irish playwright

Although until 1754 it was technically possible for a couple to make a 'common-law marriage' merely by expressing their unconditional consent to each other, generally but not necessarily in front of witnesses, the vast majority of marriages took place in the church of the Anglican parish of the bride or, less often, of the groom with the benefit of ordained clergy to perform the ceremony. This usually occurred after the reading of banns on three consecutive Sundays in the parishes of both parties.

Banns of Marriage
Banns were introduced in England and Wales in the 13th century. The reason that banns were read before a marriage could take place was so that any legal impediment could be raised in order to prevent illegal marriages, e.g. if one person was already married to someone else or the relationship between the couple was prohibited such as between a man and his niece. The banns were valid for three months; after that time had elapsed, new banns would have to be read. There was a fee to be paid for the reading of banns.

During the Commonwealth period, marriage was made a civil contract performed by a local Justice of the Peace, but banns were still required and were either read in church on Sundays or in the local market square on market days. Many marriages were not recorded during this period. Some couples found an Anglican minister who would perform a marriage ceremony for them despite the ban; it is unlikely that banns would have been read in such circumstances.

After Lord Hardwicke's Marriage Act of 1753, a marriage would be void unless banns had been read or a licence had been obtained from either the local bishop or the Archbishop of Canterbury. Members of the Royal Family were exempt from this. This Act had the result of forcing most nonconformist couples (except Jews or Quakers who were also exempt) to marry in the local Anglican church.

> Note: Banns were to be read on three successive Sundays at Morning Service or, if there wasn't one, at Evening Service.
> They were valid for three months.

Registers were produced to record the reading of banns, some giving just the details of the banns that were read, others including the later marriage details, but relatively few of these banns books have survived compared to the marriage registers themselves; some begin in 1754 when the Marriage Act came into force but most are from the mid or late 19th century. The fact that banns were read does not necessarily mean that a marriage subsequently took place since either the bride or groom might change their mind or the marriage might be forbidden, e.g. in the case of a serving soldier who did not have his officer's permission.

> Note: An entry in the Banns Book is not evidence that a marriage has taken place.

Since 1837, when civil registration was introduced, the intention to marry was also displayed on a notice board at the local Register Office or, in the case of a nonconformist marriage, at the chapel where the wedding would take place. If the couple getting married did not live in the same parish, the minister could not solemnize the marriage unless a certificate had been presented confirming that banns had been read in the other parish. Hence, the statement on some marriage certificates that the couple have married 'by certificate' rather than by banns or by licence.

A sample from the banns book of Badgeworth.
G.A. Ref: P31 IN 1/22

Marriage Licences
Marriage licences were introduced in the 14th century to permit a marriage to take place more quickly than banns allowed or for the marriage to take place away from the home parishes of the bride and groom. However, some people also chose to marry by licence as a status symbol.

To obtain a **common licence**, the couple or, more frequently, just the bridegroom would apply to the local diocese and would swear an **allegation** that there was no impediment to the forthcoming marriage. This was done either at the Diocesan Registry in Gloucester or before a surrogate elsewhere in the county. A fee would be paid for the licence and a **bond** for a specific sum of money was recorded which would have to be paid if the marriage was later shown to be against Canon (church) Law. A **special licence** would be provided by the Archbishop of Canterbury to permit the marriage to take place in any church outside of the couple's home diocese but within his province.

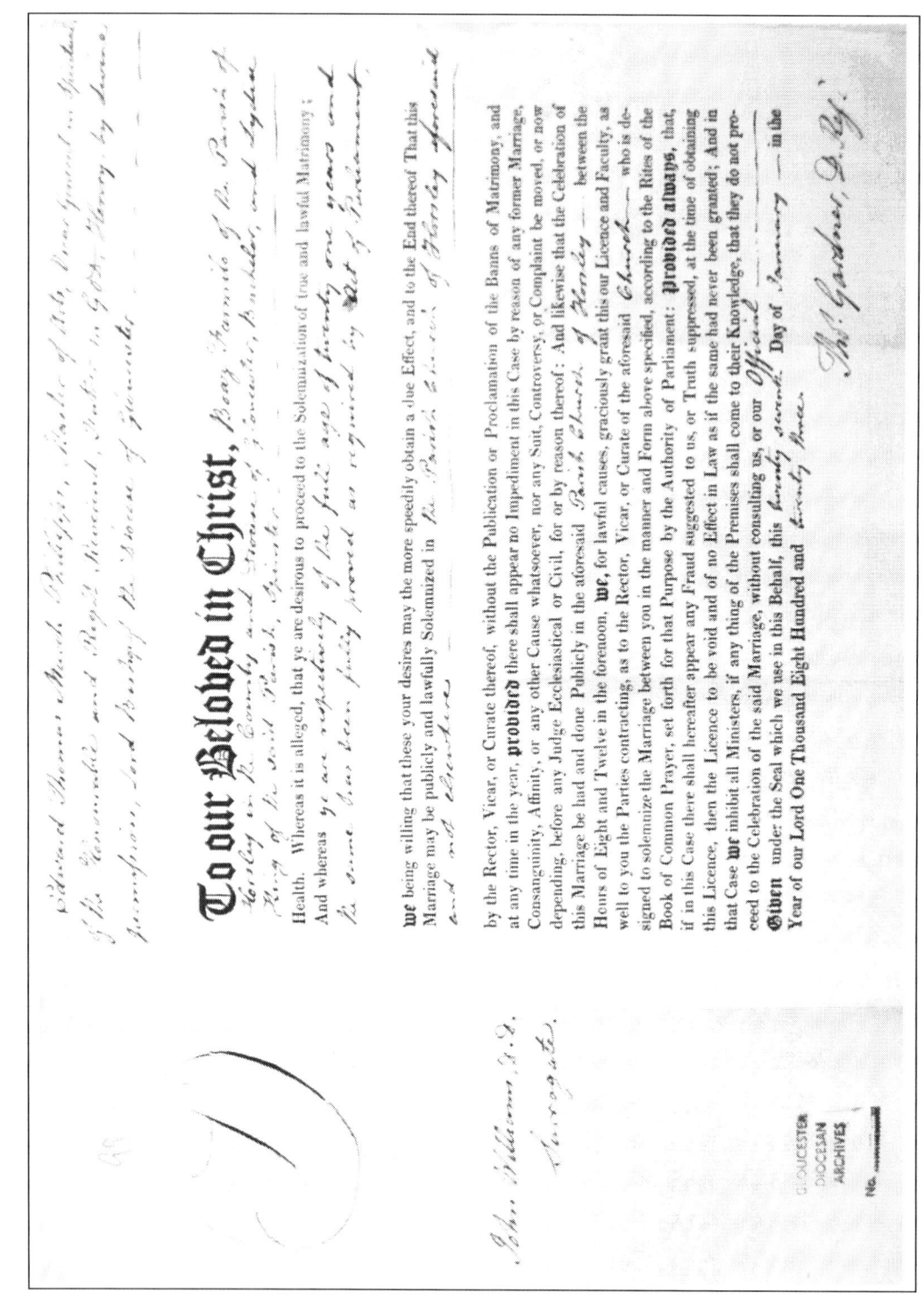

A sample marriage licence for Boaz Farmilo and Lydia King, both of Horsley, from the Diocesan collection for 1823. G.A. Ref: GDR/Q4.

8. More on Marriages

As with the probate records, the Peculiars (Bibury, Bishops Cleeve, Deerhurst and Withington) were authorised to record allegations and affidavits and to issue their own marriage licences and bonds. Some of these remain for the peculiar of Bibury. 26 such licences, allegations or bonds are held at the Gloucestershire Archives and can be found using G.A. Ref: D296B/F16.

Groom	Bride	Year	Parish	Type
Thomas Hignell	Mary Moulder	1769	Bibury	Licence
John Staite	Sarah Hewer	1811	Barnsley	Licence
William Alfred Glover	Maria Clappen	1813	Barnsley	Licence
Revd. John Hughes of N. Tidworth, Wilts (35)	Mary Coxwell (30)	1808	Bibury	Licence, Bond & Allegation
George Long	Elizabeth Porter	1772	Bibury	Licence
Richard Harding (34+)	Mary Ayliff (36+)	1771	Bibury	Allegation & Bond
Samuel Turner	Esther Moulder	1776	Barnsley	Licence
Giles Cripps	Ann Essex	1781	Barnsley	Licence
Charles Whitehead	Betty Driver	1778	Barnsley	Licence
William Smith	Mary Wheeler	1780	Winson	Licence
Richard Bridgeman	Mary Poole	1781	Barnsley	Licence
James Shurmer	Ann Strange	1781	Barnsley	Licence
Thomas Keene (w)	Elizabeth Sessions	1781	Barnsley	Licence
John Ivine	Hannah Poole	1787	Barnsley	Licence
Thomas Clapham	Sarah Paish	1789	Barnsley	Licence
John Trinder	Mary Moulder	1790	Barnsley	Licence
Humphrey King (21)	Mary Wilson (21)	1807	Barnsley	Licence & Allegation
Thomas Clapham	Ann Hatherall	1801	Barnsley	Licence
William Hewer	Hannah Evans	1794	Barnsley	Licence
Thomas Jackson (21)	Amy Cole (23)	1808	Winson	Licence, Bond & Allegation
James Ireland	Elizabeth Hawker	1792	Barnsley	Licence
Edward Larner of Tewkesbury	Ann Tressell	1792	Barnsley	Licence
Solomon Webb	Mary Timpany of Kensington	1793	Barnsley	Licence
William Garne (24)	Marianne Waine (19)	1809	Aldsworth	Allegation & Bond
William Wilson	Phoebe Reeves	1811	Barnsley	Licence
John Mills of Ablington	Elizabeth Keble	1767	Barnsley	Licence

A list of the documents relating to applications for a marriage licence made to the Peculiar of Bibury.
G.A. Ref: D296B/F16.

Apart from the occasional individual licence remaining in a family collection, nearly 140 licences for the Diocese of Gloucester exist in collection GDR/Q4; they cover the period from 1713 to 1823 but the vast majority of them are for the last two years, 1822-1823. However, there are many allegations still in existence.

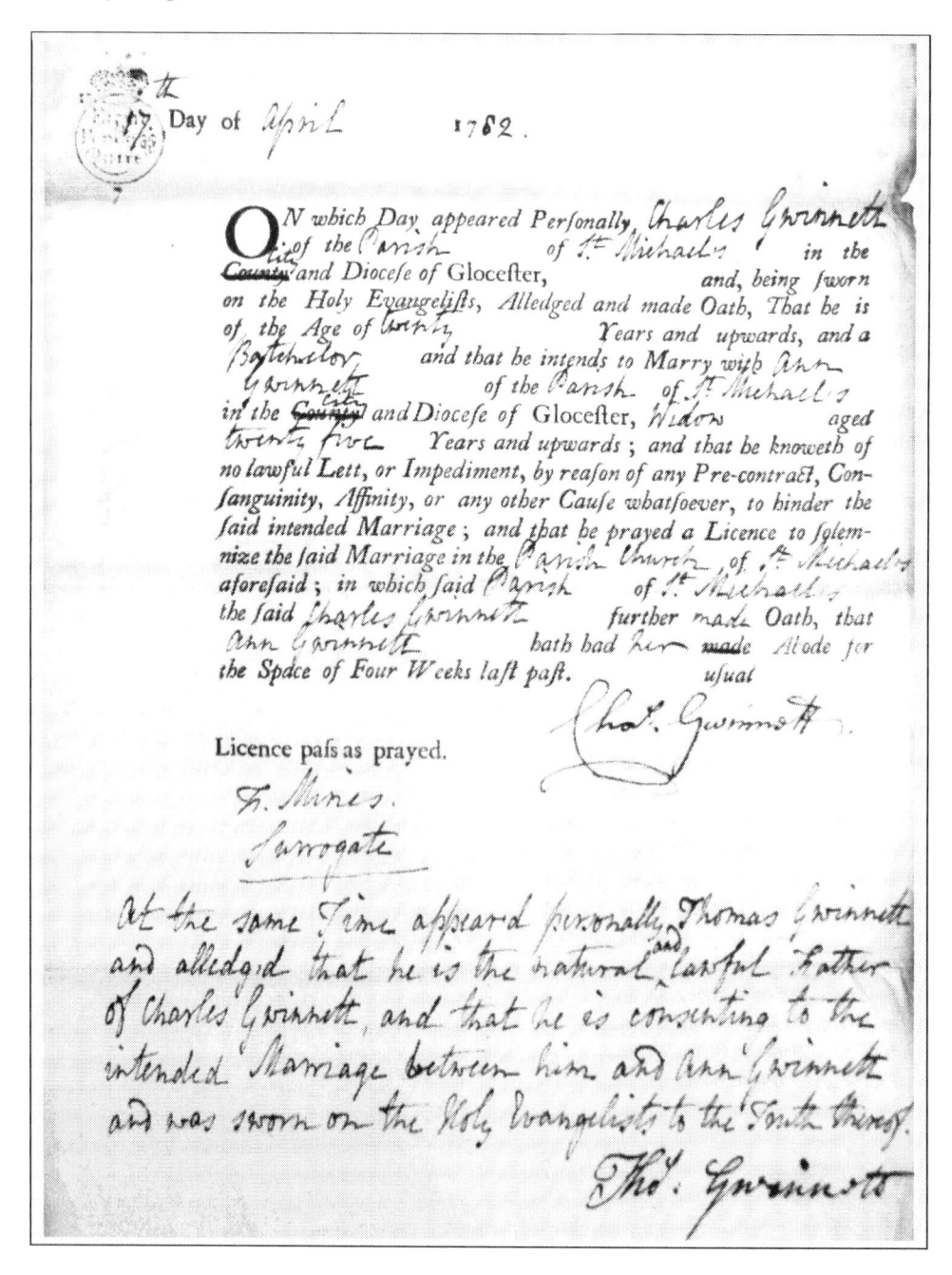

The marriage allegation of Charles Gwinnett, 1782.
G.A. Ref: Q2/35/75

8. More on Marriages

The marriage allegations usually recorded:

- The names of the bride and groom
- Their occupations
- Their marital status
- Their abode
- Their age
- Where they might marry.

Ages were often fairly precise but not always; they were usually described as being, for example, '24 years and upwards' meaning between 24 and 25 years old but there was no guarantee that the person was not much older. Ages of widows and widowers might be given as '21 years and upwards' which could mean anything over the age of 21, the age of majority. One person thus described was later found to be in his sixties at the time. As with the sample allegation, if either of the couple was under the age of 21, a parent had to give consent.

Allegations sworn at the Diocesan Registry before 1748 are held in volumes in the GDR/Q3 series; they cannot be photocopied but can be photographed. Those recorded there after 1748 are on loose sheets in bundles covering six month periods so photocopies may be obtained. They are in the GDR/Q2 series.

Two volumes of *Gloucestershire Marriage Allegations* edited by Brian Frith and published by the Records Section of the Bristol and Gloucestershire Archaeological Society (in 1954 and 1971 respectively) cover the periods 1638 to 1680 and 1681 to 1700 and include surrogate allegations up to 1694. The books each have an index to the names of the brides and grooms as well as one to the bondsmen. The name in the index leads to the page giving the name of the couple planning to marry and the date of the licence. You then need to find the church in which they were wed.

> Sept. 21. Robert Farmer, Hardwick, clothworker, and Alice Gyles, Aston, [? Aston Ingham], Herefords.
> Sept. 27. Mathew Parsons, Westerleigh, coal-miner, 26, and Elizabeth Weane, Chipping Sodbury, 23 : Bdm. John Clarke, Chipping Sodbury, apparitor.
> Sept. 28. Laurence Gwinnett, Shurdington, gent., 25, and Katherine Gregory, Alston, p. Cheltenham, 20.

Some entries from Gloucestershire Marriage Allegations for the year 1666.

Marriage licence allegations obtained after 1700 and up to 1837 are indexed on paper slips in Gloucestershire Archives. Each slip gives the name of one party, the year of the allegation and the reference required to locate the original document.

Discover Gloucestershire Ancestors

There are two large volumes on the open shelves in Gloucestershire Archives containing indexes to marriage licences covering the periods from 1830 to 1854 and from 1876 to 1906. Both have a rough index (e.g. names beginning with A are grouped together but not in strict alphabetical order). They list:

- When sworn
- Date of licence
- By whom sworn
- Name of bride and groom
- Their residences
- Their marital status
- Their age
- Where to be married.

The earlier volume (G.A. Ref: GDR/Q5/1) has over 8000 entries and the later volume (G.A. Ref: GDR/Q5/2) has over 3200 entries. The volume between 1854 and 1876 seems to be missing.

People living in the south of Gloucestershire would frequently go to Bristol to be married and would obtain their licences from the Bristol Diocese. To aid your search for these early marriages, there is a book entitled *Marriage Bonds for the Diocese of Bristol, 1637 – 1700* transcribed by Denzil Hollis and edited by Elizabeth Ralph, published by the Records Section of the Bristol and Gloucestershire Archaeological Society, 1952. It contains similar entries to those in the two Gloucestershire Marriage Allegation books.

At the Bristol Record Office, there is a manuscript index to licence bonds and allegations for the period from 1700 to 1800 and a card index covering 1804 to 1827 with references leading to the documents. However, these allegations held at Bristol Record Office only cover the parishes that fall within the City of Bristol or the Deanery of Bristol; they do not cover the parishes in the east of the Bristol Diocese. These appear to be included in the collection of allegations held at Gloucestershire Archives.

> *Note: Licence allegations for marriages in the eastern part of the Diocese of Bristol are held in Gloucestershire Archives not in Bristol Record Office.*

Two other indexes, not held in Gloucestershire, which should be considered when looking for that elusive marriage licence allegation are the Vicar General's Marriage Allegations and the Faculty Office Allegations, issued by the Archbishop of Canterbury. Although most of these referred to couples from the London area, they also include some people from Gloucestershire, so should be checked.

The Vicar General's Index, covering the period from 1694 to 1850, includes over 350,000 entries for allegations from couples from different dioceses but this index contains only surnames and the date of the licence. The Faculty Office Index which contains over 300,000 entries for couples from different provinces (Canterbury or York) between 1701 and 1850 does

8. More on Marriages

include forenames as well as surnames and the licence date. The original documents are held at the Lambeth Palace Library but the indexes can be accessed online and a copy purchased at the pay per view website British Origins on www.origins.net

Two corresponding pages from the Marriage Licence book.
G.A. Ref: GDR/Q5/1

Irregular and Clandestine Marriages

Despite the fact that marriages were supposed to take place in the parish of either the bride or the groom unless covered by a Bishop's licence, some marriages took place in a different parish. These were **irregular marriages** held by **marriage-mongers** or **marriage brokers**, clergymen who specialised in performing marriages for a fee, regardless of where the couple originated. A look at the registers for certain parishes will show that many of the marriages which took place there were for couples without residential qualifications. Such Gloucestershire parishes included:

- Bagendon
- Hampnett
- Hempsted
- Lassington
- Newington Bagpath
- Oddington

as well as many of the Gloucester City parishes, where the extra-parochial locations of South Hamlet and Littleworth were often given as the residence of the couple. Likewise, some Bristol parishes frequently held marriages for those from outside the city.

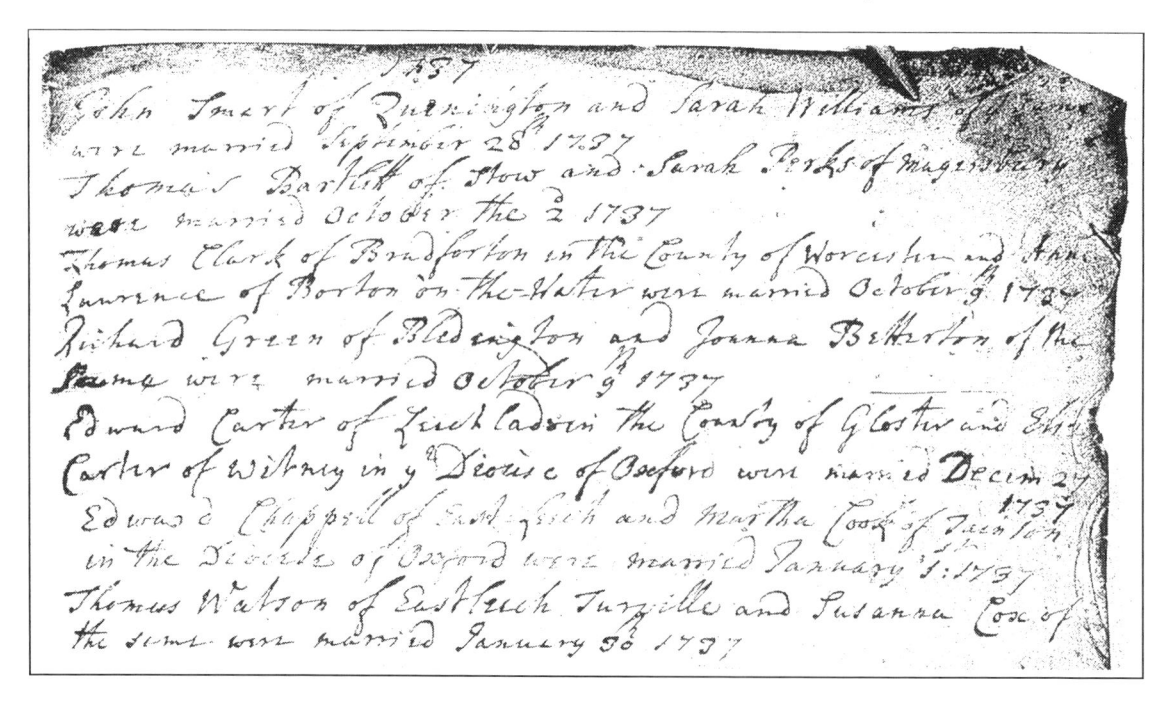

A copy of the marriage register for the parish of Hampnett. The married couples came from: Quenington, Stow on the Wold, Maugersbury, Bretforton (Worcestershire), Bledington, Lechlade, Witney and Tainton, (Oxfordshire) and Eastleach Turville.
G.A. Ref: P159 IN 1/2

8. More on Marriages

Hardwicke's Marriage Act of 1753 was brought in to prevent irregular or clandestine marriages which, although legally binding, did not comply with ecclesiastical law. A regular marriage was one that:

- Took place in the home parish of one of the participants or took place by licence
- was officiated by an authorised clergyman (see following example)
- was held between the time from 8am to noon
- was not held during certain closed seasons, e.g. between Rogation and Trinity Sundays.

A note in the Newnham register reads: 'The unnumbered entry between 321 and 322 concerns the same parties as No. 322. The marriage was apparently repeated on May 25th on the discovery that "Thomas White, Curate" was an impostor.' This was the "Sham Parson", Robert Peacock, also known as Revd. Thomas, William Whitefield, or William Whitmore. Thomas White was charged with fraud, found guilty and executed 'over the Lodge at the County Gaol' on 3rd September 1814.

G.A. Ref: P228 IN 1/6.

All other marriages were **irregular marriages**. A **clandestine marriage** was an irregular marriage which involved a degree of secrecy as well. The latter could occur in several circumstances. The groom might:

- be an apprentice contracted not to marry
- be marrying an under-age bride without parental consent, especially a rich bride
- marry a widow left money by her husband on condition she did not remarry
- already be married and therefore committing bigamy
- be too closely related to the bride to permit a church wedding.

The most famous location for clandestine marriages was the Fleet Prison where clergymen imprisoned for debt were willing to officiate at weddings, for a fee, the prison being outside the jurisdiction of the church. The Fleet registers start from the late 16th century but marriages occurred there long before that time. Approximately a quarter of a million marriage records have survived though many have been lost. Although most of the Fleet marriages were of people from London, there were a few Gloucestershire (and Bristol) people married there. Some clandestine marriages in the Fleet during various periods between 1680 and 1754 have been indexed on CD by Mark Herber, available from S&N Genealogy Supplies, but many remain unindexed.

Date	Groom	Groom's Abode	Bride	Bride's Abode	Note
1726 Aug 22	Richard Dimmery	Bristol	Jane Reason	Nottingham	Spinster. Certificate dated 1722
1727 Dec 27	John Dixson	Bristol	Martha Willson	London	Mariner
1728 Apr 12	John Cornish	Bristol	Ann Camell	Chalk, Kent	Bachelor / Widow
1728 May 11	John Williams	Ireland	Ann Lewis	Bristol	Bachelor / Widow
1728 May 28	William Wheeler	London	Joanna Johnson	Bristol	Mariner & Bachelor / Widow
1728 Aug 11	Charles Hudson	Beckford	Prichard Andrews	Canterbury	'sheare brushmaker'
1729 Oct	Edward Waine	Kentsford (Kempsford?)	Margaret Crowser	Harksum (Hexham?)	Labourer
c. 1753	Edward Hartland	b. Stroudwater	Martha		He aged 50+

Clandestine Gloucestershire and Bristol marriages held in the Fleet.

Marriage Settlements

A marriage settlement was a legally binding agreement between the parties involved in a marriage, and, frequently, their parents as well. In most cases, the couple or their parents were wealthy or owned land. Some settlements involved a sum of money, others property and some both. A father might settle a sum of money on his son or daughter (and her husband) so that they had sufficient income to live a suitable lifestyle, to buy a house to live in or to set up a business.

One type of marriage settlement was a bond so that, when a woman was widowed, the money she had provided on marriage or the monetary equivalent of the land she had brought to the marriage, was repaid. Another settlement would guarantee to pay the dowries, etc., of his wife's children by her first marriage which would otherwise not be paid as all she had inherited from her first husband became the property of her second husband. Other settlements involved payment of a sum of money to a trustee for the wife's use, so that the husband had no power over it.

A search in the Gloucestershire Archives catalogue using the words 'marriage settlement' returns over 2000 items. The vast majority of these are in personal collections though some are in council collections as they refer to property later held by them.

A Marriage Settlement for John Collett and Ann Hanman.
G.A. Ref: C/DC/S 52

Adultery
Although most marriages began in a hopeful way, not all of the couples lived happily ever after! A common cause of marital breakdown was adultery. The parish was concerned for the morals of its congregation and the churchwarden would report any lapses to the Bishop. The participants would then be summoned to appear before him. The records concerning such cases are held in the papers of the Consistory Court with Gloucestershire Archives reference GDR/B4/1. There are almost 500 of them.

A copy of the Consistory Court document dated October 1704 summoning Lawrence Gwinnett to appear before the Bishop to explain himself, having been caught 'in incontinency with Margaret Clifford, the wife of James Clifford of Charlton Regis in the open field.' The outcome is unknown.
G.A. Ref: GDR/B4/1/2196

8. More on Marriages

Divorce

If a marriage did break down and the couple wished to end their partnership, they would usually just separate as divorce was rare and difficult to come by. Before 1858, a private Act of Parliament was needed before a couple could divorce and, as this was very expensive, few people could afford to end their marriage in this way; only about 300 divorces occurred by the time the new laws came into being.

By virtue of an order from the Lord Bishops Court of Gloucester, the Sentence of Divorce between John Collet junior and Mary his wife was pronounced in the parish …. of Upp. Slaughter the twenty second Sunday after Trinity … 1685 the said sentence being confirmed by the Dean of the Archdeaconry and the Court of Delegates the reason they give is because of their incestuous marriage shee being the naturall and lawfull sister of his former wife deceased. By virtue of the same order this sentence of divorce was commanded to be here registered that it may be kept upon record.

Jos. Stone, Minister
Richard Perrett
John Hunt
Churchwardens

This sentence was decreed by Rich. Parsons, Dr. of Laws, and Chancellor of the Diocese of Gloucester. 1687.

G.A. Ref: P297 IN 1/2

Alternatives to divorce were annulment by the church authorities or legal separation. For most people, however, it was a case of enduring an unhappy marriage. As the marriage had taken place in church, it was the church which normally officiated when a marriage broke down. The parties could apply to the Bishop for an annulment which could be on the grounds of:

- the marriage having been bigamous
- the marriage being incestuous as in the case above
- that either the bride or groom was under the age of 21 at the time and had not had parental consent to the nuptials.

A legal separation could be granted if one partner was guilty of cruelty or adultery; if this occurred, neither partner was free to marry again but legally lived apart. In reality, few people resorted to either legal separation or annulment.

January 1858 saw the formation of a new Court for Divorce and Matrimonial Causes which made it easier to obtain a divorce, though it was still a difficult and expensive process for many people as most cases had to be heard in London. The number of cases of divorce increased. By the 1920s, registries were set up around the country and the petitions could be heard in more locations making it easier for those who lived outside of the capital.

> A BRISTOL CASE IN THE DIVORCE COURT.—In the Divorce Court, on Thursday, before Lord Penzance, the case of Gwinnett v. Gwinnett was heard. It was a petition by the husband for a judicial separation on the ground of his wife's desertion. The Hon. Mr. Thesiger appeared for the petitioner. In stating the case, he said the petitioner held a position in the Custom-house, Bristol, and he was married to the respondent on the 22nd December, 1852. He at that time was 38 years of age, and the respondent was 37. They lived together at Bristol until the year 1857, when the respondent left her husband and went to reside with her uncle, who also lived at Bristol. The petitioner had made several attempts to induce her to return to him, but had failed to do so, and therefore instituted these proceedings. George Gwinnett, the petitioner, having given evidence, the Court granted a decree for a judicial separation on the ground of desertion.

Article from the *Bristol Mercury* dated 11 June 1870.

Records of divorces before 1858 should be found in the ecclesiastical records, e.g. Consistory Court records, located at the county archives. By entering the surname in the online catalogue or checking the Personal Name Index (the latter is available only at the Archives), you should be able to see if any documents relating to a divorce remain. Some divorces took place in the London Consistory Court; the records for these are held at London Metropolitan Archives.

8. More on Marriages

Later records of those divorces which took place between 1858 and 1937 are held in the National Archives, reference J77 and indexed in J78. Not all of them have survived. Indexes can also be found online on the FindMyPast website. Since 1937, records of divorce are held at the Principal Registry of the Family Division, First Avenue House, 42-49 High Holborn, London, WV1V 6NP. These files are closed for a hundred years unless permission is granted by PRFD. There is also a fee to access these records. Their web address for information is: www.hmcourtsservice.gov.uk

In more recent times, in the mid-twentieth century, the local newspapers were a good source of information on divorce cases. Each time the Divorce Court was in session, lists of divorce decrees were given in the newspapers, including the name and address of the two participants and the reason for their separation, e.g. adultery, desertion or presumption of death. The more lurid cases were reported in some detail.

Bigamy

Because of the difficulty of obtaining a divorce, couples would quite frequently split from each other and go their own way. This would sometimes lead one of them to contract a second marriage whilst the first spouse was still living. In most cases, this would take place in a different part of the country so that the news would not reach his or her earlier parish.

Bigamy was a more common occurrence than may be thought but it is not that easy to spot. You may find an ancestor who has described himself as a widower when he 'married' but have been unable to locate a death for his first wife before that date or even, maybe, located her death after his second 'marriage'. Checking the signatures in the marriage registers or on the marriage certificate or noting the names of the informants on a death certificate might help to confirm that you have the same person in each case.

Bigamy was obviously against the practices of the church. Early records of bigamy will be found in the Consistory Court documents but few seem to have survived for the Diocese of Gloucester. However, it was not until 1861 that it became a criminal offence. Few people were actually caught and charged with the offence.

One group of people who quite often committed bigamy were the convicts who were already married when they were transported to Australia or elsewhere and who had no chance to return to this country but settled down to live honest lives once their sentences were over. Take the case of Joseph Pullen of Marshfield. Born in 1795, he married Charlotte Cox in 1820 but, one year later, after committing several crimes, he was transported to Van Diemen's Land (now Tasmania) where he served his seven year sentence. Rather than returning to his native land, he settled down and married again in 1831, this time to Ann Turner, and raised a family. He died in 1844, still a comparatively young man. Incidentally, Charlotte also married again.

More recent cases would have been reported in the local newspapers. One such case, in 1900, concerned a man by the name of John Kinsella who was caught having married at least four unsuspecting women!

A FOUR-FOLD BIGAMIST
MARRIED TWICE IN CHELTENHAM
FIVE YEARS PENAL SERVITUDE

At the Central Criminal Court, on Tuesday, John Kinsella, alias Frederick Hall, was indicted for feloniously marrying Mary Beale, Marion Jennings, Agnes Lane and Mary Ann Dormer, in each case his wife then being alive; also for stealing money and goods belonging to three of the women named. Prisoner pleaded guilty to the charges of bigamy but not guilty to the charges of larceny.

Mr Matthews, for the Treasury, referred to the peculiar and extraordinary character of the bigamy charges. In 1894, the prisoner married his cousin and resided at Manchester where he was employed as a tailor. He was discharged but was subsequently found concealed on their premises and was sentenced. With his wife, he went to live at Leeds, and in 1898, he deserted his wife.

In 1899, there appeared a matrimonial advertisement in a Gloucestershire paper and meeting in this way a young woman named Beale, he married her at Cheltenham on January 6th. A few days later, he left her, having obtained all her property, and contracted a marriage with Marion Jennings, at Cheltenham. He obtained her jewellery and left her, and under the pretence of marriage he seduced a domestic servant and obtained from her £20 under the pretence of purchasing a business.

In September, he married, in the name of Reginald Wilkinson, Agnes Lane at Kingston, and obtained from her £40 and jewellery which he pledged at once for £11. Nineteen days after this wedding, he married, at Reading, Mary Ann Dormer. It was impossible to imagine a more heartless and cruel bigamy case, or a case of a more aggravated kind. The women the prisoner had deceived and robbed could ill afford to lose what to them was considerable property, and in fact their all. Besides the bigamous marriages actually contracted, the prisoner had made arrangements to marry three other women. His whole object seemed to be to rob the women of their property.

The Recorder: He seems to have made a regular business of this. Mr S. Jones, for the prisoner, pointed out that most of the ladies with whom his client had contracted bigamous marriages were considerably older than himself. That was no excuse but it showed that the prisoner was not taking advantage of young girls of no experience to trifle with them. In nearly every case, the women consented to marriage after a few days' acquaintance.

The Recorder said it was difficult to conceive of a worse case than this. The prisoner had made it a regular business to get hold of these foolish women, to take all they had in the world and then to decamp. He had, apart from robbing them, done great injury to these women by jeopardising their characters and inducing them to believe he was in a position to make honest wives of them when he was not. He must go to penal servitude for five years.

Gloucester Journal, 15 December 1900

8. More on Marriages

Finally, you may be able to find out more about your ancestor's marriage by checking the local newspapers. If a woman deserted her husband, he might wish to publicly disown her and any debts she might incur. A notice would be placed in the press wherever he thought she might go.

> Whereas Katharine, the Wife of Henry Cofter of Heddington in the County of Wilts, hath Eloped from him: This is to give Notice to all Persons not to truft her on his Account; for he will not pay any Debts contracted by her fince the Third of this Inftant June. Witnefs my Hand,
> Henry Cofter.

Advertisement from the *Gloucester Journal* of 13th June 1731.

In the early days, only the really famous/important people would have been mentioned in the local press but as time progressed, this changed. First of all, notices appeared stating who was getting married, where and when.

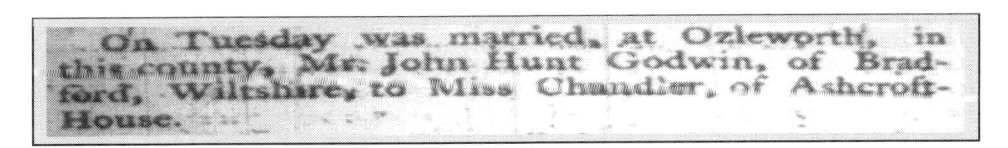

> On Tuesday was married, at Ozleworth, in this county, Mr. John Hunt Godwin, of Bradford, Wiltshire, to Miss Chandler, of Ashcroft-House.

Advertisement from the *Gloucester Journal* dated 12th January 1801.

In the 1930s, even my own parents, who were just an ordinary couple, not even particularly well known in their neighbourhood, had two columns in the local newspaper detailing their marriage at the Bethel Congregational Church in Queenborough on the Isle of Sheppey. The clothes worn by the bride, her bridesmaids and the mothers of the happy couple were described in detail. My mother:

> 'looked handsome in a full length frock of Jubilee blue satin, the skirt being gracefully shirred at the hem. The bodice was adorned with an original draped neckline, outlined with silver lame and finished with a diamante clasp, the wide bishop sleeves being shirred at the top. The lace gauntlet gloves gave a smart finish. She wore a smart blue picture hat and carried a bouquet of pink carnations and ferns.'

The article, describing the wedding of Sidney Blinkhorne to Alice Elizabeth Sosbe, provided a wonderful opportunity to find out more about the families of the happy couple and their relations. If I hadn't already known, I would have learned the names and addresses of the parents of the bride and groom, and the names of the bride's sisters and that one of the bride's grandmothers had died before 1935, as she placed her bouquet of pink carnations on to the grave. The article also told me that they would start their married life living at 37 High Street in Cinderford where my father was working.

The Wedding of Sidney Blinkhorne to Alice Elizabeth Sosbe in 1937

There followed a list of over 50 people who had given the couple wedding presents, together with a note of the gift. The parents of the bride and groom gave them furniture, most of the rest of their friends and neighbours gave them items to help them set up house together. I now know that the canteen of cutlery that I still have came from Uncle Dick and Aunt Lou, on my mother's side of the family, but I haven't worked out yet who 'Little Sherley Hare' was who gave them the biscuit barrel!

Chapter 9

More on Deaths

*'To every man upon this earth
Death cometh soon or late'*

*Lord Macaulay
1800 – 1859, poet*

Discover Gloucestershire Ancestors

There is a tendency, when researching family history, to concentrate on births, baptisms and marriages in order to progress your tree back farther but deaths, burials and related records can be very informative as well and can help to fill out the picture of your ancestor's life. Death can be an important time in the lives of an ancestor's survivors, too – did they inherit some money or property, did they move away and emigrate or did they, perhaps, get married once their parental responsibilities were removed? One of the most important things to do is always to check to make sure that the person you have been following did not die as an infant! You would not be the first researcher to follow a person through to adulthood and marriage only to find later that he or she died in infancy! So you need to locate your ancestor's burial place and to be sure that it is the correct one.

> *Note: Always check to make sure that the person you are researching did not die in infancy.*

Possible means of legally disposing of bodies include:

- burial in a churchyard
- burial in a nonconformist burial ground
- burial in a private cemetery
- burial in a civic cemetery
- burial in a military cemetery or burial at sea
- cremation.

The method chosen depended upon the religion and wishes of the deceased and his family, the situation of the death and the period in which the death had occurred. Until the middle of the 18th century, only the first two options were available. Soon thereafter, private companies opened up cemeteries where people could be buried for a fee. One such private cemetery was opened in 1762 near Lawford's Gate in Bristol but the only one for which records exist at Bristol Record Office was the Howland's Burial Ground which opened in 1804.

However, by the middle of the 19th century, churchyards were becoming full and demand for space was growing. The authorities were beginning to worry about the danger of spreading disease following various cholera epidemics so the Burial Act was passed by Parliament in 1853 to reduce burials in towns and cities, to close the churchyards and to set up civic cemeteries outside of the population centres. Burial Boards were established as the public authority to provide and oversee civic cemeteries. Some of the Bristol and Gloucestershire churchyards were closed at this time. A subsequent act in 1879 permitted cemeteries to be non-denominational, thus overcoming nonconformists' refusal to be buried in consecrated ground.

> *Note: Many churchyards in the cities of Gloucester and Bristol were closed to further burials from 1854 onwards when public cemeteries were opened.*

9. More on Deaths

From 1837 onwards, you can find the date of death from the General Register Office Death Indexes and order your ancestor's death certificate but, once you have received it, you will discover that it does not tell you where he or she was buried. So the search begins to try to locate the site of the grave, assuming the deceased was not cremated. If the death took place before civil registration in 1837, then you should be able to find a burial record in the parish registers for the deceased person's home parish - but life is not always that simple.

Most burials took place in the parish churchyard or local nonconformist burial ground so you should check the local parish registers first but people did move around and, if they died away from home, were usually buried where they died as transporting the body back to the home parish was expensive and beyond the means of most families. Finding a burial in such circumstances thus becomes a problem.

"An Act to amend the laws concerning the burial of the dead in England beyond the limits of the metropolis, and to amend the Act concerning the burial of the dead within the metropolis" made for the protection of the public health, no new burial-ground should be opened in the city of Gloucester, without the previous approval of one of Her Majesty's Principal Secretaries of State, and that burials should be discontinued therein, with the following modifications, viz:

> To be discontinued forthwith in the following churches and chapels: the *Cathedral, St Aldate, St John the Baptist, St Michael with St Mary-de-Grace, St Mary de Crypt with St Owen, St James, St Nicholas, St Mary-de-Lode, St Catherine, St Luke and Christ Church*; in the *Independent Chapel, the Wesleyan Chapel, the Baptist Chapel, the Unitarian Chapel, St Margaret's Chapel* and in *St Mary Magdalen's Hospital Chapel*, and within five yards thereof.
>
> In *Christ Churchyard* burials to be confined to vaults and brick graves, in which each coffin shall be embedded in charcoal and entombed.
>
> Burials to be discontinued from and after the thirty-first December, one thousand eight hundred and fifty-five, in the Cathedral Precincts and (except in existing vaults and brick graves, in which each coffin shall be embedded in charcoal and separately entombed), in the churchyards of *St Aldate, St John the Baptist, St Michael with St Mary-de-Grace, St Mary de Crypt, St Nicholas, St Mary-de-Lode, St Catherine, and Christ Church(Spa)*; and also discontinued from the same date in the Burial-grounds of the Infirmary, of the Independent Chapel, of the Wesleyan Chapel, of the Baptist Chapel, of the Unitarian Chapel, and of St Michael.
>
> In the *Churchyards* of *St James* and *St Luke*, and in the new burial ground of *St John's*, one body only to be buried in each grave, and no grave to be ever re-opened. The regulations for new burial-grounds to be observed in the said two churchyards, and in the *Wootton Cemetery*, near Gloucester.

Extract from an Act of Parliament relating to the closure of Gloucester City churchyards for burials, dated 11th December 1854.
G.A. Ref: GBR/L4/6/3

Burial Indexes

To find a burial in a Gloucestershire parish or in a nonconformist burial ground, once you have searched the more obvious local registers, there are some indexes available to help you with your search. The International Genealogical Index (I.G.I.) contains very few burials, but Gloucestershire Family History Society has produced on CD an index and transcript for burials within the Diocese of Gloucester; this includes some of the nonconformist burial grounds from registers held at Gloucestershire Archives. The period covered is from 1813 to 1851 and, in the case of some parishes, even later. The CD is available from the GFHS, and can be purchased either online or at their Family History Centre. Although most indexes either begin or end at 1837 when civil registration began, this one covers the extended period up to 1851. So, for instance, if you can locate an ancestor on the 1841 census but not on the 1851 census, you can check to see if he or she was buried in the intervening ten years.

Surname	Forenames	Date of Burial	Age	Abode	Parish
Gwinnett	Agnes	28 May 1830	91	Cleeve	Bishops Cleeve
Gwinnett	Ann	19 May 1833	65	Crickley Hill	Cowley
Gwinnett	Ann	23 Mar 1839	69	Withington	Withington
Gwinnett	Charles	28 Jul 1822	59	St Mary de Crypt	Barnwood
Gwinnett	Charles	17 Aug 1843	10	Charlton Kings	Charlton Kings
Gwinnett	Eliza	5 Feb 1847	4	Union	Painswick
Gwinnett	Elizabeth	14 Jan 1836	76	Rodmarton	Rodmarton
Gwinnett	Elizabeth	10 Sep 1848	5	St John the Baptist	Gloucester
Gwinnett	George	19 Nov 1847	40	St John the Baptist	Gloucester
Gwinnett	Hester	18 Jul 1831	68	Gloucester	Sandhurst
Gwinnett	Isaac	24 Feb 1822	48	St Mary de Lode	Gloucester
Gwinnett	Jemima	22 Jan 1849	60	Cowley	Cowley
Gwinnett	John	16 Jan 1847	2	Union	Painswick
Gwinnett	John	7 Dec 1849	93	St Mary de Crypt	Gloucester
Gwinnett	Julia	22 Feb 1844	1	Painswick	Painswick
Gwinnett	Mary	19 Mar 1833	25	Cleeve	Bishops Cleeve
Gwinnett	Mary	29 Jul 1843	66	Cheltenham	Prestbury
Gwinnett	Mary	30 May 1844	66	Foxcote	Withington
Gwinnett	Robert	12 Jul 1836	34	Dumbleton	Dumbleton
Gwinnett?	Sarah	1 Dec 1829	83	Wotton St Mary	Barnwood
Gwinnett	Sarah	8 Oct 1836	38	Woodmancote	Bishops Cleeve
Gwinnett	Theodore	20 Apr 1827	54	Cheltenham	Prestbury
Gwinnett	William	9 Nov 1834	18	Cowley	Cowley
Gwinnett	William	14 Nov 1851	76	Union	Painswick
Gwinnett	William H.	8 Feb 1818	5m	St John the Baptist	Gloucester

The Gloucestershire Family History Society has also produced some CDs containing transcripts of nonconformist registers and the second of these CDs contains burials for 13 Gloucestershire nonconformist chapels. They are:

Burial Ground	Period Covered
France Meeting, Chalford Hill, Independent Chapel	1785-1837
Blakeney Baptist Chapel	1834-1837
Bourton on the Water Baptist Chapel	1776-1788, 1790-1837
Chedworth Independent Chapel	1800-1837
Cheltenham Chapel of Protestant Dissenters	1810-1837
Cirencester Coxwell Street Baptist Chapel	1735-1839
Dursley Wesleyan Methodist Chapel	1812-1837
Gloucester Barton Street Chapel	1785-1836
Gloucester Northgate Street Wesleyan Chapel	1830-1837
Gloucester Southgate Street Independent Chapel	1786-1837
Littledean Independent Chapel	1821-1837
Mitcheldean Independent Chapel	1784-1837
Oakridge Methodist (Wesleyan) Chapel	1909-1983

Bristol and Avon Family History Society has produced similar indexes on CD to the burials in the Diocese of Bristol and nonconformist burials in South Gloucestershire and the City of Bristol between 1754 and 1837. These are available for purchase. They also have an online burial index which includes burials in the southern part of the county. Check out: www.bafhs.org.uk

The third option is the National Burial Index which is now in its third edition and can be purchased from the Federation of Family History Societies. Whilst not offering complete coverage of the country, it has over 18 million burial entries for England and Wales, from the 16th to the 21st century, including over 180,000 burials for Gloucestershire. Their website is at: www.ffhs.org.uk

If your ancestor was a serviceman who died in one of the wars, you should be able to locate his death and burial place, if it is known, on the excellent Commonwealth War Graves Commission website. This will give you name, rank and service number of the person, the regiment he or she served in, date of death and age, the name of the cemetery and, usually, the next of kin. See: www.cwgc.org

There is also an excellent website based upon the book *Leaving all that was Dear* by J Devereux and G. Sacker which covers Cheltenham soldiers killed in the Great War. The website is at: www.remembering.org.uk. The book is one of several appearing recently to record the sacrifice made by our soldier ancestors.

Burial Grounds

If you have still not located the burial place of your ancestor, you need to know where else you might look besides the more obvious churchyard or cemetery. To help with your search, GFHS volunteers have listed all of the known burial and memorial sites 'whatever size or denomination, from AD 1000 onwards, although many of the established parish churchyards are older' that have been found in the county of Gloucestershire. The index, called MICAT, was updated in 2002. Whilst not absolutely complete, it is the most comprehensive list in existence and should not be ignored. The list, which stretches to 20 pages, can be found on the GFHS Memorial Index CD available via the GFHS website. A sample entry, for the village of Chedworth, is shown below, listing details of the parish church, the nonconformist church and the war memorial..

CHEDWORTH: (Lower) Congregational Chapel & Graveyard Ref: SP 1694 1111
Pancake Hill (1752 - 1980)
Some buried at Northleach Independent.

Nonconformist Chapel and Meeting-houses (Royal Commission on Hist. Mon. of England) 1985: PHILIPPS Revd. Stephen (d. 1836) and two wives (Mary d. 1829, Mary d. 1839).

CHEDWORTH: St Andrew Ref: SP 051 121
Rudder, *History of Gloucestershire*, 1779: p333 1779 SELY, WALL I
Bigland, *Memorial Inscriptions* 1781: + List B
Bristol and Gloucestershire Archaeological Society Transactions v55 p143 1932 SCLY
J & N Jones & Nash memorial inscriptions of 1957: List of 98 memorials
Verey's *Pevsner's Gloucestershire*, 1970: Several & Photograph
Golding 1995: List (Copy with GFHS)

CHEDWORTH: War Memorial Ref: SP 0697 1111

Cemeteries
When someone was buried in a cemetery, a notice of interment was provided and sent to the Burial Board. It contained:

- name of the deceased
- parent's name, if child
- home address
- age
- date and place of death
- date and time of burial
- officiating minister
- grave reference
- if consecrated ground
- type of grave, e.g. vault
- if bought in perpetuity
- if already purchased
- depth of grave
- undertaker's name
- signature of next of kin

Most cemeteries retain their own records but some have been deposited at Gloucestershire Archives. For instance, registers of pauper graves and purchased graves for the New Cemetery at Coney Hill, Gloucester, are there.

Notice of Interment for Ellen Verrinder dated 1873. The document is included by courtesy of Stroud District Council.
G.A. Ref: DA16/205/19

Year	Date of Burial	Forenames	Surname	Age	Sex
1857	4 Oct	Anthony	Bubb	37	M
1857	4 Oct	Samuel	Wildings	4 months	M
1857	18 Oct	James	Bishop	27	M
1857	21 Oct	John	De Bar	73	M
1857	3 Nov	William	Miles	3 months	M
1857	4 Nov	Henry	Herbert	76	M
1857	7 Nov	James	Bethel	76	M
1857	9 Nov	Henry	Tedstill	25	M
1857	13 Nov	John	Brown	50	M
1857	15 Nov	Rosehannah	Harris	2 weeks	F
1857	19 Nov	William	Rawlings	43	M
1857	22 Nov	James	Ralph	14	M
1857	26 Nov	Hannah Priscilla	Ball	6	F
1857	26 Nov	Catherine	Huggins	6 months	F
1857	7 Dec	Frances Susannah	Frampton	16 months	F
1857	10 Dec	Charlotte	Barnes	10	F
1857	22 Dec	Charles	Veal	28	M
1857	26 Dec	Harriet	Cole	19 months	F
1857	29 Dec	Ellen	McCarthy	22	F
1857	31 Dec	William	Hyde	55	M
1857	31 Dec	Thomas	Piffe	62	M
1858	10 Jan	John Elliott	Lane	65	M
1858	10 Jan	Martha	Lewis	68	F
1858	12 Jan	Dennis	Haire	3	M
1858	12 Jan	Elizabeth	Godfrey	70	F
1858	19 Jan	Daniel Capel	Veale	65	M
1858	20 Jan	Elizabeth	Walker	4 weeks	F
1858	24 Jan	Tramp	Not known	80	M
1858	24 Jan	Eliza	Churchill	34	F
1858	27 Jan	Hannah	Hyde	84	F
1858	27 Jan	Esther	Beard	56	F
1858	5 Feb	Mary	Cole	9 weeks	F
1858	6 Feb	Harriet	Meadows	2 months	F
1858	22 Feb	Mary	Lacey	1 day	F
1858	25 Feb	Joseph	Webb	75	M
1858	26 Feb	Margaret	Lacey	37	F
1858	28 Feb	John	Holland	20	M
1858	3 Mar	Ann	Woodward	78	F
1858	15 Mar	Caroline	Wightwick	2	F
1858	17 Mar	James	Drake	54	M

Transcript of the first entries in the Pauper's Burial Register for Coney Hill Cemetery.
G.A. Ref: GBR/L4/4/3a

9. More on Deaths

There are currently cemeteries in at least the following locations:

Gloucestershire

Bishops Cleeve	Blockley	Brimscombe
Charlton Kings	Cheltenham	Churchdown
Chipping Campden	Cinderford	Cirencester
Coleford	Dursley	Gloucester
Kemble	Lydney	Moreton in Marsh
Newent	Northleach	Painswick
Sapperton	Stow on the Wold	Stratton
Stroud	Tewkesbury	Winchcombe
Wotton under Edge		

South Gloucestershire and Bristol

Almondsbury	Arnos Vale	Avon View
Brislington	Canford	Filton
Greenbank	Henbury	Kingswood
Mangotsfield	Marshfield	Mayshill
Ridgeway Park	Shirehampton	South Bristol
Thornbury	Westerleigh	Wickwar

The Gloucestershire Family History Society has begun to transcribe the burial registers for Gloucester Cemetery. To date, they are up to 1901 and the CD is available to purchase but there are still many registers to transcribe. Their index includes:

- Surname of deceased
- Forenames of deceased
- Date of burial
- Description e.g. wife of X
- Age at death
- Gender
- Last residence
- Place of death
- Number of grave
- Situation of grave
- Officiating minister
- Volume and Page reference

Tewkesbury Historical Society has recently produced a booklet and an accompanying CD giving the history of their local cemetery. It includes, among many interesting articles, information relating to the cholera epidemics in the town and an index with plan of all the burials there since it was opened in 1857. The CD contains details of all those buried in the cemetery, a map showing the location of each tomb and some photographs of headstones.

Surname	Christian Names	Date of Burial	Description	Age	Sex	Last Residence, Parish and City or County	Place where death occurred	No. of Grave	Situation of Grave	Officiating Minister	Vol. + Page No
Gwilliam	Ann	12 Jan 1863		66	Female	St Nicholas, City of Gloucester	White Swan Lane	6113	Consecrated Ground	Hugh Fowler, Headmaster of the Kings School, Gloucester	1/122
Gwilliam	Henry William	4 Aug 1863		2 wks	Male	St John the Baptist, City of Gloucester	3 Hare Lane	7698	Consecrated Ground	John Emeris, Perpetual Curate of St James	1/150
Gwilliam	Ann	20 Dec 1863		50	Female	St Nicholas, City of Gloucester	Deacon Street	5508	Consecrated Ground	William H Hutchinson, Curate of St Mark	2/4
Gwilliam	Mary Ann	5 Apr 1868		65	Female	St John the Baptist, City of Gloucester	33 Sherborne Street	8354	Consecrated Ground	Barry Chas Browne, Rector of St John the Baptist	3/16
Gwilliam	Philip	29 Apr 1870		73	Male	St John the Baptist, City of Gloucester	3 Brothers Place	8354	Consecrated Ground	John Emeris, Perpetual Curate of St James	3/141
Gwilliam	Frederick Thomas	5 Feb 1871		15 mths	Male	St Catherine, City of Gloucester	1 Wellington Terrace	6654	Consecrated Ground	John Emeris, Perpetual Curate of St James	3/197
Gwinnell	David	26 Jul 1866		11	M	St Mary de Lode, City of Gloucester	Clare Street	5253	Consecrated Ground	John Mayne, Asst Curate St. Mark	2/138
Gwinnett	Hester	23 Dec 1863		3 mths	Female	St Catherine, City of Gloucester	Park Street	5327	Consecrated Ground	C Naylor, Curate of St Mark	2/4
Gwinnett	Sophia Elizabeth	15 Jul 1867		81	Female	St John the Baptist, City of Gloucester	6 Worcester Street	5007	Consecrated Ground	John Emeris, P C of St James	2/180
Gyde	Louisa Bridget	24 Feb 1860	(w) of Henry Gyde	65	Female	Hamlet of Barton St Michael, City of Gloucester	Hampden Place	10187	Consecrated Ground	John Emeris, Perpetual Curate of St James	1/56
Hacker	Elizabeth Ann	31 Jan 1867		48	Female	Barton St Mary, County of Gloucester	Regent Street	5694	Consecrated Ground	John Emeris, Perpetual Curate of St James	2/162
Hacker	Mary Ann	15 Apr 1868		5 mths	Female	Barton St Mary County of Gloucester	31 New Street	1772	Unconsecrated Ground	William Collings, Minister of Brunswick Rd Chapel	3/17
Hackney	Jane	14 May 1858		7	Female	Parish of St Nicholas, City of Gloucester	Quay Street	9388	Consecrated Ground	W Balfour, Incumbent of St Nicholas	1/13

A sample printout from the developing GFHS Gloucester Cemetery Index.
© Gloucestershire Family History Society 2011.

Crematoria

Cremation became legal in 1884 but was not very popular until quite recently. Although most people are cremated today, only 10% of the population was being cremated by the middle of the 20th century. Records of cremation are similar to those of burial. None has yet been transcribed or deposited in Gloucestershire Archives or Bristol Record Office so you need to contact the crematorium for information on those who were cremated. Some will have had memorial plaques displayed in the crematorium grounds but others will have no lasting memorial site at all.

There are seven crematoria in Gloucestershire and Bristol. They are located at:

- Arnos Vale
- Canford
- Cheltenham
- Forest of Dean
- Gloucester
- South Bristol
- Westerleigh

A website, www.deceasedonline.com is being developed which provides some burial and cremation records. The index is free to search.

Monumental Inscriptions

Many a happy hour has been spent, wandering around a country churchyard, looking at the headstones, trying to find an ancestor's grave. Some churchyards have been cleared, with the stones displayed around the perimeter of the site, in others, the headstones have been lain flat to prevent accidents should the slab fall. Some have been turned into wildlife sanctuaries and are home to butterflies, birds and small mammals as well as our ancestors whilst some churchyards are now very overgrown and neglected.

Gravestones and memorial tablets give us tangible evidence of our ancestors' lives. Important people in the parish were often buried inside the church or just outside the church door but those graves with tombstones on the floor will have suffered from the passage of hundreds of feet over the years. Family tombstones are often grouped together making the search much easier. But don't just look at headstones. Check the stained glass windows for dedications, look at the plaques around the church walls and you may even sit and pass the time of day on a bench placed in the churchyard in memory of your ancestor.

It should be remembered that not all headstones actually refer to a burial; some are just memorials to the person who has been buried or cremated elsewhere. Equally important, you should be aware that not all people could afford any kind of headstone; a simple wooden cross used by the poorest of folk, would have disintegrated by now so no marker will be found. For the paupers who could not even afford to pay for the burial and were buried by the parish, they may well be interred in large, common graves where no headstone would mark their passing.

Over the centuries, the stones have been affected by the weather, many have become faded and difficult to read; they may be covered with ivy or brambles making it almost impossible to read the inscription. We are extremely fortunate in Gloucestershire, therefore, to have a work affectionately known as 'Bigland'. Its full title is: *Historical, Monumental and Genealogical Collections, relative to the County of Gloucester, printed from the Original Papers of the late Ralph*

Bigland, Esq., Garter Principal King of Arms. This major work was edited by the late Brian Frith, M.B.E., and published in four volumes by the Bristol and Gloucestershire Archaeological Society, from 1989 onwards.

The Reverend Ralph Bigland (1711 - 1784) was a herald of the College of Arms who became Garter King of Arms in 1780. In 1737, he married Ann Wilkins of Frocester in Gloucestershire and his interest in the county was awakened. He began gathering information in 1750 with the intention of producing a new county history, but died before anything was printed. After his death, his son and others continued his work.

Bigland and his helpers copied coats of arms and transcribed inscriptions from monuments throughout the county; many, if not most, of these are now illegible. Thus we have access to the monumental inscriptions that we can no longer read covering a period up to 1790. Additional historical information is given for each parish including details of the manor, the incumbents, and other interesting features. Engravings showing many of the churches are included.

Most parishes within the county are included in the Bigland volumes. The parishes which were not included were those in the City of Gloucester itself and these have since been incorporated into a book by the Reverend Thomas Dudley Fosbrooke (1770 - 1842). Later, Henry Yates Jones Taylor (1826 - 1906) was to record more city memorial inscriptions.

Fosbrooke was appointed curate at Horsley church in 1794. In his book *An Original History of the City of Gloucester* first published in 1819, he gives a general history of the city of Gloucester and then takes each church in turn, beginning with the Cathedral, recording a little of their history, their incumbents and patrons and, most importantly for family historians seeking ancestors, the inscriptions and epitaphs to be found in the church and churchyard. Some dissenting meeting houses are included.

As an example, for St. Mary de Crypt church, in Southgate Street, he gives the alternative names of Christ Church, St. Mary in the South, St. Mary Within the South Gate, St. Mary of South Gate or simply, St. Mary's of Gloucester. After that follows the history and description of the church before listing the incumbents and patrons since the 12th century. He then records the inscriptions in the chancel, without the chancel, in the body of the church, both as memorials and gravestones set in the floor and finally, those in the graveyard.

Amongst others, recorded in the body of the church, he lists: Elizabeth Morris, a faithful servant, who lived with Mr. Samuel Wilse, of this parish, near 26 years, died June 14, 1772, aged 81 years: Arthur Lysons, of this city, died 1st March 1597 and Anne his wife 9 June 1619: John Purlewent, of this city, and Bridget, his relict; he died June 3rd, 1672, aged 70, she August 13, 1701 aged 100: Richard Gough, goldsmith, August 31, 1701, aged 71.

The work by Henry Taylor, entitled *Memorials and Citizens of Gloucester* has been transcribed by volunteers and is available on CD from the GFHS. It contains articles about many leading citizens of Gloucester, some pedigrees, genealogical information of

9. More on Deaths

all kinds and a multitude of monumental inscriptions. So, from the churchyard of St. Mary de Crypt, he records:

To the Memory/ of/ John Gwinnett/ who died Dec 4 1849/ aged 93 years/ He died in the Faith of his/ Saviour and in sure hope of resurrection and life to come/ Also of Urania Gwinnett/ who died April 28 1859 aged 76 years/ "I know that my Redeemer liveth"/ Also of William Gwinnett/ who died May 20 1860 aged 97 years/ For over with the Lord/ Also of Urania Mary Morris George born Feb[y] 23rd died April 5th 1844./ It is well with the child

As you can see from the photograph, without this entry from Taylor's work, it would be impossible to know the full inscription on John Gwinnett's tomb as the bottom section has eroded.

Many family history societies have transcribed the monumental inscriptions from tombstones, tablets and war memorials and Gloucestershire FHS is no exception. It has produced a CD which holds copies of inscriptions from nearly 150 churchyards, some nonconformist burial grounds and other memorials which can be purchased via their website.

A sample entry, offering additional genealogical information, gives:

> 246 Headstone type C5 with pedestal, kerbs and lead letters. This is now face down.
>
> Parish Records: Theodore Gwinnett buried April 20th.1827 aged 54, Mary buried July 29th. 1843 aged 66
>
> SACRED
> TO THE MEMORY OF
> WILLIAM HENRY GWINNETT,
> FIFTH SON OF THEODORE AND MARY GWINNETT,
> FORMERLY OF BROCKHAMPTON PARK,
> AND ALBION HOUSE CHELTENHAM,
> BORN 9TH MARCH 1809,
> DIED AT GORDON COTTAGE CHELTENHAM,
> 30TH JULY 1891.
> ALSO OF
> ROSA MATILDA, WIFE OF THE LATE
> THOMAS GILL PALMER,
> AND YOUNGEST SISTER OF THE ABOVE
> BORN 13TH MAY 1812,
> DIED AT ROYAL CRESCENT CHELTENHAM,
> 5TH JULY 1893.

Often you will get a plan of the churchyard or burial ground with the location of each grave, to enable you to find your ancestor's tomb more easily. Such a plan exists for Shortwood Baptist burial ground, along with a graveyard book telling you who was buried in each plot. In some transcriptions, the type of grave is also given to aid recognition. Some transcripts of monumental inscriptions have been made by parishioners and remain in the church for visitors to see. You should never forget, however, that some transcripts are wrong. Apart from the inevitable error in any transcript, there is a greater risk of mistakes with reading from headstones because of the difficulty of reading the original due to erosion and other factors.

> *Note: Always remember that memorial inscription transcripts may be wrong due to the poor state of the headstone.*

Many of the city graveyards have been closed to new burials since the mid nineteenth century and have since been cleared so that the area could be developed. At the time of clearance, some councils recorded information of those interred and copies of these were sent to the National Archives. For instance, there is an entry for Abbotswood in Cinderford in the RG37 category of records. A list still exists at Gloucestershire Archives for the graves moved from St. Mary de Lode, in Gloucester. The remains from there were transferred to the Gloucester Cemetery.

9. More on Deaths

A website which provides some Gloucestershire memorial inscriptions is the Wishful Thinking site at: www.wishful-thinking.org.uk/genuki/GLS/MIs.html

If your ancestor was a serviceman who died in one of the wars, you may be able to find details, not only from the Commonwealth War Graves Commission website, mentioned earlier, but also from one of the developing War Memorial websites, such as the United Kingdom National Inventory of War Memorials at www.ukniwm.org.uk or the Royal British Legion Roll of Honour website at: http://www.roll-of-honour.com where the information is organised by county.

A small booklet by Gwen Martin entitled *A Guide to some Memorials and Monuments in Gloucester Cathedral* gives information on 49 people recorded at the Gloucester Cathedral including Ralph Bigland, John Stafford Smith who wrote the music for the American National Anthem, the prison reformer George Onesiphorous Paul and the two local poets, F.W. Harvey and Ivor Gurney. A complete list of legible memorials in the Cathedral may be inspected at the information desk or bookstall.

Memorial Cards

You may be fortunate, in your family mementoes, to have one or more memorial cards. These cards were usually supplied by an undertaker during Victorian times. Some were sent out in black-edged envelopes as notification of a death or invitation to the funeral of the deceased. Others were merely in memory of the deceased person. Several years ago, a National Memorial Card Index was being kept which, at that time, held over 6000 names covering the period from 1845 to 1990, but this does not seem to have appeared online.

Sample Memorial Cards for Fryer Close and his wife.

Undertaker's Records

Linked to the burial of the deceased, there are still some undertaker's records that can contain useful information for the researcher, although only a few have been deposited at Gloucestershire Archives. Consider, for instance, the notebooks of J. W. Lewis of Stroud, undertaker, which cover a period from 1885 to 1937. He recorded the name of the deceased, his or her address, where and when the funeral would take place, who would carry the coffin and finished with a list of mourners and friends, some of whom were given a place of abode.

June 20 / 1895 Funeral of the late **Mrs Thomas Phipps** of The Parklands, Cainscross To be interred at Cainscross Church On Monday June 24th 1895 At 2.30. Procession to leave the house at 2 o/clock. **Officiating Clergyman**: Revd. E. W. Place, B.A. **Sexton**: G Chandler, Cainscross Lane **Bearers**: Mr Wm. Phipps, Stokenhill Farm, nr. Stroud Mr Wm. Phipps, Holcomb Farm, nr. Stroud Mr Rich. Hill, Callowell Farm Mr Geo. Chandler, Rodboro. --- **Mourners**: Wesley Whitfield, Cainscross Mr M. L. Feibusch(?), London	**Mourners and Friends:** Mr Saml Phipps, Redhouse Farm, Westrip Mr Jno. Phipps, King's Farm, Tunley nr Cirenr Mr Jno. Phipps, Parklands, Cainscross Mr Thos. Phipps, West End Farm, Arlingham Mr Jas. Merrett, St Augustus Farm, Arlingham Mr Wm. Hill, Stonehouse Mr Jos. Hill, King Street, Stroud Mr Jno. Hill, Butcher, Bath Road, Cheltenham Mr H. Holmes, Stonehouse Mr P. Phipps, The Dell, Painswick Mr W. Knight, Dudbridge Mr S. Butcher, Dudbridge Lane Mr C. Curtis, Cainscross Mr E. Barnard, Ebley Mr E. Wathen, Stroud Mr W. Gaskins, Cainscross Mr C. Merrett, St Augustus Farm, Arlingham Mr Wm. Merrett, St Augustus Farm, Arlingham Mr Jno. Pimbury, Sparkbrook, Birmingham ** Mr Aug. Pimbury, Kings Norton, Worcestershire Mr J. Alf. Pearce, Chemist, Cainscross ** Mr J. Wyndham, Cainscross ** These entries were crossed out.

A transcript of a page from the notebook of J. W. Lewis of Stroud, undertaker.
G.A. Ref: D2265/1/1

9. More on Deaths

Newspapers

The local or even the national newspapers can help you find out more about your ancestor's life and death. At the simplest level, you may well find a death notice that was placed in the local newspaper by the family, to inform people of the death of the deceased and the funeral arrangements. Similarly, nowadays, you find In Memoriam notices to register remembrance of those who died in previous years.

If the person who died was well-known locally, you may find that a journalist has actually written an obituary, recording the background and achievements of the deceased. These were particularly popular from the second half of the 19th century.

> **DEATH OF MR. W. H. GWINNETT.**
>
> Cheltenham has sustained a sad loss in the death of Mr. William Henry Gwinnett, one of its oldest and most esteemed townsmen, which occurred on Thursday at his residence, Gordon Cottage, North-place. The deceased gentleman was out walking about a fortnight since, and it is only within the last ten days that he has been laid aside, but no serious consequences were apprehended. Indeed, on Wednesday, when he was to have taken the chair at the Grammar School distribution of prizes, he was better, and the end came somewhat unexpectedly. The deceased was a J.P. for the county, and held many public appointments. He has been Chairman of the Conservative Club from its inauguration in 1881, and has held the position of leader of the Conservative party in Cheltenham since the death of the late Sir Alexander Ramsay. He was also Chairman of the Board of Governors of the Grammar School, Chairman of the Gas Company, Chairman of the County Bank, and of the Trustees of the Delancey Fever Hospital, of which he was the hon. treasurer. He was also a member of the Council of Cheltenham College, and a distinguished Mason. His decease, so comparatively sudden, has come as a shock not only to the party with which he was more particularly identified, but to the town at large. His fairness, generosity, and sound judgment won him many friends and sympathisers. The flags at both the Conservative and Liberal clubs were put half-mast.

Obituary for W. H. Gwinnett from the *Gloucester Journal* 1892

The obituary may be followed by a funeral report. Sadly, as William Henry Gwinnett was a bachelor, this gave little information on his relatives, mentioning only his sister. Again, placed by the family, there may be a note of 'Thanks' to those who attended the funeral and sent condolences. Obituaries are gradually appearing online at: www.deceasedonline.com

If your ancestor died without having left a will, you may find advertisements from solicitors, executors or administrators seeking beneficiaries, creditors and debtors, to enable them to deal with the estate of the deceased.

Likewise, if your ancestor died suddenly, through natural causes, accident, suicide or murder, you may be lucky enough to find full details of the coroner's inquest in the local newspaper. These can be particularly interesting and informative. (More details can be found in the chapter on Coroners' Records.)

Gloucestershire Archives have a card index to Birth, Marriage and Death notices in *Gloucester Journal* from 1880 to 1914. They also have a card index to items of local and national interest in the newspaper from 1859 onwards which includes some obituaries.

Other places that you might find obituaries and details on the death of an ancestor include:

- parish magazines which began in the late 19th century
- the *Gentleman's Magazine* (1731 – 1870)
- regimental magazines; contact: www.glosters.org.uk for information
- the *London Gazette*, online at: www.gazettes-online.co.uk

Death Duties
By the Legacy Duty Act of 1796, a tax, was imposed on some bequests in wills. These 'death duties' or 'estate duties' were the equivalent of the current Inheritance Tax. They were originally imposed on only those estates that were valued at more than £20. The requirements of the Act were extended in 1805 also in 1815 and again in 1853. To begin with, close relatives were not included if they inherited money but this changed over the years.

As these were national records, the Death Duty Registers (about 8000 of them) are held at the National Archives in series: IR 26 and IR 27. They have been indexed in Volume 177 of the List and Index Society publication and, currently, the period between 1796 and 1811 can be searched online. Death Duty records between 1904 and 1931 have been destroyed.

Each entry in the register includes:

- Date of probate and sum involved
- Name and description of deceased
- Name and place of abode of Executor or Executrix
- Name of Legatees, distinguishing Residuary Legatee
- Degree of Kindred
- Amount of Legacy or Annuity
- Particulars of the several Specific Legacies, Bequests in Trust – and of the Residue
- References to the Registers
- Amount of duty paid
- Any observations.

The entry in the Death Duty Register for John Butler of Sandhurst whose will was proven on 2nd October 1809 named his executors as William Barton and John Daniell and included the following list of beneficiaries and their legacies. Further details from the entry mentioned that Hester Gwinnett was the wife of William Gwinnett and that Susanna Workman was the wife of John Workman. Altogether, the information from this sort of register entry can add quite a lot of information to the family tree.

Legatee	Kinship	Legacy	Value	Duty Paid
1. Martha Daniel	Niece	£500	£500	£12 10s
2. John Daniel	Nephew	£500	£500	£12 10s
3. Thomas Butler	Nephew	Horse & Gun	£40 16s	£1 0s 5d
4. Hannah Butt	Niece	Stock & Furniture	£165 14s	£4 2s 10d
5. Hester Gwinnett	Niece	£50	£50	£1 5s
6. Susanna Workman	Niece	£50	£50	£1 5s
7. Sarah Drew	Niece	£50	-	-
8. Hannah Berry	Niece	£50	-	-
9. Thomas Butler	Bro	Residue	£522 13s 3d	£13 1s 3d

A transcript of part of the Death Duty Register for John Butler, late of Sandhurst
NA Ref: IR 26/346

Few records of death duties exist at Gloucestershire Archives but where they do, they are listed in the online catalogue under the family name and are usually held either in family estate papers or in solicitors collections.

Inquisitiones Post Mortem
If you are seeking ancestors back beyond the introduction of parish registers in 1538, you should check the Inquisitiones Post Mortem. These records cover a period from the 13th century up until 1660. When a tenant of the Crown died, an inquiry was held into his possessions and his heirs, the aim being to establish the value of the monarch's property and who should inherit it.

The inquest was held before a named jury and summoned witnesses taken from the neighbourhood so, even if the inquiry was not into a member of your family, you may find your ancestor listed amongst the jurymen or witnesses, thus indicating that he was a resident in the area at the particular time.

Inquisitiones Post Mortem records are held at the National Archives in Kew in the series C132-142. They have been indexed and some of them have been abstracted into a series of books entitled *Gloucestershire Inquisitiones Post Mortem* by W. P. W. Phillimore and George S. Fry published in 1893.

There are six volumes for Gloucestershire covering the following periods:

Volume	Period	Volume	Period
1	1625 – 1636	4	1236 – 1300
2	1637 – 1642	5	1302 – 1358
3	1625 – 1642	6	1359 - 1413

John Newton alias Newington, gentleman

Inquisition taken at Stow-on-the-Wold, 7th August, 10 Charles I [1634] before *Anthony Daston*, esq., *Anthony Hodges*, gent., *Leonard Chamberlayne*, escheator, and *Henry Brownjohn*, gent., feodary, after the death of *John Newton*, alias *Newington*, gent., by the oath of *William Roberts*, gent., *John Shaylor, Richard Barker, Thomas Mace, John Hayward, William Gunn, Henry Collett, John Penfield, Thomas Andrewes, Richard Baker, Thomas Guy, John Pegler, John Johnson, Thomas Allen, Peter Hayward,* junior, *William Hulls, Nicholas Parrett, Richards Robert, and Thomas Hobbes,* who say that

John Newton alias *Newington* was seised of the manor of Wormington, and of all messuages, lands, rents., etc., thereto belonging; one messuage or tenement in Stoke Orchard *alias* Stoke Archer late parcel of the manor of Stoke Orchard, late in the tenure of *John Flooke*; one parcel of meadow or pasture called Ley Homsteedes in Stoke Orchard containing ½ acre; and divers lands, meadows, and pastures in Stoke Orchard to the said messuage belonging, late in the tenure of the said *John Flooke*.

All the said premises are held by the King in chief by knight's service, but by what part of a knight's fee the jurors know not, and are worth per annum, clear, 52s. 4d.

John Newton died at Wormington, 12th March last part; *Mary Gwynnett*, widow, late the wife of *Richard Gwynnett*, gent., deceased, is his sister and next heir, and was then aged 24 years and more.

Inq. P.m. 10 Charles I, p.3, No. 146.

A sample abstract from the Inquisitiones Post Mortem for
John Newton of Wormington, 1634.

As you can see, looking at all records related to the death of your ancestors can be one of the best ways of finding out additional information on them and their family. These records should not be ignored in the rush to trace your family tree back to its earliest days.

Chapter 10

Coroners' Records

'Weary the path that does not challenge. Doubt is an incentive to truth and patient inquiry leadeth the way.'

*Hosea Ballou
1796 – 1861, clergyman and writer*

In the event of a sudden or suspicious death, a coroner has to determine the cause, whether it be a natural death, an accident, suicide or murder, etc. Coroners have been in existence since the 12th century but, until the 20th century, they did not have to have a legal or even a medical qualification to do the job. Before 1926, the only qualification required was to be a landowner.

In the early days, the coroner would have a jury to assist him, made up of local people. Until the 20th century, the jury contained anything between 12 and 23 people, but by 1926, this was reduced by half. Originally, inquest findings were sent to the Court of Kings Bench and such records can now be found in the National Archives at Kew in the KB9 to KB12 series of documents. Between 1752 and 1860, the inquest records were kept with the Quarter Sessions documents. Some of these may be found in the local record office.

Recent documents relating to coroners' inquests are closed for 75 years and access is granted only to close family members on application to the relevant Coroner's Office. However, coroners had the right to dispose of their records after 15 years and many inquest records have therefore been destroyed over the years. Those that did survive the sifting process will have eventually been transferred to the local archives office. So there is no guarantee that records of the inquest that you are seeking will remain but it is well worth a look if there is one.

Before 1844, any Gloucestershire coroner could act in any part of the county except in the boroughs of Gloucester and Tewkesbury which had their own coroners. After 1844, the rest of the county was divided into four areas and each coroner then had his own district for which he was responsible. So, the six districts then were:

- Upper Division
- Stroud Division
- Lower Division
- Forest Division
- Gloucester City
- Tewkesbury Borough

For very early inquests, there are records for the Borough Coroners for:

Area	Document	Period	G.A. Ref:
Gloucester Borough	Inquisitions	1642 – 1660	GBR / G2
Tewkesbury Borough	Inquest Files	1733 – 1791	TBR/B4/10

Later Borough Coroners' records remain as follows:

Area	Document	Period	G.A. Ref:
Gloucester Borough	Inquest Files	1921 – 1974	CO 6
Gloucester Borough	Correspondence	1953 – 1962	CO 6
Gloucester Borough	Registers of Deaths	1944 – 1974	CO 6
Tewkesbury Borough	Inquest Files	1890 – 1936 1951 – 1965	CO 5
Tewkesbury Borough	Statistical Returns to Home Office	1893 – 1935	CO 5

10. Coroners' Records

Before 1844, there are surviving County Coroner records for:

Area	Document	Period	G.A. Ref:
Stroud	Register of Inquests	1831 – 1848	CO 3
Berkeley (Lower)	Register of Inquests	1790 – 1823	D260
Gloucester	Inquisitions	1791 – 1818	D1406

Between 1844 and 1966:

Area	Document	Period	G.A. Ref:
Forest of Dean	Register of Inquests	1868 – 1871	CO 4
Forest of Dean	Minutes of Inquests	1868 – 1942	CO 4
Forest of Dean	Inquest Files	1960 – 1966	CO 4
Lower Division	Inquest Files	1855 – 1874 1916 – 1935 (gaps) 1946 – 1966	CO 1
Stroud Division	Inquest Files	1857 – 1966	CO 3
Stroud Division	Register of Deaths	1844 – 1848 1881 – 1913	CO 3
Upper Division	Inquest Files	1936 – 1966	CO 2
Upper Division	Register of Deaths	1926 – 1936 1953 – 1964	CO 2
Upper Division	Daily Record Books	1917 – 1965	CO 2
Upper Division	Correspondence	1936 – 1954	CO 2

The areas were then re-organised. Between 1966 and 1974:

Area	Document	Period	G.A. Ref:
Cotswold Division	Inquest Files	1966 – 1974	CO 7
Cotswold Division	Daily Record Books	1966 – 1974	CO 7
Lower Division	Registers of Deaths	1961 – 1969	CO 8
Lower Division	Inquest Files	1966 – 1972	CO 8
West Gloucestershire Division	Inquest Files	1966 – 1974	CO 9

Another re-organisation occurred later. Since 1974, certain coroners' records exist for:

Area	Document	Period	G.A. Ref:
Cheltenham Division	Inquest Files	1975 – 1995	CO 7
Cheltenham Division	Case Papers	1974 – 1995	CO 7
Cheltenham Division	Register of Deaths reported	1974 – 1983	CO 7
Cheltenham Division	Daily Record Books	1974 – 1981	CO 7
Gloucester Division	Inquest Files	1974 – 1997	CO 10
Gloucester Division	Daily Registers	1987 – 1989	CO 10

As an example of documents available, Coroners' files for the Lower Division consist of three separate series of documents:

- Inquests
- Notices of death where an inquest was deemed unnecessary
- Miscellaneous papers, usually relating to the appointment of coroners.

The files could contain any of the following:

- Notice of death
- Inquest documents
- Jury lists
- Jury summons
- Witness list
- Witness information
- Correspondence
- Surgeon's report
- Other items e.g. newspaper reports.

In the event of a sudden death, the information would be sent to the coroner who would record it in his register of deaths. These registers are normally indexed for ease of location of a specific entry. They provide the date of death, name and address of the deceased and the place of death.

Date of Application	Name of Applicant	Date of Inquisition	Name of Deceased	Age
1841 July 4	Letter from Mr Barnett's housekeeper enclosing one from Mr Grey, Overseer	5th July 1841	Jane Gardner	35

Part of an entry in a coroner's register of inquests. This one was held in the 'Horse and Groom' in Bourton on the Hill. Jane Gardner had been 'found dead in bed'. The verdict was 'Visitation of God'.
G.A. Ref: CO3/2/2

Relevant facts would be gathered, with witnesses making their statements. If necessary, a post mortem would be organised. Then, if, after taking medical advice, the coroner decided it was necessary, an inquest, with jury and witnesses, would be held. A report, on a form called an Inquisition, would be made. Details on these are often briefer than one would like.

The Coroner's report included:

- Location of inquest
- Date of inquest
- Jurors' names
- Coroner's name
- Name of deceased
- Date of death
- Cause of death.

10. Coroners' Records

A copy of the inquisition completed following the inquest into the death of George Dando in 1855.
G.A. Ref: CO1/I/1/D/12

For those who died unexpectedly in the very south of the county, who may have been within the Bristol Coroner's jurisdiction, only early records remain. All coroners' files between 1836 and 1936 have been destroyed and those after 1936 are still within the 75 year closure period so may not be viewed except by the next of kin in exceptional circumstances.

Anyone seeking details of an ancestor's sudden death in the south of the county will need to check the relevant Bristol newspapers, such as the *Bristol Mercury*. This may be accessed online through the newspaper archives via your local library.

Inquests
If an inquest was held after the death of your ancestor, it will, assuming it occurred after July 1837, be recorded on the death certificate. The coroner would notify the registrar with the necessary information. Before 1837, there was no method of indicating that a death was sudden and unexpected, except for the occasional reference in the parish burial register.

Inquests were normally held in the parish in which the death occurred, sometimes in the local workhouse, prison or hospital but frequently in the local public house. Coroners were paid for each inquest and, after the event, could also claim travelling expenses. The early claims were recorded in the Quarter Sessions documents and would include some information relating to the deceased person; some of these coroners' accounts remain.

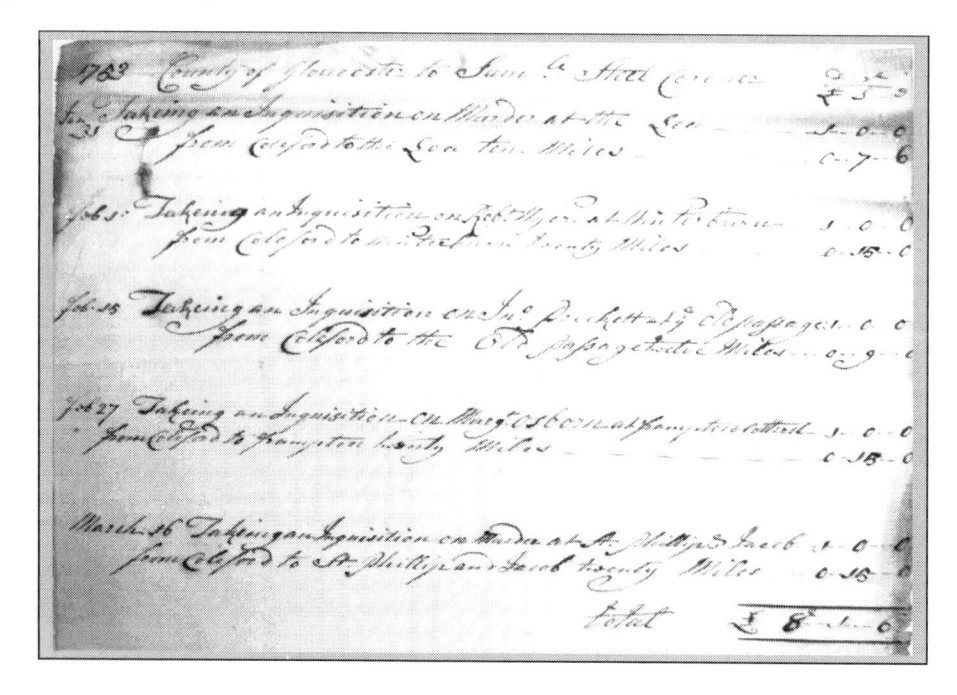

An excerpt from the expenses paid to the Coroner, Samuel Steel, in 1753.
G.A. Ref: Q/SR/1753/B

10. Coroners' Records

The coroner would require a list of potential jurors in the parish, mostly tradesmen, and the local constable or beadle would be required to organise their appearance at the selected time and place of the inquest, along with the witnesses who could help to clarify events. Once all the evidence had been heard and a decision had been made, a summary of the inquest would be produced and sent to the relevant authorities, such as the Court of the King's Bench, the Quarter Sessions, etc. If the verdict was one of negligence, manslaughter or murder, files would be sent to the Assizes for further investigation and may have led to a trial.

The inquest was often reported in very great detail in the local newspaper, sometimes including witness depositions verbatim. It is always worth checking the newspapers of the time as they give the best record of the event. You will often find names of relatives, neighbours and workmates included.

For example, the inquest on Mary Ann Weare, of Chalford, who was shot in the thigh by her husband in March 1911 and bled to death before help could arrive, returned a verdict of accidental death. It mentioned:

- her husband, William Francis Weare, a chimney-sweep
- their sons, Tom (14) and Frederick (16) and an elder son, Frank
- next door neighbour, Mary Gubbins
- neighbour Georgina Neale, wife of E.W. Neale, a stick-worker of Chalford
- John Orchard, licensee of the Railway Inn at Brownshill
- James Richard Whiting, licensee of the Mechanics Arms Inn in Chalford
- local doctor, Dr. J. M. Rogers Tillstone
- Mr. Robert Davies, foreman of the jury
- the Coroner himself, Mr. A. J. Morton Ball.

Post Mortems

Doctors have dissected corpses for thousands of years to learn more about the internal workings of human bodies and to investigate causes of death but the first funded post mortems did not occur until the 1830s. Records of autopsies are rare in the coroners' files but one such was located for the inquest into the death of George Dando, in 1855.

The inquest was held at The Horseshoes public house in Frampton Cotterell on 8th November in that year in front of coroner William Gaisford and a jury of 12 men: Abraham Huggins, Joseph Newman, Joseph Gibbs, Thomas Luton, James Offer, Isaac Williams, Gabriel Gibbs, George Mathews, Isaac Luton, Jonathan Carter, Charles Harris and James (Sha…?).

Evidence was given by several witnesses to say that George had been alive at supper time on the 5th November and found dead two days later. His neighbour, Susannah Jones, confirmed that she had not heard any movement in the house since the Tuesday and his brother, Samuel Dando, confirmed that George was in the habit of taking laudanum to deaden the pain of his rheumatism. The verdict that was returned said that George had died of natural causes and by the 'Visitation of God'.

> Edwin Day on his oath saith – I am Surgeon practising at Hambrook. I have known the deceased for many years; he was of very full habit of body and very short neck. I don't recollect having seen him alive for the last two or three months. By order of the Coroner I made a post mortem examination of his body.
>
> I found him upon a board enveloped in a sheet and on a board on the landing at the top of the stairs in his house. I had the body stripped and first examined it externally but found no marks of violence whatever. The countenance presented a very livid appearance and the integuments over the body were much decomposed and I should suppose he had been dead for two or three nights. I have heard the evidence of all the preceding witnesses and it is my opinion that he died on Monday night.
>
> I examined his head and found the brain highly congested and a considerable quantity of sereus fluid between the membranes and the right and left ventricles of the brain were full of sereus fluid. I next examined the neck; it was livid but not different from other parts of the body and there was not the least appearance of external strangulation.
>
> I next examined the abdomen. I applied a ligature to both extremities of the stomach and removed the stomach and afterwards examined its contents. I found it to contain a considerable quantity of laudanum, onions and bread. I washed the stomach and examined it minutely. There was no appearance of any mineral or irritant poison having been taken.
>
> I have no doubt that the deceased died from apoplexy accelerated by taking a quantity of laudanum. From the appearance of the stomach, I consider he had taken as much as two ounces; his whole body presented the livid appearance always attendant upon taking opium in large quantities so as to produce death.
>
> I consider the deceased was predisposed to apoplexy and he was of an age when death would be most likely to occur to a person of his full plethoric habit from apoplexy. I always considered him likely to die from apoplexy - he was exceedingly fat. I consider that his death was hastened by taking laudanum but I should not like to say that it was wholly occasioned by taking laudanum because the predisposition to apoplexy was so strong in him.
>
> An interval of four or five hours might probably elapse between his taking the laudanum and his death.

The post mortem report given by Edwin Day at the inquest on George Dando in 1855.
G.A. Ref: CO1/I/1/D/12

Accidents

Did your ancestor die in an accident? If it was a major accident that affected several people, then reports would appear in the local or even the national press and a public enquiry may have taken place as well. Take, for instance, the Charfield Railway disaster that occurred on 13th October 1928 when, in the early hours of the morning, a passenger/mail train from the north travelling towards Bristol crashed into a goods train moving in the same direction, the wreckage being hit by another goods train travelling north. After the impact, the gas used to light the carriages ignited and, according to the official report, 16 people died with over 40

10. Coroners' Records

injured. Included in the total of dead were two young boys, aged around 14 and 5, who were never identified.

One person who was believed to have been on the train was a student by the name of Goodwin Jenkins who was returning home for the weekend. His body was never identified and, in 1929, an inquest was permitted under the new Coroner's Act, the first one ever to be held without a body. A fellow traveller identified the student from his photograph and, based on that evidence, it was proved that he had indeed died in the crash.

The train driver, Harry Aldington was accused of manslaughter for ignoring a danger signal, was taken to trial and subsequently acquitted. Further details can be gained from the trial record.

So, for an accident of this magnitude, you will find articles in the local and national newspapers, records of various inquests, a trial and finally a railway enquiry, reports of which are in the National Archives in the RAIL series.

> Note: Always check the local newspapers for the report of an inquest if your ancestor died in an accident.

Some occupations were particularly fraught with accidents and one of these was coalmining. Both in the south of the county, around Westerleigh, Mangotsfield, Pucklechurch and Kingswood, and in the Forest of Dean, there were numerous coal mines. For accidents in the southern part of Gloucestershire, there is an excellent publication, *Killed in a Coalpit* by D.P. Lindegaard, published in 1988 with a supplement five years later.

In the Forest of Dean, if a man was born within the Hundred of St Briavels and had worked for a year and a day in a mine, he was entitled, by ancient rights, to be a 'freeminer'. Since 2010, in the cause of equality, women were also granted the right to be freeminers. Mines, or gales as they are known locally, were allocated by the Gaveller, a position which still exists in the Forest today.

Volunteers of the Forest of Dean Local History Society have produced a CD entitled *Roll of Honour* which is available for sale from their website (www.forestofdeanhistory.org.uk). It contains details of almost 600 mining and quarrying fatalities together with an index of freeminers and quarrymen who registered before 1960. Although some entries are undated, the records of fatalities go back at least until 1797.

Information is provided on the CD in a variety of ways. In one case, we learn that on 6th April 1819, in the Bilson Mine, four people, Thomas Morgan (26), William Tingle (19), Robert Tingle (16) and 11 year old James Meredith were killed 'by the breaking of a chain lowering them down the shaft; they were precipitated to the bottom'. By then looking at the mine itself, we get a brief history of the mine, its location and its current state.

There is a list of over 4000 freeminers dating from when registration began in 1838 and over 300 quarrymen, so even if your ancestor only worked at a particular mine and did not die in an accident, you can find useful information from this CD. Check out their website at: www.forestofdeanhistory.org.uk

Surname	Forename	Date	Age	Occupation	Mine	Cause
Kear	George	11/10/1803	20	Collier	Rising Sun Engine Pit	Fell down pit about 15 fathoms.
Kear	George	21/05/1892	56	Miner	China Engine	A stone, from the side of the main road or the level where he was engaged repairing fell unexpectedly and injured him. He was removed to Gloucester Hospital but died on his way there.
Kear	John	01/07/1901	42	Labourer	Speech House Hill	When riding up a dipple on the rope in front of the water cart struck the top resulting in his being knocked off and crushed between the cart and side of road. Bronchitis set in and he died on 3rd July from the effects of the accident.

Three sample entries from the Freeminers Roll of Honour giving details of each fatality. Copyright: Forest of Dean Local History Society, 2006.

When it comes to individual accidents, in the home, at school or at work, in the fields or on the roads, there would have been a coroner's inquest and you may find details in the newspaper but that would depend upon other newsworthy events occurring at the time and the space the editor had available.

Suicide

One of the causes of death that the coroner had to determine was that of suicide, and, if the deceased had killed himself or herself, whether they had been sane at the time. This decided whether or not the body could be buried in consecrated ground. If the person was deemed to have been a lunatic and therefore not in full control of his faculties, e.g. 'while the balance of his mind was disturbed', he could have been buried in consecrated ground with the full ecclesiastical rites. If, on the other hand, the deceased was considered to be sane at the time, the verdict was *felo de se* or self-murder. In such a case, the body was not permitted in consecrated ground. In fact, in early times, the body would most likely have been buried at the nearby cross-roads with a stake through the heart – to kill the evil spirits – so you will most likely not find an entry in the parish registers if this happened to one of your ancestors..

Such was the case until 1823 when burial at the cross-roads ceased and the body could be interred in the churchyard (though not 'buried' as the ceremony was carried out without the rites of the burial service), as was also the situation for unbaptised infants. The interment would take place between the hours of 9pm and midnight, on the north side of the churchyard and within 24 hours of the inquest being performed. Any property owned by the person who committed suicide was forfeited to the Crown. This continued to be the situation until 1870.

The Burial Law Amendment Act of 1880 extended the right to be buried in the churchyard allowing interment within 48 hours, with or without a graveside service, depending upon the beliefs and sympathies of the residing minister.

Suicide was a felony until 1961 so failed suicides could be charged with attempted suicide. One such case involved 62 year old George Bridges, a plasterer from Painswick who unsuccessfully tried to kill himself in 1901 and was sentenced to ten days of hard labour in Gloucester Gaol. This obviously cured him of attempting to take his own life as he lived for another fifteen years. Although attempted suicide is no longer a crime, it is still, in 2012, a crime to aid and abet a suicide.

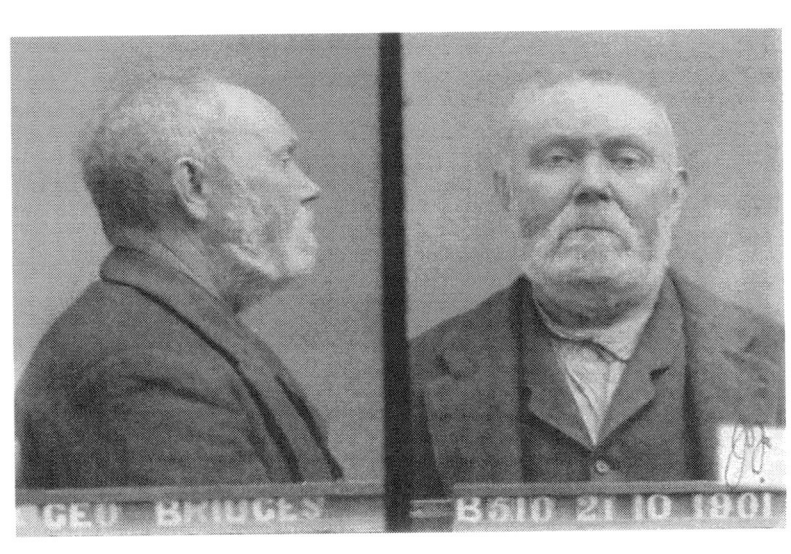

George Bridges, who was sentenced to ten days of hard labour in Gloucester Gaol in 1901 for attempting to kill himself.

G.A. Ref: Q/Gc/10/2

If your ancestor committed suicide, you may be able to locate the coroner's record of the inquest and will probably be able to find an item in the local newspaper about the case.

ATROCIOUS BURGLARY.—*John Ballinger*, aged 25, (who was brought up from the Penitentiary, where he was under punishment for stealing a scythe at Cleeve,) and *George Guy*, were charged under the following dreadful circumstances, with breaking into the dwelling-house of Sarah Gwinnett at Bishop's Cleeve, on the night of the 13th September last, and stealing a variety of articles.

Mr. Alexander stated the case. The consequences of this outrage, he said, were very serious. Mrs Gwinnett was a widow residing in a very retired situation, called Longwood, in the parish of Bishop's Cleeve, whose house was broken into by two persons, and who was so alarmed by the conduct of one of them that she jumped out of her bed-room window, by which her spine was dislocated, and she was so dreadfully injured that she languished for a short time, and eventually died, not being, during her illness, in such a situation as to be able to give any account of the circumstances of the outrage. It happened, however, fortunately for the ends of justice, that a maid-servant slept in the same room, and the jury would have the benefit of her evidence. After a few more observations, explanatory of the case, the Learned Counsel called

Thomas Gwinnett, a lad apparently about 16 years of age, who stated, he was the son of Mrs. Gwinnett. On the night of the 12th Sept. witness went to bed about eight o'clock; two younger children had gone to bed rather earlier. There were also in the house a man servant named Cartwright Buckle, and a maid servant named Ann Kent. Between twelve and one o'clock witness was awoke by a noise of hammering at the kitchen window; he got out of bed, opened his room window, and saw two men below, one of whom had a candle and lanthorn in his hand, and the other was hammering at the window bar. Witness called out "hallo," but they made no answer; he then proceeded to dress himself, and while doing so he heard the steps of two persons coming up the stairs; one of them he heard proceed into his mother's room, and the other staid at the top of the stairs, opposite the door of the servant Buckle's room. The man who went into his mother's room, afterwards came out of that, and entered witness's room; his face was blackened all over; he opened a box and threw the things about the room; he swore a great deal, and asked where the money was kept? Witness said he did not know; he took some half-pence out of the box, and then burst open the servant's box, which was in the same room, with a chissel, and took out something, saying with an oath, he had got two shillings. He said no more and went out; he was dressed in dark clothes, with long skirts to his coat. While he was in the room, witness heard the man who was staying outside say "Hie on, jolly tar." He said this several times, and also said "Money we want and money we'll have." Witness knew the voice to be that of John Ballinger; he had known him five or six years; he had worked for his (witness's) mother frequently. As they were going away, the house clock struck one.

Cartwright Buckle examined. He was in the service of the late Mrs. Gwinnett; on the night of the 12th Sept. he was awoke by two persons coming up stairs one of whom stationed himself opposite witness's door, and swore he would blow any one's brains out who should attempt to interrupt them, and he (witness) heard the "click" of a gun or pistol; the other went into Mrs. Gwinnett's room, where he staid some time, and afterwards went into her son's room; the person at the head of the stairs also said "hie on, jolly tar;" witness thought it was the voice of John Ballinger. The men went away about one o'clock, and then witness and the other inmates went down stairs to assist Mrs. Gwinnett. Before going to bed, witness had fastened the doors and windows; when he went down he found the bar of the kitchen window broken, and the casement opened, which was large enough for a man to get through.

Anne Kent examined. She was servant to Mrs. Gwinnett, and slept with her; they went to bed about ten o'clock; between twelve and one they heard a noise at the kitchen window; Mrs. Gwinnett got out of bed, opened her room window, and called out "for God's sake, what are you at?" to which a man outside replied, "d—n you, we'll soon let you know what we be at." Soon afterwards two persons came up stairs, one of whom came into the bed-room; her mistress met him at the door and cried out for mercy; a man on the stairs said, "D—n her, blow her brains out if she do'n't get out of the way." Mrs. Gwinnett retreated towards the window, which was a casement, and the man who came into the room followed her, and presented something at her, but witness did not see that he had any thing in his hand; Mrs. Gwinnett then threw herself out of the window; the man went back to the door and returned with a candle; witness then saw a pistol in his hand; witness was standing near the window; he laid hold of her and threw her on the bed, put the pistol to her head, and said he would blow her brains out if she moved; he then asked her if she was the mistress, and demanded the keys; she replied she was not mistress, and that she had not any keys. While this was doing, she heard her mistress cry for assistance; the man also heard her cry out, and exclaimed "d—n her, she is out of the window, we'll go down to her." He then went down, and witness heard him ask her for her money and keys; she said she had none, and the man again came up stairs into the room, searched under the bed, and found Mrs. Gwinnett's pocket, from which he took her keys and some silver; but previously to finding this, he burst open a box in the room with a chissel. He was in the room altogether near a quarter of an hour. He had the same voice as that which answered her mistress outside the door; his face was blackened; he carried the candle in his hand about the room; he was a tall stout man, with largish whiskers, and was dressed in a long dark coat with black waistcoat and dark corduroy trowsers; it was the prisoner Guy. [Guy's appearance in the dock did not by any means correspond with this description of his stature; he was rather slight made, about 5 feet 6 or 7 inches high, and had small whiskers.] Witness heard Ballinger's voice on the stairs; she knew his voice from having frequently heard him speak. After the men were gone away, she went down stairs to assist her mistress, and found her lying on the stones beneath the window; she was not able to move; she never recovered, and died in a fortnight afterwards.

In her cross-examination by Mr. Talbot, she admitted that she had never known Guy or seen him to the best of her knowledge before that night, and that then his face was blackened; that she was present the next day but one when Guy's lodgings were searched, and that nothing belonging to Mrs. Gwinnett was found there.

John Herbert proved that he was at the Plasterers' Arms, Winchcomb, on the evening of the 12th Sept. and saw the prisoner Guy and another man named Yearp there; they came in about eight o'clock and went away about a quarter to nine. Guy was dressed in a similar manner to that described by the last witness. The Plasterers' Arms is about three miles from Longwood.

Benjamin Stack, proved that "hie on, jolly tar," was a common expression of the prisoner Ballinger, but, he added, that the same expression was frequently in the mouth of other persons in the village.

John Gwinnett produced an iron chissel, found in the house after the departure of the prisoners. Witness stated he was brother to the deceased Mrs. Sarah Gwinnett, who was a widow, and about 36 or 38 years of age.—There was no evidence to connect the chissel with either of the prisoners.

Mr Talbot ably addressed the jury in behalf of Guy, commenting upon the barren nature of the case against him, and stating that it was in his power to prove most distinctly an alibi in his favour.

The Learned Judge, without having the witnesses called, directed an acquittal for Guy. Ballinger called a witness for whom he worked at the time in question, who proved that he left his work in the evening of the 12th, about eight o'clock, and came again next morning between five and six. The jury, after consulting together for two or three minutes returned a verdict of not guilty in his case also.

Article on the trial relating to the murder of Sarah Gwinnett in 1836.
Gloucester Journal, 8th April 1837.

10. Coroners' Records

Murder and Executions

If the coroner decided that a death was the result of murder, the police or, in earlier times, the village constable were required to locate and arrest the perpetrator and the case was then taken to the Assizes. Thus it was following the death of Sarah Gwinnett in 1836.

On 13th September 1836, Sarah Gwinnett, a widow with two children still at home, was asleep in her lonely farmhouse on the outskirts of Bishops Cleeve, when two men broke into her home. The men, with blackened faces, threatened the family and Sarah was so terrified that she jumped from an upstairs window. According to an entry in the *Cheltenham Gazette*:

> 'After Mrs Guinnett had jumped from the window, the robbers came to her in the garden, and while lying on the ground they kicked her in the back and head in the most brutal and ferocious manner; and, conceiving their victim dead, they threw her into a plantation. It is sincerely hoped that justice will meet these most heartless ruffians.'

Six weeks later, the newspaper reported:

> 'The daring burglary in the house of Mrs Guinnett of Cleeve, and the brutal violence perpetrated by the villains must be fresh in the memory of our readers. We have now the melancholy task of announcing that the unfortunate lady died on Thursday last from the injuries she received, she experienced the most dreadful agony during the time she lingered.'

As the death occurred in Bishops Cleeve, before 1844, the inquest could have been held by any of the county coroners of the time. Records for the relevant period only remain for the Stroud coroner, John Ball. Although most of these refer to deaths in the Stroud area, they do cover deaths from other locations in the county, but unfortunately not for this one.

Two men, John Ballinger and George Guy, the former at least a seasoned criminal, were arrested and indicted for the burglary and appeared before the Crown Court of the Oxford Lent Assizes in April 1837. There the proof of identification failed and the men were acquitted.

However, many other people were convicted of murder in Gloucestershire in the past and subsequently hanged. Before 1792, executions were carried out on the gallows at Over just outside Gloucester and these were not just for people convicted of murder but for many other crimes as well, including arson, rape, highway robbery, burglary and stealing. Records of the 18 men hanged at Over are included in *The Murderers of Gloucestershire* by Bryan White, former Senior Officer at the Gaol, the first recorded as being on 2nd April 1786. Only two of them were convicted of murder.

From 1792 onwards, the hanging took place 'over the drop at Lodge Gate' at Gloucester Gaol. For the next 75 years, the executions were public spectacles when people gathered outside the gaol and the Lodge Gates were opened so that the crowd could view the proceedings. Between 1792 and 1864, 105 such hangings took place in public; the convicts and their crimes are listed in Bryan White's book.

From 1872 onwards, the executions, arranged by the County High Sheriff, were held in private. Seventeen more people met their fate at Gloucester Gaol before hanging was abandoned, the last being Ralph Smith of Swindon hanged for murder on 7th June 1939. Of the 140 executions, only eight were of women. The youngest was a 16 year old boy, John Baker, hanged in 1821 and the oldest was 70 year old John Evans executed in 1793. Both had been convicted of burglary. Corresponding ages for women were 21 (Harriet Tarver for murder) and 69 years of age (Dinah Riddiford for burglary). By law, all executed prisoners were buried within the precincts of the prison in which they had been held.

It was the coroner's duty to investigate all deaths of people held in prison, whether they were criminals or merely debtors and had to do so even in the case where the death was obviously one of natural causes.

Your ancestor may have met with a sudden or tragic death but the surviving coroners' records can hold fascinating detail of their lives to enrich your family history. If you can locate such a record for your ancestor, it will be well worth a look.

Chapter 11

Petty Sessions, Quarter Sessions and Assizes

'All human life is there.'

*Henry James
1843 – 1916, writer*

The records pertaining to the Petty Sessions and Quarter Sessions are often said to be ignored by family historians yet they contain a wealth of information, with both criminal and administrative detail; they help to expand your knowledge of the lives of your ancestors. The disappointing thing about these records is that they are not often indexed and, therefore, are very time-consuming to search.

With the gradual demise of the manorial and ecclesiastical courts over the centuries, a new system was introduced to carry out local administrative tasks and to provide a basic justice system. At parish level, this involved a local magistrate or Justice of the Peace (JP) hearing minor cases or dealing with relatively trivial administrative matters at sittings called Petty Sessions. In towns, the Mayor and Aldermen sometimes took on the role of magistrate and jury. A Recorder could be paid to deal with the paper work if necessary; this would have been a local lawyer.

Justices of the Peace were first introduced in the 14th century and were chosen from local property owners; they were unpaid and generally untrained. It wasn't until the early 20th century that the property qualification was dropped. Even when the offence had occurred on the JP's own land, he would still give judgement.

Any cases which were not resolved locally or appeals against sentences and decisions made at the Petty Sessions were transferred to the Quarter Sessions, when a group of local magistrates sat four times a year, at Easter, Trinity, Michaelmas and Epiphany. The Petty Sessions were a way of reducing the workload for the Quarter Sessions by filtering out the less important issues that occurred between the three-monthly sittings.

The Petty Sessions could be held in any convenient location; for example, in 1798, some sessions were held at local inns, such as the King's Head Inn in Cirencester, the Bear Inn in Newnham and the Swan Inn, Thornbury; some were held in the nearby House of Correction or Gaol, e.g. Lawford's Gate House of Correction or Horsley Bridewell; other sittings took place in lawyers' offices, such as those of Messrs Wilton, some possibly in a special room kept for the purpose and some sessions were even held in the Justice's own home.

The responsibilities of the magistrates included:

- Overseeing poor law cases, dealing with disputes on settlement, removal and bastardy
- Supervising issues dealing with local highways, defence and taxation
- Taking oaths, such as those for new magistrates
- Enforcing laws against Catholics and other nonconformist groups
- Dealing with licences including those for alehouses
- Overseeing trade issues involving apprentices, craftsmen and guilds
- Hearing minor criminal cases such as poaching, vagrancy, assault and petty theft.

The magistrate could convict and fine offenders or send them to the local House of Correction, where they would go anyway if they were unable or unwilling to pay the fine.

11. Sessions and Assizes

Many of these tasks have since been handed to the local authorities but magistrates do still deal with minor criminal offences today.

In Gloucestershire, the earliest Petty Sessions were held in the nearby town or main village of the local Hundred or group of Hundreds. As the population grew and new regulations were introduced, particularly those for poor law supervision and alehouse licensing, more divisions were introduced until, eventually, a major revision of the system was made in 1840. In the mid 20th century, there were 31 divisions, later reduced to 7 divisions towards the end of the century. More recently, the divisions have been grouped together again, so by the 21st century, they were reduced to the five divisions of Cheltenham, Gloucester, North Avon, North Gloucestershire and South Gloucestershire. Finally, in 2004, all divisions were abolished and replaced by the single Petty Sessional area of Gloucestershire covering the whole county; the individual courts are still held in the towns as before but the administration is now carried out centrally.

Gloucestershire Archives has some Petty Sessions records for the following divisions, each of which has its own code, as shown. Most of the Petty Sessions records available at Gloucestershire Archives fall into these categories and references to the documents will begin with PS followed by the relevant code. So, for Petty Sessions records relating to Northleach, you would look for the code PS/NO in the Archives online catalogue to see what records exist and the period covered by them.

Code	Division	Code	Division
AV	Avon North	NC	North Cotswolds
BE	Berkeley	NE	Newent
CA	Campden	NG	North Gloucestershire
CH	Cheltenham	NM	Newnham
CI	Cirencester	NO	Northleach
CO	Coleford	SD	Stroud
CR	Cross Hands	SG	South Gloucestershire
DU	Dursley	SO	Sodbury
FA	Fairford	TH	Thornbury
FD	Forest of Dean	TT	Tetbury
GC	Gloucester City	TW(B)	Tewkesbury Borough
GL	Gloucester (county area)	TW(C)	Tewkesbury (County Area)
LA	Lawford's Gate	WH	Whitminster
LY	Lydney	WI	Winchcombe
MO	Moreton-in-Marsh	WO	Wotton-under-Edge
NA	Nailsworth & Horsley		

Most of the Gloucestershire Petty Session records that survive come from after the 1840 re-organisation although a collection of the Slaughter Hundred records survive in the Whitmore family collection (G.A. Ref. D45), covering the period from 1633 to 1700. There is also a series of files containing notes of Petty Session convictions in the Quarter Sessions collection. For these, the basic details of each case have recently been recorded in a book entitled *Calendar of Summary Convictions at Petty Sessions, 1781 – 1837* edited by Irene Wyatt. Each entry gives the reference to the document, the name of the offender and nature of the offence, the names of the magistrates and possibly the occupation and abode of the offender, the name of the victim and the penalty imposed. For example:

Q/PC 2/53/A/98.
19 October 1833
John Gwinnett. Assaulting Thomas Tarling at Bishop's Cleeve. J.E.Viner, JP and T.J.Baines, JP, at Cheltenham. Fine £1 and 9/6 costs. Offence committed 17 October 1833.

The different types of Petty Session records kept at Gloucestershire Archives include:

- Minutes – of courts, special meetings, Justices meetings, etc.
- Letter Books
- Petty Cash Books
- Adult court
- Juvenile court registers
- Papers including Depositions, Informations, Complaints
- Justices' orders
- Convictions
- Registers of summary convictions
- Probation Care Committee
- Fines and Fees
- Security Books
- Register of Bail
- Register of Enforcement
- Poor Law Papers
- Bastardy Books – applications for summonses
- Settlement cases
- Register of Adoptions
- Register of Family Panel Court and Domestic Court
- Register under Vaccination Act
- Register of Alehouse Licences
- Register of premises under Explosives Act (1875)
- Register of Clubs under Licensing Act; Register of Music and Dancing Licences
- Register of Gaming Permits
- Register of Persons authorised to kill hares
- Plus a variety of miscellaneous documents.

Not all of these records are available for all divisions so you need to check the online catalogue for the individual division in which you are interested. Most of the records are closed for 30 years but the more sensitive Registers of Adoptions are closed for 100 years. Some examples of these documents follow.

11. Sessions and Assizes

COUNTY OF GLOUCESTER, TO WIT.

THE INFORMATION AND COMPLAINT of *George Watts* *Overseer of the Poor of the Parish of Slimbridge in the said County* taken upon Oath this *twenty fourth* day of *January* in the Year of our Lord One Thousand Eight Hundred and Thirty *four* before *me* of His Majesty's Justices of the Peace of and for the County of Gloucester at *Slimbridge* in the said County of Gloucester

WHO SAITH That *Jonathan Frankis formerly of the Parish of Leonard Stanley now or late of the Parish of Arlingham in the County of Gloucester being the reputed Father of a Male Bastard Child born in the Parish of Slimbridge aforesaid of the body of Sarah Jones Singlewoman hath neglected and refused to pay the Sums of Money which by an Order of Filiation made upon him the seventh day of August one thousand eight hundred and twenty nine by two of His Majesty's Justices of the Peace for the said County he hath been ordered to pay towards the maintenance of the said Child and against which Order no appeal hath been made — and that there is due from the said Jonathan Frankis upon or by virtue of the said Order the sum of Two Pounds nine shillings which hath been demanded of him and which he hath refused to pay, the same*

Sworn before me

J. C. Dunsford   *George Watts*

There is no record of this maintenance order in the surviving Overseers of the Poor papers for Slimbridge so this Petty Session record of 1834 requiring Jonathan Frankis to pay towards the upkeep of Sarah Jones's illegitimate child would enable a researcher to locate the previously unknown father of the child.
This example came from the Petty Sessions 'Informations' section.
G.A. Ref. PS/BE/P1/2

Date	Name and Address of Person Bound.	Principal or Surety.	Sum in which Bound.
1881 March 29	William Henry Wragge	Principal	20
April 4	Daniel Morley	Principal	10
"	John Morley	Surety	10

Undertaking or Condition.	By Deposit of Money with the Clerk of the Court, or by oral or written Acknowledgment.	By whom taken.	Further Proceedings and Remarks.
To keep the Peace towards Sarah Anne Wragge for six months	Oral acknowledgment	Henry Godfrey Esquire Cheltenham	
To keep the Peace towards Ellen Morley for 3 months	Oral acknowledgment	Captn Ford Cheltenham	
For Daniel Morley to keep the Peace towards Ellen Morley for 3 months	Oral acknowledgment	Captn Ford Cheltenham	

These two pages from the 1881 Cheltenham Security Book list those people who were bound over to keep the peace and put down money which would be forfeited if they didn't. In the second example, Daniel Morley deposits £10 to ensure he keeps the peace with Ellen Morley and a relative, John Morley, contributes another £10.

G.A. Ref. PS/CH/F4/1

11. Sessions and Assizes

A sample of the Ale Licences granted in 1832 at Fairford, found in the Bibury Justices Book.
G.A. Ref. PS/FA/RA1/1

The Informations file for the Gloucester Petty Sessions gives details of the discharge of debtor John Norris from the County Gaol in 1812.
G.A. Ref. PS/GL/M1a/1

Quarter Sessions

When cases were too complex or too important to be dealt with at the Petty Sessions, or when decisions which had been made there were challenged, the case was held over to be dealt with at the Quarter Sessions. As the name suggests, the Justices of the Peace met four times a year, at Easter, Trinity, Michaelmas, and Epiphany, each court convening within 21 days of the 25th of March, June, September and December, respectively. If, however, there was too much work to be handled in these sessions, the JPs could meet in between times to deal with outstanding cases. Gradually, as the workload increased, aspects of the work were split off and dealt with by separate committees, e.g. licensing.

As with the Petty Sessions, the Quarter Sessions dealt with a wide range of topics including criminal matters such as assault, poaching, theft, forgery, horse stealing, highway robbery, arson, rioting, machine breaking, and even, occasionally, murder. The JPs also handled administrative matters such as:

- the welfare of the poor
- neighbourhood disputes
- slander
- military matters involving deserters and pensions
- industrial disputes and wage rates
- pricing of commodities
- trading standards
- planning matters
- road and bridge maintenance issues
- licensing of innkeepers
- licensing of gamekeepers
- tax collection issues
- the taking of oaths
- religious observance.

Records from the Quarter Sessions are similar to those of the Petty Sessions, the cases in the former just being more complex, serious or important than those in the latter. Quarter Session records relating to settlement examinations, removal orders and bastardy bonds are almost exactly the same as those found in the parish chest archives so examples will not be repeated here. However, it should be emphasized that they are a great source of reputed fathers of illegitimate children, often not found in the overseers of the poor papers, and should therefore not be ignored.

> *Note: The Quarter Sessions records frequently include the names of reputed fathers of illegitimate children not found elsewhere.*

Needless to say, the number of documents found in the Quarter Sessions collection is vast. Some of these records are more useful to family historians than others but all of them are interesting. They range from items referring to the officers of the court themselves to those for both the rich and the poor people of the county.

11. Sessions and Assizes

At each Quarter Session sitting, there would be several Justices together with a jury. The names of those involved would be given at the start of the records for that session. At the Epiphany Sessions in 1662, held in the Boothall in Gloucester, the following were the attending Justices of the Peace:

> Edmund Bray, bart., Edward Bathurst, bart., John Stephens, Thomas Horton, Thomas Estcourt, Thomas Master, John Fettiplace, Richard Cockes, Nicholas Rutter, Richard Daston, Phillip Sheppard and Duncombe Colchester, esquires.

They were joined by Henry Hampson, gent., who acted as Clerk of the Peace. The Clerk dealt with the paperwork involved with the courts and was one of the few public officials to receive a salary. The position would normally have been held by a local lawyer who would have a better grasp of the law than the justices themselves and would be able to give advice if required.

There could be two juries at the Sessions, the Grand Jury and the Petty Jury. The qualification for being on the jury was a property one and was for men only. A refusal to serve or not appearing when requested without good cause was punishable with a fine. Finding an ancestor's name on the list of jurymen at the Quarter Sessions indicated that he had attained a certain standing in the community. The Grand Jury at the Epiphany Sessions in 1662 comprised:

> Sydenham Payne, gent., Edward Willet, Oliver Dowle, William Dutton, William Rutter, Edward Wathen, John Freeman, Anthony Poole, Anthony Keene, William Pace, John Nelme, Stephen Symonds, John Watt, John Brock, Richard Greene, Richard Hyett, James Robins, James Bradford, William Cole, Robert Martyn and John Dowdeswell.

The first stage of the court process was the presentment of complaints. These could be made by the chief constable, the parish constable, overseers of the poor or a private individual. The court would determine whether or not there was a case to answer. If there was not enough evidence or if the complaint was found to be malicious, the case was rejected as not being a 'True Bill'. If, however, the case continued and the accused pleaded guilty, he or she would be sentenced immediately. Otherwise, the defendant would be sent to gaol while information on the case was gathered, to await the next Quarter Sessions or to be bailed on a recognizance, usually in the region of £20 to £40.

The most common entries found in the Indictment books in the 1660s appear to have been for those who were keeping an alehouse or tippling house without having been licensed. The Quarter Sessions records give the following names, for 6th December 1660.

Name	Abode	Occupation	Notes
John Henley	Late of Clifton	Labourer	
Robert Mabbut	Cromhall	Labourer	In margin. 'Licensed'
Thomas Freame	Cromhall	Labourer	
William Hicks	Cromhall	Labourer	

Name	Abode	Occupation	Notes
Sarah Cooke	Cromhall		
[Anthony Archerly]	Stroud	Barber	Deleted
Elizabeth Grime	Woodchester		
Richard Balston	Hanham	Labourer	
Elinor Lewellin	Hanham	Widow	
George Morgan	Newent	Labourer	
Thomas Sandy	Newent	Labourer	
Roger Masters	Bisley	Labourer	
John Hunt	Bisley	Labourer	
George Parsons	Bisley	Labourer	
Ralph Townesend	Ashton-under-Hill	Labourer	
Christopher Perrine	Shipton Moyne	Labourer	
Edward Hopkins	Shipton Moyne	Labourer	
Lewis Jenkins	Woolaston	Labourer	
George Davis	Woolaston	Labourer	
William Mortimer	Moreton	Labourer	
Richard Hewes	Moreton	Labourer	

Entries from records of the Epiphany Quarter Sessions 1660.
G.A. Ref. Q/SIb

Once the indictment had been made, the constable would be instructed to summon the defendants and witnesses to attend at the next Quarter Sessions.

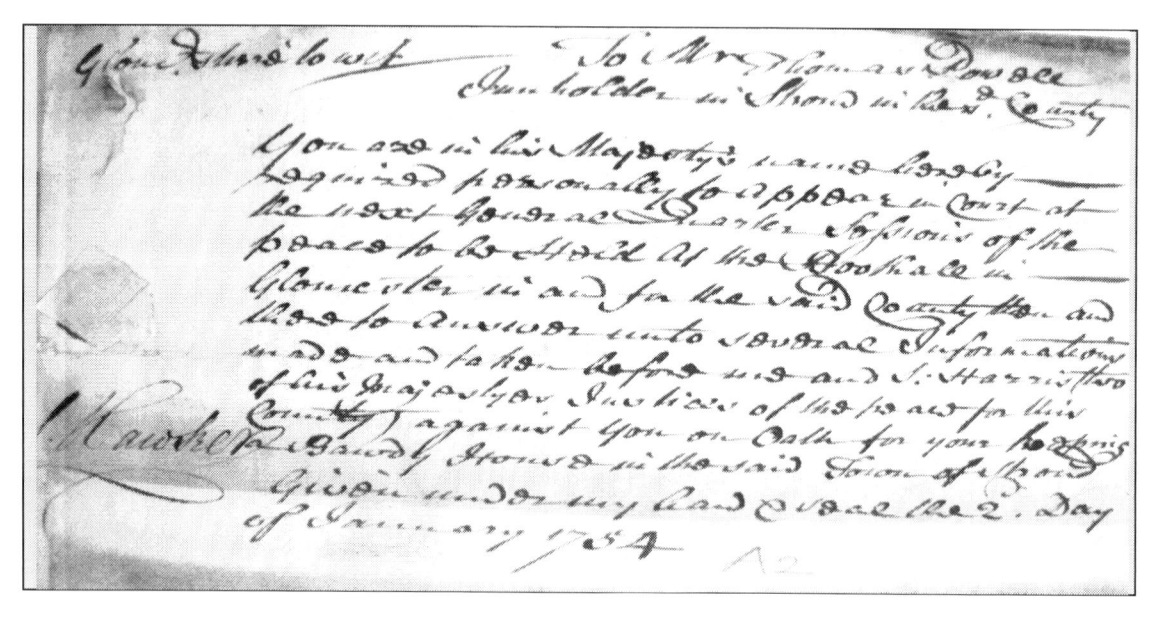

Thomas Powell, innkeeper, of Stroud, was summoned to appear at the Quarter Sessions in 1754 to answer to a charge of keeping a bawdy house.
G.A. Ref. Q/SR/1754

11. Sessions and Assizes

Until the early 18th century, people were required to attend church every Sunday and anyone who didn't who did not have a good reason for their absence would be listed in the Sessions records. There were many entries in the Indictments Book for 'non-attendance at church'. The following, all from transcripts of G.A. Ref. Q/SIb, were indicted at the Epiphany Quarter Sessions for non-attendance at church from 1st September 1660 for three months:

f.1v Elizabeth Hulands, senior, Elizabeth Hulands, junior, Mary Hulands, James Hulands, Charles Kilmaster, Richard Cradock and Elinor Harding, all of Harnhill.

Working or gambling on a Sunday was also against the law and people were frequently brought before the court for disobeying.

f.26 Agnes Mann, late of Cirencester, widow, for selling butcher's meat on 4th January 1662/3 being Sunday and other Sundays at Cirencester in contempt of the Lord's Day.

f.68 Samuel Lane and Thomas Bostine, junior, both late of Mitcheldean, labourers, for playing at unlawful games called cards, dice and tables at Mitcheldean, 6th January 1664/5, being Sunday at the time of divine prayer.

People were often charged with some form of bad or malicious behaviour. The following charges show the variety of charges made during the 1660s.

f.35v Hester Warner, late of Stroud, widow, for being a common swearer, brawler and disturber of the peace and for sowing discord among her neighbours at Stroud, 1st May 1663, and at other times. [In margin – quashed]

f.25v William Constable, late of Cirencester, mercer, for certain false and scandalous words uttered at Cirencester on 29th September 1662 to John Hodges, clerk viz. 'He demanded why one might not be buried in the Highway as well as in the churchyard;' the said John Hodges answered 'Noe, it was consecrated'; the said William Constable replied 'What because Pope Nicke or the Bishop as you call him hath spread his wings over it.'

f.26 Elianor Townsend, wife of Richard Townsend of North Cerney, labourer, for uttering scandal of Robert Oliffe at North Cerney on 21st September 1662, viz., 'that he, the said Robert, did ravish her the said Elianor.'

f.4 John Manning, late of Littledean, mason, Thomas Manning, late of Littledean, mason, John Richbill, late of Littledean, saddletreemaker, James Heane, late of Littledean, collier, William Davis, late of Littledean, collier, and Thomas Workeman, late of Ruardean, butcher, for assembling at Abenhall unlawfully and riotously with weapons and making an assault on John Chinn, gent, being then chief constable of the Hundred of St. Briavels and in execution of his office, 29th September 1660.

The Justices of the Peace also had the authority to control commodities, such as the weight of bread and the measure of ale, to set wages and ensure they were paid, and to supervise masters and apprenticeships. No one could trade until they had completed a full apprenticeship, usually of seven years.

> f.49v Giles Newman, late of Prestbury, yeoman, being constable of Prestbury and having an order from the general sessions of the peace to cut down and destroy tobacco, for neglecting the order, 1st June 1664.

> f.30v Thomas Manninge, late of Nympsfield, butcher, for putting 'gutts and garbage' on the highway at Nympsfield, 17th April 1663. He appeared and was discharged. Fined 2/6 paid to the sheriff.

> f.10v Arthur Hillman, late of Painswick, labourer, for the illicit exercise of the art or mistery(sic) of Mill wright (in which he was never apprenticed for seven years) at Painswick on 29th June 1661 and for three months afterwards. He appeared. Quashed.

The highways and byways of the county were important for trade and travel and each parish had to maintain the roads and bridges within their area. They did not always do this as they should and would be called before the court to explain their failure and, frequently, to be fined.

> f.69 Robert Gregory, Thomas Bubb, Thomas Hall, James Coale and John Rider, husbandmen, and Richard Wood, labourer, being inhabitants of the parish of Barnwood and occupying several plow lands, for not finding men fit for labour, or carts and horses to repair the highways when summoned by Giles Snowe and William Swayne, overseers of the highways in the parish, for 6 days during the month of May last past. [1665]

Taxation was another aspect of parish life which the officials had to deal with and which the Justices of the Peace supervised.

> f.23 Richard Bower, late of Rockhampton, yeoman, being tithingman of Rockhampton, for not returning the names of those who pay Hearth money within the parish, 13th November 1662.

Minor criminal offences, such as poaching, were also dealt with at the Quarter Sessions:

> f.65 The jury present Peter Mifflin alias Peeters, late of Cirencester, barber, for hunting and taking 12 partridges worth 4/- with nets and setting dogs, 29th September 1664.

Once an indictment had been made, the evidence gathered and the witnesses summoned to appear, the case was heard at the next Quarter Sessions. The result of each case was recorded in an Order Book. Generally speaking, the entries in the Order Books are much briefer than those in the Indictment Books but as full records for a particular case may not have survived,

11. Sessions and Assizes

it is always worth checking both Indictment Books and Order Books when seeking information on your ancestor. In many instances in the Order Books, it is not clear exactly what the charge was.

Some sample entries follow, from the abstracts of Order Book, G.A. Ref. Q/SO 1 (covering the period from the Easter Sessions of 1672 to the Michaelmas Sessions of 1681), showing aspects of life during the period.

- f.21 Seamen: lists required under Letters from Privy Council of seamen in each parish, whether at home or abroad, with ages. High constables to return to the Clerk of the Peace at the next general assizes.

- f.21 Frampton Cotterell – Bastardy: Jn. Ellery, labourer, reputed father of female child of Ann Rodman, wid., having fled from the parish, the churchwardens and overseers have entered by warrant into his leasehold cottage; order that Jn. Tyler, snr, Jn. Hughes, Th. Poole, Jn. Millett, Jn. Prigge and Jn. Thurston of Frampton Cotterell hold the cottage for maintenance of child.

- f.29a License to Jn. Driver and Richd. Maior, falconers and servants of Edw. Rich, Esq., to shoot birds for hawks' meat.

- f.49 Discharge under Act of Pardon for Jn. Hayward, Wm. Millett and Josiah Carrier, prisoners in Gloucester Castle for several years for contempt.

- f.50 Order to restore to Wm. Hall and wife Mary, committed to Gaol on suspicion of murder, their goods or value as appraised, for their relief in Gaol; Court being of the opinion that seizure of goods by Coroner or any other person, before owner's conviction, is contrary to law.

- f.61 Nicholas Carter committed to the Bridewell for hard labour having returned to South Cerney after removal order to Somerford Keynes, Wiltshire.

As with the Petty Sessions, the Justices of the Peace could fine someone, order them to be flogged or branded or send them to jail. More serious cases could be forwarded to the Assizes for trial and sentencing.

- f.12v Aaron Jakes, late of Tetbury, labourer, for taking and carrying away a pewter cup worth 4d belonging to Sarah Sale at Tetbury, 1st January 1661/2. He was found guilty and flogged.

- f.110v William How, senior, of Longney, husbandman, for taking and carrying away 2 ewes and 2 lambs, worth 20/- belonging to William Pace at Longney, 24th Jun 1666, William Pace and John Chaplin prosecuting. He appeared and pleaded not guilty. He put himself on his country. Guilty. Read and was branded.

[The phrase 'put himself on his country' meant that he requested trial by jury. Apparently, the jury found him guilty.]

Others who were found guilty of the charge were bound over to 'keep the peace' and paid a recognizance to encourage them to do so. Books of Recognizances, similar to those from the Petty Sessions, may tell you what your ancestor did to breach the peace and what it cost him if he failed to behave himself in future. Sometimes, someone would opt to join the Army rather than be sent to prison.

The Justices of the Peace were, themselves, required to take oaths of allegiance to the monarch at the beginning of a new reign and their declarations are entered in the records. At times, similar oaths were also taken by the clergy, prominent people and landowners. If your ancestor became a Justice of the Peace, his name should appear in the oaths of allegiance records. Occasionally, the signature of a woman was included in the list but the vast majority of signatures were those of men.

But oaths of allegiance were not restricted to those who became magistrates or held important positions in the community. The Protestation Oath of 1641 was one requiring all males over the age of 16 to swear allegiance to the Church of England. 1696 saw the Association Act when loyalty to William III was required. These were organised on a parish basis and formed a basic early census for each area.

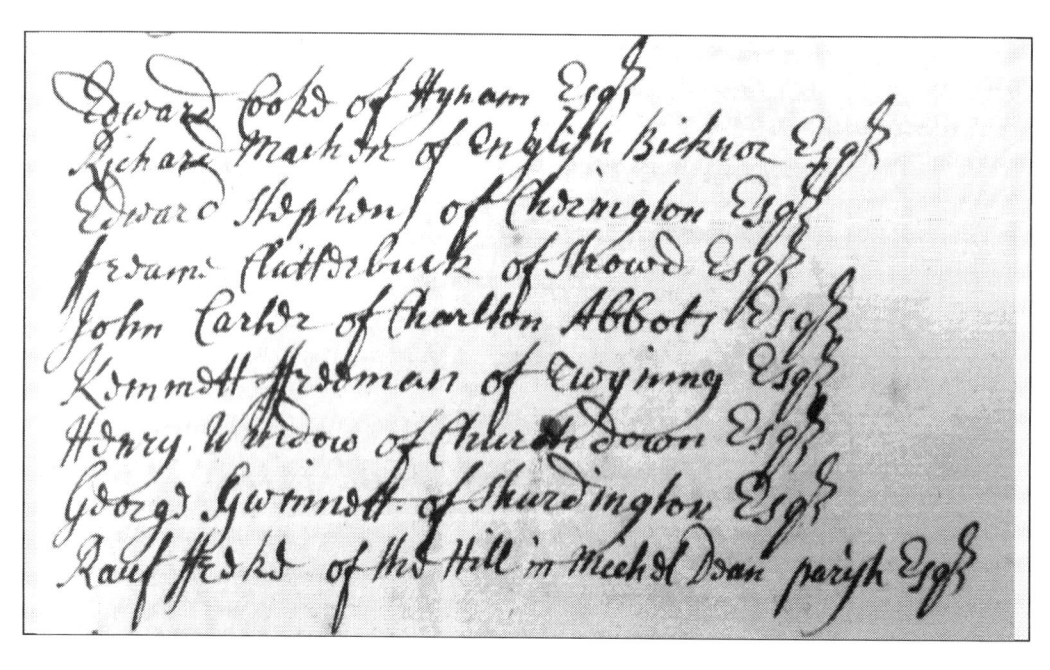

George Gwinnett of Shurdington was included in a list of names of those taking the Oath of Allegiance to King George I in 1715.
G.A. Ref. Q/SO/4/2

During times of religious upheaval, Roman Catholics were identified and their names recorded on lists of Papists. Their estates were also subject to sequestration. My search over many years failed to find information on a marriage, children and burial for one Lawrence Gwinnett in the late 17th and early 18th century; when his name was discovered on a list of Papists, it became clear why he had not been located in the parish registers! Gloucestershire

11. Sessions and Assizes

Archives has a list of papists for 1715 in Q/SO/4/2 and records relating to Papists' estates in Q/RNc.

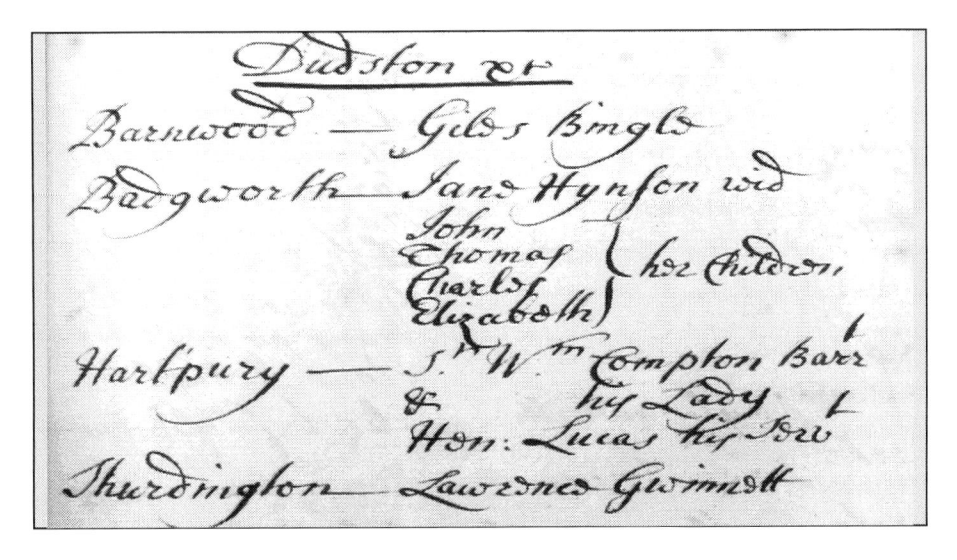

A few pages after George Gwinnett was recorded as taking the Oath of
Allegiance, his brother, Lawrence Gwinnett, appears on a list of Papists.
G.A. Ref. Q/SO/1/2

All officials, such as the mayor and aldermen, had to prove that they had recently taken communion by producing a sacrament certificate; this ensured that nonconformists could not hold important positions.

Part of a sacrament certificate confirming that Richard Horsman of Chipping
Campden did receive the sacrament on 30th September 1781 in the parish church.
G.A. Ref: Q/SR/1781/D

207

Discover Gloucestershire Ancestors

Nonconformists did, also, appear in the Quarter Sessions records with declarations made by dissenting ministers, imprisonment for being a Papist or payment for reporting one, as well as applications for licences for dissenters' meeting houses and registers of such houses.

f.229a   Papists – Th. Osbourne, committed for maintaining Pope's supremacy, to remain in gaol until next assizes. [G.A. Ref. Q/Sib]

It was not just the minister who applied for a meeting house licence but several of the important officials of the church as well so you may be able to identify your ancestor as a nonconformist from such an application.

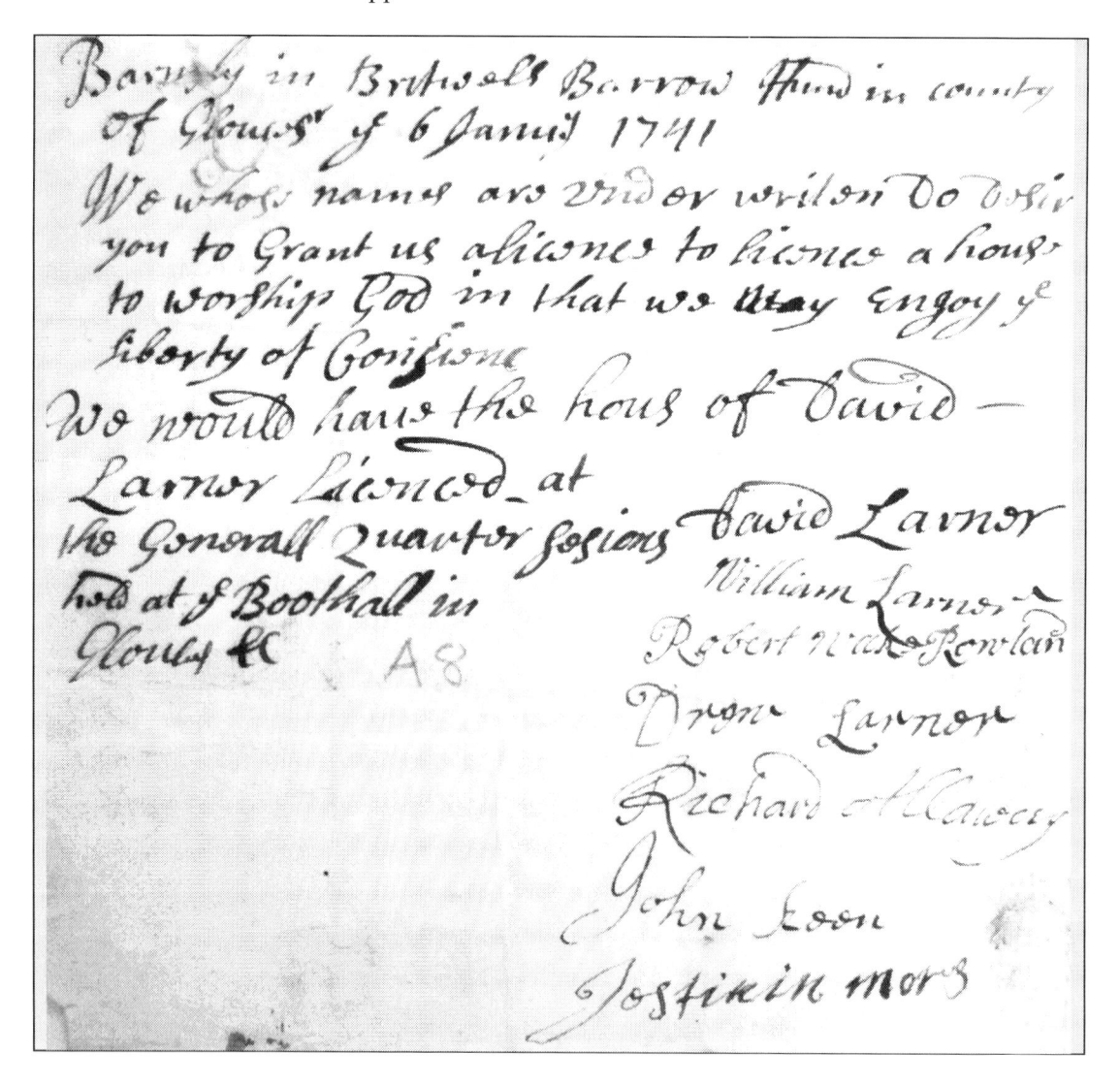

Application to the Quarter Sessions for a licence for a dissenters' meeting house in Barnsley in the Brightwells Barrow Hundred in 1742.
G.A. Ref: Q/SR/1742

11. Sessions and Assizes

There are three collections of Quarter Session records held at Gloucestershire Archives, those for the County as a whole, those for Gloucester Borough and those for Tewkesbury Borough. The collection of records for Gloucestershire County Quarter Sessions all begin with the letter Q and are followed by a code as shown below. The records for Gloucester Borough Quarter Sessions all begin with the code GBR G3 followed by the relevant code whereas those for Tewkesbury Borough Quarter Sessions documents all start with the reference QT.

These three collections of records of the Quarter Sessions, held at Gloucestershire Archives, are organised under the categories shown below. So, for example, the records relating to the court in session documents would begin with Q/S or GBR G3/S or QT/S depending upon the location where the quarter session was held. Using these codes when searching the online catalogue can help to narrow down your search.

Code	Topic
J	Justices of the Peace
S	Court in Session
A	Administration
F	Finance
R	Registration, Enrolment, Deposits
C	Clerk of the Peace
Y	Police Records
G	Gloucester Gaol & Houses of Correction
X	Probation Records

The category, J, relating to Justices of the Peace, is relatively small and contains commissions of the peace when a justice was nominated by royal commission and oaths taken by the Justices, some swearing that they had the necessary property qualification and others being oaths of allegiance to the monarch. This section is only likely to be of interest to those whose ancestors were Justices of the Peace.

The Court in Session collection, with code S, covers the widest range of items, including all documents relating to the various criminal and administrative cases heard in the Quarter Sessions court, of which examples have been given here. The collection includes indictments, writs, juries, lists of officials, depositions, order rolls, recognizances, presentments, fines, appeals, prisoners and transportation bonds as well as items relating to less interesting items such as highway and footpath diversions. This category includes some of the most useful and informative records for family historians.

The code, A, relates to documents dealing with the administrative function of the Justices of the Peace. One aspect of this was the planning, erection, maintenance and repair of buildings which belonged to the county, such as Shire Hall, the Judges' Lodgings, militia storehouses, reformatories and various houses of correction and gaols. Other items refer to weights and measures, highways, licensing of alehouses, victuallers, slaughter houses and asylums, and to the police force.

Documents relating to the financial aspects of the work done at the Quarter Sessions have codes beginning with Q/F. This covers all aspects of the Coroner's work such as fees and expenses, securities, fines from courts, county rates and police accounts.

The Registration section, code R, is another large collection of documents and includes appointments of officers, elections, electoral registers and poll books, land tax and other tax assessments, inclosures and encroachments in the Forest of Dean, canals and turnpike trusts, water works and drainage systems, freemasons, places of worship, banks and friendly societies, and much more. You may find reference to your ancestor in most of these but rarely are details of family relationships given.

The Clerk of the Peace records (code C) covers all correspondence dealt with, accounts and fees, agendas for meetings, attendance records, expenses and bonds, parliamentary returns and miscellaneous other items. As with the previous category, few family details will be found here but it is always satisfying to find a mention of one's ancestor, however brief. Information on the codes Y (Police records), G (Gloucester Gaol and the Houses of Correction) and X (Probation records) will be dealt with in the next chapter on Punishment.

Assizes
Some cases were deemed more serious than the minor crimes dealt with at the Petty and Quarter Sessions. Cases of murder, treason, rioting, arson, counterfeiting, major theft and bigamy, for example, were sent to the Assizes by the local magistrates. Occasionally, the coroner would also pass a case on if there were any suspicious circumstances. These assizes had been in existence since medieval times but were abolished in the 1970s and replaced by the current crown courts.

The assizes were held regularly, twice a year, around February/March and July/August. An additional session could be held in between times if the gaols became too full, such as during times of rioting; anyone unfortunate enough to be arrested in, say, September, could be held in gaol for many months until the next assizes were due.

Judges from Westminster presided over these trials and, because they travelled around to the different locations to hold court, the assizes were organised into 'circuits'. The Gloucestershire assizes were part of the Oxford Circuit along with Herefordshire, Worcestershire, Berkshire, Shropshire, Staffordshire and, of course, Oxfordshire itself. Bristol, as a privilege of an ancient charter, had, until 1832, the right to hear its own criminal cases so assize records for the city up to that time are held at Bristol Record Office. The most serious cases may have been transferred to the Old Bailey in London which has a database of trials, to be found at: www.oldbaileyonline.org

As with the quarter and petty sessions, assize records may include:

- Indictments (containing the plea, verdict, sentence, abode, where arrested)
- Depositions (sworn statements of witnesses who must appear in court or pay a fine)
- Calendar of prisoners (name, crime, age, literacy, abode, date gaoled)

11. Sessions and Assizes

- Calendar of sentences (printed after assize)
- Gaol delivery calendars (names of convicted prisoners, brief details of crime)
- Order books and minute books

The vast majority of records from the Assizes are held at the National Archives at Kew (in the ASSI series) although many of them have not survived. Those that exist for the Oxford Circuit as a whole cover the period from 1558 to 1971 but the Gloucestershire crown and gaol books begin in 1657, the indictment files from 1662 and depositions from 1719; those records made before 1732 are in Latin. They are not indexed by personal name so you need to know approximately when the case came to court to locate the record you are seeking. You then have to search through every entry until you find what you are seeking.

Between 1805 and 1892, the Home Office recorded information on people charged with indictable offences in registers held at the National Archives in Class HO27. Family History Indexes (www.fhindexes.co.uk) has produced CDs containing the name, alias, age, date of trial, crime, sentence and reference for each case, organised by county. Approximately a third of those accused were found not guilty. A similar index to these national Criminal Registers can be accessed on the Ancestry website.

A couple of weeks before they were due to start, local newspapers would announce the date of the forthcoming assizes. A list of potential jurors was drawn up. For example, for the Lent Assizes to be held in 1836, a list of 65 people was drawn up of jurors to be 'summoned, impanelled and returned to try the issue between John Doe (on the demise of Rose Riddell), plaintiff and Thomas Newell, defendant, on a plea of trespass and ejectment'.

The people shown on the jury list were:

1. Benjamin Antill of Nelson Street, Stroud, grocer
2. George Anstey of Dirham and Hinton, innkeeper
3. William Bishop of Painswick, mealman
4. Edward Gittins Bucknall of Rowcroft, Stroud, silversmith
5. Joseph Bailey of Gyde's Terrace, Cheltenham, broker
6. William Beckett of Winchcomb, baker
7. William Britton of Oldland Hamlet in Bitton, mechanic
8. Thomas Burchill of Doynton, farmer
9. George Bartlett of Eastington, grocer
10. Stephen Maynard Colchester, of Ashelworth, farmer.
11. William Clissold of Miserdine, maltster
12. Samuel Henry Clissold of High Street, Stroud, seedsman
13. Henry Collett of High Street, Cheltenham, grocer
14. William Churchill of High Street, Cheltenham, ironmonger
15. William Carter of Brockthrop, farmer
16. James Eley of Berkeley, saddler
17. Joseph Evans of Charlton Kings, nurseryman
18. Samuel Fry of Oldland hamlet in Bitton, clock and watch maker
19. Samuel Gabb of Cam, farmer

20. William Gardner of Spoonbed in Painswick, grocer
21. Robert Gardner of Gratton Terrace, Cheltenham, coal merchant
22. George Greenwood of Horton, farmer
23. Richard Grinnall of Winchcomb, farmer
24. James Gage of Oldland Hamlet in Bitton, bacon factor
25. Thomas Grant of Frampton Cotterell, hatter
26. John Griffin of Eastington, builder
27. John Hathway of Cam, farmer
28. William Hill of Coaley, farmer
29. Richard Herbert of Edge in Painswick, farmer
30. John Holland of High Street, Stroud, grocer
31. James Harris of Brockthrop, farmer
32. William Hall of Winchcomb, slatter
33. Abner Howes of Oldland Hamlet in Bitton, furrier
34. William James of Elmore, farmer
35. Henry Margaret of Bath Place, Cheltenham, baker
36. Thomas Mills of Highnam, Over and Linton, miller
37. James Merrett of Upton Saint Leonards, farmer
38. Jeffrey Matthews of Dirham and Hinton, farmer
39. Thomas Marshall of Littledean, bailiff
40. Thomas Newman of Winchcomb, carpenter
41. William Pritchard of Pittville Street, Cheltenham, pastry cook
42. Thomas Powell of Tresham Tithing in Hawkesbury, mealman
43. Samuel Parker of Frampton Cotterell, hatter
44. Elmes Pain of Coleford Tithing in Newland, mason
45. Joseph Pole of Oldbury Tithing on Thornbury, farmer
46. Robert Pool of Kingstanley, butcher
47. Thomas Roberts of Ashelworth, farmer
48. Thomas Rodway of Miserden, yeoman
49. George Ratcliffe of Tresham Tithing in Hawkesbury, farmer
50. Joseph Robins of Littledean, mason
51. George Seaborn of Berkeley, baker
52. John Savage of Coaley, farmer
53. Richard Slader of Portland Square, Cheltenham, cabinet maker
54. James Snelling of Manchester Street, Cheltenham, painter
55. Robert Smith of High Street, Cheltenham, shoemaker
56. John Smith of Horton, farmer
57. Isaac Tucker of Doynton, farmer
58. John Trotman of Oldbury Tithing in Thornbury, fisherman
59. Thomas Turner of Frampton on Severn, butcher
60. William Vick of Elmore, farmer
61. Amos Vimpany of Moreton Valence, yeoman
62. William Williams of Northfield Terrace, Cheltenham, carpenter
63. James Waite of High Street, Cheltenham, turner
64. William Wood of Littledean, maltster
65. John Whittington of Coleford Tithing in Newland, farmer

G.A. Ref: D333/X7

11. Sessions and Assizes

Once the assizes began, a list of prisoners to be tried was given.

Prisoners' Names, Ages, Causes of Commitment, &c.

1 FREDERICK BAKER, aged 22,...R. W. WELL.. Committed August 15, 1845, by J. Dowling, esq. Mayor, and W. M. Meyler, esq. for *stealing*, on the 4th day of August, within the said City, *one mare*, of the value of ten pounds, the property of Henry Cox.

The first entry on the Calendar of Prisoners taken for trial at the Lent Assizes held in Gloucester on Saturday, 4th April, 1846. Frederick Baker was accused of stealing a mare.
G.A. Ref: D3620/2

Despite the fact that official assize records are held at Kew, entering the word 'assizes' into Gloucestershire Archives online catalogue brings up a list of nearly 200 documents that pertain to the assizes in one way or another. These may be in the diocesan, quarter or petty session collections or in family or solicitors' records and include judge and jury lists, calendars of prisoners, briefs for the prosecution counsel, and other legal documents relating to various trials, but these are usually individual records that have survived rather than whole collections.

Usually the best way to discover the details about any case held at the assizes, even minor ones, is to look at the local newspapers for reports of the trial. At the start of the Assize period, the newspaper would print the names of judge and jury, together with the introduction to the court by the judge. For example, at the Lent Assizes in 1870, the judge said

> 'he was happy to be able to congratulate them on the state of the calender; there was nothing in it which called for any observations from him. It was unusually light.'

This was followed by very full reports of the events that occurred in court including witness statements and the sentence given, assuming the accused was found guilty (see article on following page).

Filmed copies of the old newspapers can be accessed at Gloucestershire Archives while some newspapers referring to the cases held at the assizes can be found on the Internet in the Times Online Archive by entering Oxford Circuit and Gloucester.

From the *Gloucester Journal*, 2nd April 1870.

After listing the names of the Judge and Grand Juries, and reporting the introduction given to the court by the judge, commenting on the lightness of the calendar before him, each of the individual cases were reported. Below is one such case, showing much more details than the basic assize records hold.

STEALING A PURSE

George Carr, aged 20, described as a tailor, was charged with stealing a purse and money from Elizabeth Duffett Maggs, at Berkeley, on the 23rd March. Mr Browne prosecuted.

The prosecutrix was at the Berkeley Road Station, on the day of the Berkeley Steeple-chases, and whilst on the platform, was hustled by the prisoner and another man. She had her purse in her right pocket. Prisoner was on that side, and she felt her pocket lightened by the removal of her purse, which a minute before was there. The other man was on the other side. No other person was near on her left side. The purse contained 2l 10s in gold and a little silver. The prisoner passed up the station yard. She told her husband and the police, and the prisoner was brought back. She said "That is the man." The police tried to search the man but he ran away and the constable followed. He was brought back with the handcuffs on. He was very violent. No one but the prisoner could have touched her pocket from the time she felt her purse to the time she missed it.

Mr Maggs, husband of the prosecutrix, said that when his wife called his attention to the loss of her purse, he saw the prisoner who went away. He collared the other man and the prosecutrix said "You have got the wrong man," upon which he, with the policeman, chased the prisoner who was brought back.

P.C. Wilkes said he was on duty at Berkeley Road Station on the 23rd March, and on Mr Maggs' information he went after the prisoner who ran away across the fields. He came in the course of the chase to a swampy land where he saw something on the ground in the shape of money. He overtook the prisoner in a minute or minute and a half. The latter said "I won't be took," and struck the witness on the breast. Mr Maggs came up and assisted and the prisoner was handcuffed and brought back to the station, where he was searched, but nothing was found upon him. Witness afterwards searched the swampy place, but found nothing. In reply to the judge, witness said he attempted to search the prisoner before he ran away but the prisoner said "I won't be searched."

The prisoner, who said he went from Bristol to the Berkeley Steeple-chases, protested his innocence and said that when he surrendered the constable took him to the public house and made a "laughing stock" of him, saying "I will give him running me; I will make his tea sweet enough for him and hot enough." "I," added the prisoner, "knew what that meant".

The jury retired to consult and, after an absence of nearly half an hour, they acquitted the prisoner.

Chapter 12

Gaols and Houses of Correction

'These melancholy mansions of oppression and distress'.

Sir George Onesiphorus Paul
1746 – 1820, prison reformer

Petty offences such as vagrancy were often punished instantly by whipping the offender up and down the local streets or by placing the miscreant in the stocks for a few hours, where he or she was contained by sitting them down and placing their feet through holes in hinged wooden boards or metal devices which were then locked to prevent them from escaping. A slightly more severe punishment involved the pillory where the offender stood in a bent position to receive his punishment, his head and hands being secured in a similar manner to that in the stocks. The whole point of this type of punishment was humiliation as many local people would come to taunt the person and frequently pelted him or her with rotten fruit, eggs and other unpleasant substances.

More serious offences resulted in more drastic punishments involving the imprisonment, transportation or execution of the convicted. A sentence of incarceration meant either a stay in a nearby house of correction, used for the punishment of relatively minor cases or confinement in a gaol for the more serious offences. In both instances, the sentence usually included hard labour and, possibly, a beating of some kind. In later years, the young were sent to reformatories.

The stocks outside Painswick church.

Houses of Correction
A house of correction was also known as a bridewell. The original bridewell was built in the St. Bride's Well district of London in the 16th century to house and train the poor and idle but it was gradually used to hold criminals as well until that became its sole purpose. Until the 18th century, there seem to have been at least seven houses of correction in Gloucestershire and Bristol, situated at:

- Berkeley
- Cirencester
- Gloucester
- Lawford's Gate, Bristol
- St Briavels
- Tewkesbury
- Winchcombe.

In 1777, in his book, *The State of the Prisons*, the prison reformer John Howard wrote of the **Berkeley** House of Correction that it was:

> 'quite out of repair. Only one room for men and women, eighteen feet four inches by fifteen feet four, and seven feet nine inches high; the window (near four square feet) not glazed; no straw; no chimney; court not secure. Nothing has

12. Gaols and Houses of Correction

been laid out on this prison these twenty years. The sensible old keeper lamented the bad effects of close confinement in idleness, upon the health of even young strong prisoners. Many such, he said, he had known quite incapable of working for some weeks after their discharge. He told me, that some years ago his prisoners used to grind malt for a penny a bushel; and the justices would not license any victualler whose malt was not ground here: but that of late years they have done no work at all. No allowance. Keeper, Francis Norman: his salary, £20; but he pays out of it £6 to the poor of the parish for ground rent.'

Howard was concerned that prisoners of all ages and sexes were mixed together, leading to babies being born in the house; that prisoners had no work to do while they were confined, that there was limited opportunity for exercise and that gaol fever was rife.

The **Cirencester** House of Correction was slightly better than the Berkeley one in that it had two rooms for prisoners, one room for the men and one for women. However, everything was in desperate need of repair and the courtyard, intended for use by the prisoners for exercise, was not secure.

The **Gloucester** bridewell was originally held in the few rooms that remained in the ruined Gloucester Castle but was transferred in 1707 to a building at the East Gate in the city. Twenty years later, it was located at the workhouse and, fifty years after that, John Howard noted that the bridewell seemed to have returned to the castle. It appears to have been moved around a few more times before becoming part of the Gloucester City Gaol.

Lawford's Gate House of Correction, built in 1716, had four rooms but two of these, containing the luxury of a bed of sorts, were kept for prisoners who could afford to pay for them. Again there were no chimneys and, although there was a pump outside for the use of the prisoners, the yard was not secure so they were kept in their rooms. There would normally have been only a handful of prisoners held there at any one time.

Of **St Briavels** House of Correction, John Howard wrote that there were two rooms, one each for men and women, in a bad state of repair. There was 'no courtyard, no water, no food allowance and no firing'. This bridewell, owned by Lord Berkeley, was a Debtors' Gaol. It is hardly surprising that, of the two men held there when Howard visited the bridewell, one was sick and had not been outside for a year.

Tewkesbury, as a borough, had its own house of correction and gaol which, originally, was in a barn in Barton Street, then in the bell tower at the front of Tewkesbury Abbey. Later, in 1817, it was transferred to Bredon Road at the end of the High Street and enlarged. As many as 80 prisoners were held in the gaol at one time but this number reduced and, in 1841, the numbers were so low that the council requested prisoners be transferred to Gloucester henceforth. Howard did not mention the Tewkesbury House of Correction in his book.

The last of these Gloucestershire houses of correction was at **Winchcombe** and it was no better than the others. Previously held in the cellar, the prisoners had been transferred to the attics where, due to the lack of security in the yard outside, they were kept all the time.

> An early Calendar of Prisoners awaiting trial in Winchcombe House of Correction
> 1766.
> G.A. Ref: Q/SG/1766

John Howard's survey of prisons was to change the life of those who spent time in prison and was to inspire Gloucestershire's High Sheriff, Sir George Onesiphorus Paul, to examine the state of local gaols and to do something to improve them and the lot of the prisoners held within. From 1783, Paul determined to close down the existing bridewells, and open new ones, only one of which, at Lawford's Gate, was to be on the same site. So new houses of correction were built at:

- Horsley
- Lawford's Gate
- Littledean
- Northleach.

The new House of Correction at **Horsley** was completed in 1790 when the first keeper was appointed for a salary of £50 plus a share of anything the prisoners earned. Records of prisoners from that early time do not appear to have survived. The registers of prisoners held at Gloucestershire Archives cover the period from 1825 to 1860 (G.A. Ref: Q/Gh/10/1 – 5). Other documents include memoranda of convictions from 1828 to 1835, quarterly accounts (up to 1878), provisions accounts and diet books. The Horsley House of Correction was closed in 1878 and was then sold.

The Diet Book for Horsley (G.A. Ref: Q/Gh/8/1) gives details of the number of prisoners in the gaol on a particular day, lists the number fed, how many were on bread and water, and notes those who have arrived or departed that day who had special requirements. For example, on 13th April 1828, three men were committed to the Horsley House of Correction.

12. Gaols and Houses of Correction

Item	Details
Date	13th April 1828
Names	Samuel Cook, Isaac Walkley, Stephen Lamb
Committed	3
Discharged	0
Number Fed	30
Oatmeal	2lb 5½oz
Salt	15oz
Potatoes	34
Bread and Water	6
Number of Prisoners	36

It would appear that, of the 36 prisoners in Horsley House of Correction on that day, six of them were on bread and water only.

The House of Correction at **Lawford's Gate** was also built in 1790 with 32 cells for inmates. Unfortunately, during the riots that occurred in Bristol in 1831, the bridewell was burned down and most of the records relating to the prisoners destroyed with it. The only remaining documents held at Gloucestershire Archives listing prisoners are memoranda of convictions dating from 1828 to 1835. However, the Keeper's Journal gives some details of those who were held in the house of correction.

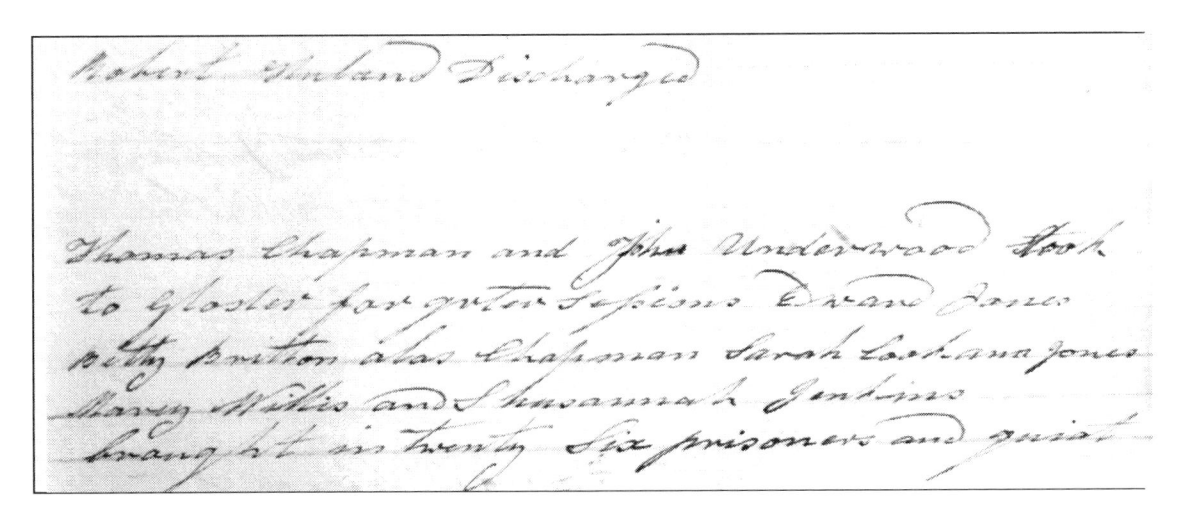

The Lawford's Gate Keeper's entry on 15th October gives details of prisoners
arriving and departing in 1820.
G.A. Ref: Q/Gla/1

Littledean's House of Correction, built at the same time as the others, is still standing and in use today as a museum. This bridewell has the most complete set of records of any of those in Gloucestershire. As well as the memoranda of convictions that exist for each of them, Gloucestershire Archives also holds, for the Littledean bridewell, journals of visiting justices, chaplains and medical officers, punishment books, order books, minute books, day books, diet books and account books as well as eight prison registers covering the period from 1791 to 1923. By looking at each of these, you can discover many details of your ancestor's life and find out about life in a bridewell in the 19th century.

The Littledean House of Correction is still standing today but is in private ownership and is no longer used to hold prisoners.

The medical journal included names of the patients, what was wrong with them and the treatment given by the surgeon. The prisoner's medical complaints were varied; the entries indicate that quite a few of them were suffering from gleet, a symptom of some form of venereal disease, as well as the more common aches and pains and every day coughs and colds.

A few entries from the 1845 surgeon's journal of Littledean House of Correction.
G.A. Ref: Q/Gli/18/3

Some prisoners suffered from more serious conditions, e.g.

12. Gaols and Houses of Correction

18th November
Richard Essex
Paralysis of the left side.
This man was taken about the middle of the night and the governor became aware of it this morning and made me acquainted with his state. I have bled him and he is now suffering with cold shivers. He is to take a tablespoonful of brandy.

Those prisoners who did not behave themselves whilst in the house of correction were subject to punishments that were recorded. The punishment book for Littledean (G.A. Ref: Q/Gli/12) shows details of the prisoner, the offence and the punishment, such as:

Item	Details
Date of punishment	7th May 1849
Name of prisoner	James Gwilliam
Age of prisoner	19
Class of prisoner	3
Prison offence and when committed	Talking to another prisoner and being very insolent to the officer when spoken to respecting it
Punishment awarded	24 hours Dark Cell
By whose authority	The Keeper
Date punishment began	7th May 7:30 am
Date punishment ended	8th May 7:30 am
When/How often punished before	Once when in Northleach
For what offence	Crowing in the morning

Even the boisterousness of the young was punished!

Item	Details
Date of punishment	23rd November 1847
Name of prisoners	Thomas Lawrence, Charles Burford, James Townley, William Townsend, Jesse Burford
Age of prisoner	12, 10, 13, 11, 12 (respectively)
Class of prisoner	3
Prison offence and when committed	For dancing in their cells yesterday morning, for singing when at work, and damaging the rules and writing on the walls of their cells.
Punishment awarded	Extra food stopped from each one day and to be locked up
By whose authority	The Keepers
Date punishment began	Breakfast time 23rd November
Date punishment ended	Breakfast time 24th November
When punished before	1st & 11th November 1847
For what offence	Larceny & Fighting, Larceny & Fighting, Larceny, Larceny, Larceny

Records which remain for the **Northleach** House of Correction include a visiting justice's journal, cash book, one register of prisoners covering the period from 1791 to 1816, an apothecary's journal, and two surgeons' journals recording events between 1818 and 1841.

The apothecary's journal covers the period from 1800 to 1818 and records treatments given to various prisoners. On 18th November 1800, the apothecary, Thomas Child, wrote:

> Visited all the prisoners and found them in good health except for Jeremiah Haly whom I found very weak and poorly in consequence of his necessary medical treatment. Ordered him as follows: viz. every morning gruel as the other prisoners, every Thursday and Sundays ¾lb mutton and 1lb potatoes, Mondays and Fridays 1½oz of rice, and 1½oz oatmeal, Tuesdays 2lbs potatoes and Saturday 3 ounces of oatmeal.
>
> [G.A. Ref: Q/Gn/5/1]

The visiting justices kept an overall eye on life in the bridewell and made recommendations for the health and containment of the prisoners.

On 29th July 1836, visiting Justice, J.E. Witts, recommended the purchase of a strait jacket for the future containment of lunatic prisoners.
G.A. Ref: Q/Gn/2

12. Gaols and Houses of Correction

Tewkesbury and Gloucester Gaols

Tewkesbury Gaol came under the authority of Tewkesbury Borough Council and the records relating to that gaol are held in the TBR series. Most of the records for the gaol again relate to its building and maintenance but there is one volume of prisoners' records covering the period between 1815 and 1854 (G.A. Ref: TBR/A13/1). It gives details of each prisoner's name, age, occupation, religion and level of literacy as well as the crime and sentence.

Item	Example
Date of Committal	16th March 1854
Number	12
Names	Benjamin Els.
Literacy Level	No [i.e. Cannot Read or Write]
Age	16
Parish	Tewkesbury
By Whom Committed	Nathaniel Chandler, Esq.
Trade	Labourer
Crime	Charged with feloniously stealing a quantity of rope, the property of Thomas Alton of the Borough of Tewkesbury.
When Tried	16th March 1854.
Result of Trial	Remanded until 17th March 1854.
When Discharged	17th March 1854 for want of evidence.
Behaviour in Prison	Very well
Religion	Wesleyan dissenter
Remarks	[Blank]

In the front of this volume, there is a list of the nine prisoners who, on 21st December 1816, were transferred from the old prison to the new building. They were: Henry Newton, John Evans, Mary Nicholls, Sarah Hale, Ann Skipp, Ann Harvey, Sarah Woodhouse, Maria Evans and Ann Bayliss.

There were two goals within the city of Gloucester, the City Gaol (which at some time incorporated the Gloucester House of Correction) and the County Gaol, the latter holding the more serious criminals. The new **City Gaol** was completed in 1781 and was the epitome of good prison design at the time, with separate quarters for men, women, and debtors, exercise yards for each group, a kitchen, chapel, bath and toilet facilities, a black hole and, at a later date, a treadwheel. This gaol served the city until 1858 when it was closed due to its unsuitability on the grounds of size, security and sanitation. Thereafter the criminals were sent to the county gaol.

The City Gaol came under the authority of Gloucester Borough so records relating to the inmates will be found either in their GBR series or in the QS series for quarter sessions, though few of these records appear to have survived. Most of the documents in Gloucestershire Archives refer to the prison itself, its building, maintenance and sale, rather than to the prisoners or staff in the gaol. There is one list of prisoners held in the city gaol in 1820 and some weekly returns for the years 1821 and 1822 but little else.

Discover Gloucestershire Ancestors

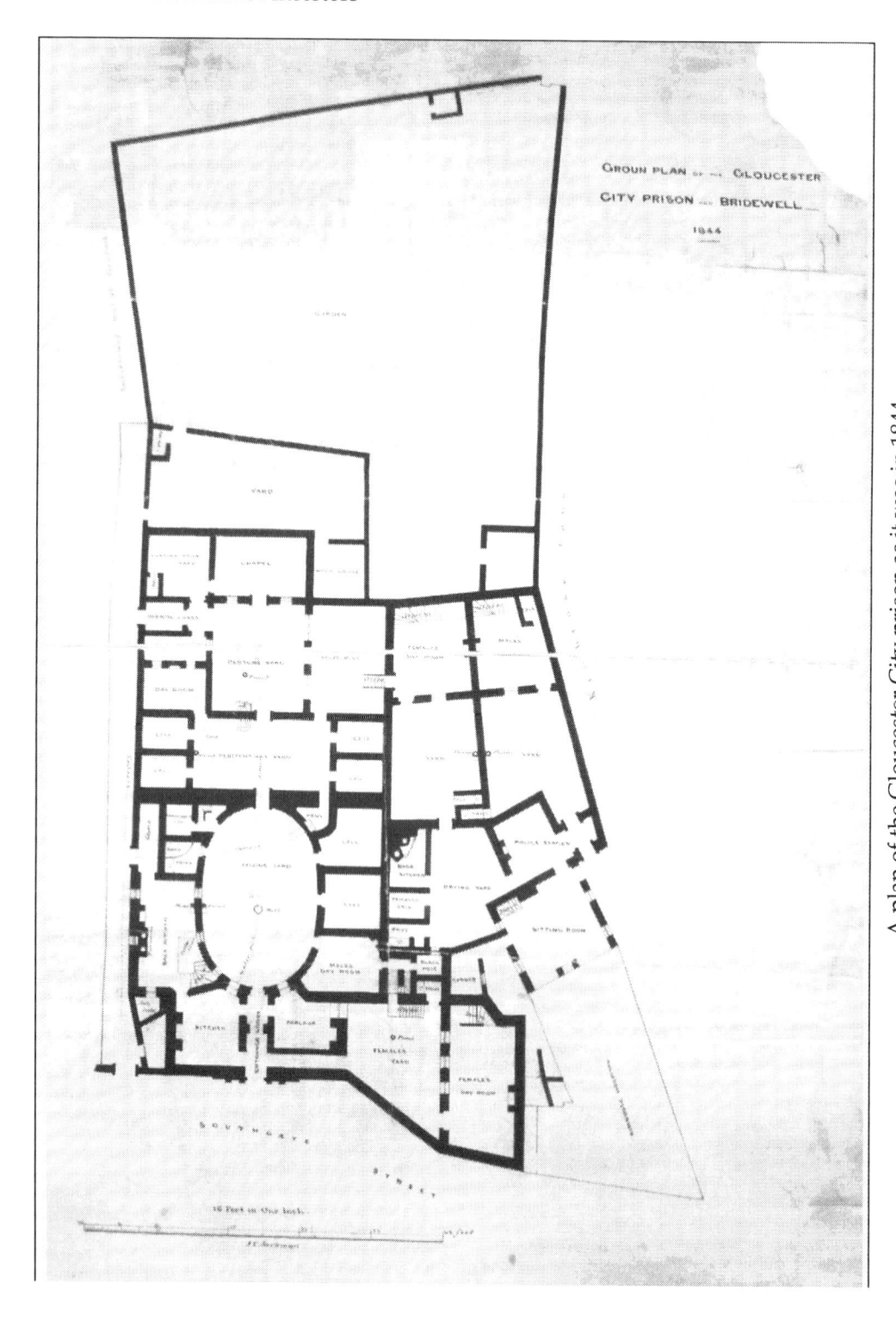

A plan of the Gloucester City prison as it was in 1844.
G.A. Ref: GBR G3/AG1

12. Gaols and Houses of Correction

A list of the prisoners held in Gloucester City Gaol in 1820.
G.A. Ref: GBR G3/AG2

From the 12th century onwards, Gloucester Castle was used as the **County Gaol**. This continued in use, in increasing states of disrepair until the end of the 18th century when Sir

George Onesiphorus Paul, the county sheriff, ordered a new gaol to be built. Demolition began in 1787 and the new prison was ready to open in 1791, on the same site.

In 1826, a new debtors' prison was built on to the gaol and at the end of the 1840s, a new convict prison was built on the same site. Under the Prisons Act of 1878, control of the prison was transferred away from the local magistrates and given to the government. Around 1915, the gaol became a male only prison and any remaining female prisoners were transferred elsewhere. After several more improvements and alterations, the gaol is still in use today.

An entry from the Governor of Gloucester County Gaol's Journal for 10th April 1809. Each day he recorded the temperature, the behaviour of the prisoners, the visitors and the names of the prisoners who were discharged as well as those who were delivered to the gaol.
G.A. Ref: Q/Gc/3/5

12. Gaols and Houses of Correction

There is a large range of documents that can be found relating to the county gaol. These include: journals of magistrates, governors, surgeons and chaplains, gaol calendars, registers of prisoners and punishments, store books, cash books, order books, day books, baker's books, copies of the prison rules and some albums of photographs of prisoners. The half-yearly returns to the Treasury (G.A. Ref: Q/CR/28/1) provide information on where your ancestor was sent to a penitentiary, with lists of prisoners transferred to other gaols. These were Millbank, Pentonville, Leeds, Leicester, Nottingham, Northampton, Wakefield, Parkhurst, Bedford and Reading.

> **PRISONERS confined in the Coun.**
> *Some for limited Times, and others till they can be transpo*
>
> 1. *William James*, aged 28, Convicted Feb. 25, 1789, for 12 months imprisonment, unless he shall sooner pay the sum of 10l. and 10s. and also for six months more, unless he shall sooner pay 2l. 10s. and 10s. Charges, &c. for cutting down oak trees, &c. — *By S. Hayward, E*
> 2. *Robert Cavey*, aged 24,
> 3. *Robert Cheshire*, aged 34, } Convicted March 12, 1789, of felony; for one year's imprisonment to hard labour, — *By Judgement of Assize*
> 4. *Peter James*, aged 43, Committed April 29, for 6 months imprisonment, unless he shall sooner pay the sums of 5l. and 14s. 6d. being convicted of cutting down an oak timber tree in his Majesty's Forest of *Dean*. — *By S Hayward, Esq.*
> 5. *James Paine*, aged 32, Committed July 11, for one year, unless he shall pay a fine of 20l. being convicted of attempting to kill a fallow deer. — *By C. J. Selwyn, Clerk.*
> 6. *Hester Vevars*, aged 18, Convicted July 16, of felony; for seven years transportation beyond the Seas. — *By Order of the Court of Quarter Sessions.*
> 7. *John Fletcher*, aged 21, Condemned at Summer assizes, 1789, and reprieved; to be transported for seven years. — *By judgment of assize.*
> 8. *Charles Pearce*, aged 17, Convicted at the same Assizes of an attempt to commit beastiality on a cow; to be imprisoned two years. — *By Ditto.*
> 9. *John Wood*, aged 26, Convicted at the same assizes of felony; to be imprisoned one year. — *By Ditto*
> 10. *John Evans*, aged 62, Convicted at the same assizes of felony; to be imprisoned two years. — *By Ditto.*
> 11. *Thomas Etheridge*, aged 26, Convicted at the same assizes of felony; for seven years transportation beyond the seas. — *By Ditto.*
> 12. *Stephen Turner Rimer*, aged 31, Convicted at the same assizes of felony; to be imprisoned one year. — *By ditto.*
> 13. *Richard Waite*, aged 24, Committed Aug. 12, 1789, for three months; convicted of using engines for the destruction of the game. — *By Sir John Guise, Bart.*
> 14. *Martha Churches*, aged 40, Committed Sept. 21, for one month; convicted of neglecting to perform a certain piece of work she had undertaken. — *B. Hyett, and N. Winchcombe, Esqrs.*
> 15. *William Weavin*, Convicted of manslaughter at summer assizes, 1789; three months imprisonment. — *By judgement of assize.*
> 16. *James Swain*, aged 26, Committed Oct. 2, convicted of stealing a beech tree; for six months, or until he shall pay the penalty of 2cl. and 6s. charges. — *By N. Winchcombe, Esq.*
> 17. *John Bishop*, aged 45,
> 18. *Richard Humphris*, aged 33,
> 19. *Solomon Hill*, aged 23,
> 20. *Henry Prosser*, aged 64,
> 21. *William Blackwell*, aged 36, } To take their Trials at the next assizes for different felonies.

A list of the prisoners confined in the County Gaol in Gloucester shown in the Gaol Calendar in 1789.
G.A. Ref: Q/SG/2

Prisoners

Apart from finding out whether or not your ancestor was held in a particular gaol, there are records which give you more information about the individual person. Gloucestershire Archives has a collection of volumes (G.A. Ref: Q/Gc/5 and Q/Gc/6) holding details of prisoners held on remand between 1815 and 1880. These volumes contain information on the offence and trial as in other records but they also hold personal descriptions and details of the character and habits of each prisoner. Each entry is spread across two pages. One such entry is as follows.

Item	Details
Date	20th November 1846
Number	1466
Name	Richard Gwinnett
Late Residence	Painswick
Trade	Farm Labourer
Age / Height	40 / 5ft 4½in
Hair colour / Eyes	Dark brown / Light Grey
Visage / Complexion	Long / Dark
Other marks	Mole on left arm near the elbow. White spot on right arm near the elbow. Left leg has been fractured.
Cause of commitment	Charged on the oath of Thomas Stephens with stealing at Painswick on the 14th day of March 1846 a sack bag, his property. Also stealing a sack bag on 30th September 1846, the property of Joseph Chandler. Also stealing a sack bag on 19th October the property of Jno. Skinner.
By whom Committed	J. Mills, Esq. and W. H. Stanton, Esq.
By which court to be tried	Quarter Sessions
By what court tried and when	Epiphany Session, 5 January 1847
Event of Trial	Guilty
Sentence Passed	2 indictments. Two calendar months with hard labour for the first offence and four calendar months more for the second offence, the last sentence to commence from the expiration of the first.
Expiration of term	5th July 1847
When discharged or removed	5th July 1847
By what authority	Time expired
Previously known character, habits and connexions	Native of Painswick. Married 7y. "I worked for Mr Holbrow of Spoonbed but the last time only 3 days and Shipway 2 weeks. I go to Painswick Church."
Convicted before and how often	Once
Conduct in prison	Orderly
Remarks	Tried Lent Assizes 1832 for stealing faggots. Guilty and had 14 days in the penitentiary.

Transcribed from the Register of Prisoners, 1844-1849. G.A. Ref: Q/Gc6/1

12. Gaols and Houses of Correction

Photography began in the middle of the 19th century and, in 1870, the governor of Gloucester Gaol ordered photographs to be taken of some of his prisoners. Gloucestershire Archives holds four photograph albums (G.A. Ref: Q/Gc/10/1 – 4) with pictures dating from 1870 and ending in 1935; the period covered is patchy and the later album is not yet available to the public as it is covered by the 100 year disclosure rule.

The first volume is entitled 'County Gaol: Return of Habitual Criminals' so it would appear to only include those prisoners who offended more than once. It contains the records of 282 prisoners, one per page, only 82 of whom were photographed. These photographs were taken between 10th April and 9th July 1870, the first being that of one Henry Winniatt. Each page recorded a register number, date when sent to gaol, name and aliases, age on discharge, height, hair and eye colour, complexion, where born, marital status, trade, distinguishing marks, destination on release, offence for which convicted, when and where convicted, sentence, date when the sentence will end, previous convictions and any other remarks.

The second album (G.A. Ref: Q/Gc/10/2) contains nothing but photographs, taken between 1899 and 1915. Only the prisoner's name, number and a date are in this album; no further details of the individual person are given.

Henry Winniatt, sentenced to six months with hard labour for stealing an overcoat.
G.A. Ref: Q/Gc/10/1

The final album (G.A. Ref: Q/Gc/10/4) contains photographs taken at various times between 1882 and 1906. Again, only name, number and date are recorded with each photograph.

The albums contain photographs of men, women and children, the oldest, William Lord, a man of 80, the youngest a boy of 7 years of age, Edgar Kilminster.

The albums do not contain photographs of every prisoner held in Gloucester County Gaol during the periods mentioned but all the photographs taken before 1906 have been copied and are available from the Gloucestershire Family History Society on a Rogues Gallery CD. There are nearly 800 photographs all together. Approximately half of them, with some additional information relating to their lives and crimes, appear in my book *Victorian Prisoners in Gloucester Gaol – A Rogue's Gallery*.

Reformatories

Until the middle of the 19th century, all child offenders who were sent to prison were incarcerated along with the adult criminals, possibly in cells containing both men and women. They frequently underwent hard labour and, in Gloucester County Gaol at least, often suffered the birch. These children could be as young as 6 or 7 years old.

This situation continued for most child convicts but, from 1850 onwards, reformatories were introduced with the aim of separating the youngsters from the bad influence of the older convicts and giving them education and training in the hope that they would settle down to a better life on release.

Possibly the first 'approved' school in the world was established at Hardwicke in Gloucestershire in 1852. The Hardwicke Reformatory, as it was known, was in use for the next 70 years.

Around the same time, reformatories were established in the Kingswood area, near Bristol, one for boys at Kingswood Reformatory and one for girls called the Red Lodge Reformatory. Any surviving records for these are held at Bristol Record Office.

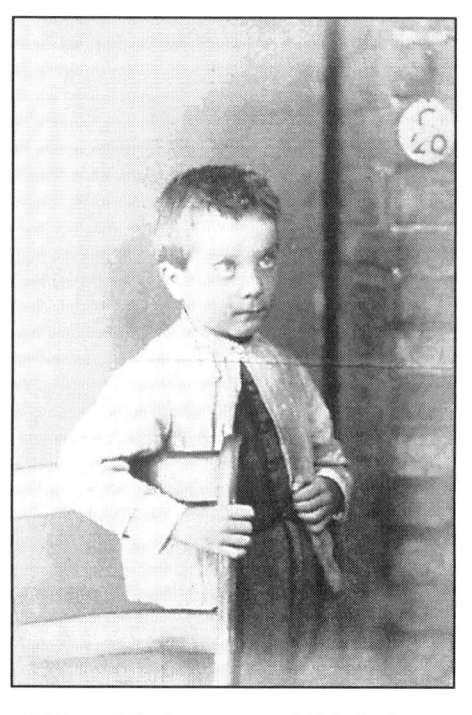

Edgar Kilminster, aged 7, jailed in 1870 for a week with hard labour and 12 strokes of the birch.

Some of the boys and staff at the Hardwicke Reformatory.
D3549/25/2/2

A list of the Hardwicke Reformatory boys who spent time in
Gloucester Royal Infirmary in 1909.
G.A. Ref: D3549/25/2/21

Transportation

As an alternative to the death penalty and to overcome increasing crowding in prisons in the early 17th century, transportation overseas became quite a common form of punishment for the more serious crimes and, in today's terms at least, for some of the not so serious offences, too. It continued for over 200 years, formally ending in 1868 although it had more or less ceased in reality ten years before. Sentences to transportation were either for life or for a specified period of time, usually 7 or 14 years.

Initially, people were sent to the West Indies to work on the plantations or to the newly formed American settlements. However, with the start of the American War of Independence in 1775, transportation to America ceased. Prisoners were still sentenced to transportation but were held in prisons and on prison hulks until new arrangements could be made to send them to Bermuda, Gibraltar or Australia, where they were used to help build the infrastructure of these developing countries. By 1788, Australia had become the main destination for convicts with penal settlements in New South Wales, Van Diemen's Land (Tasmania) and Western Australia.

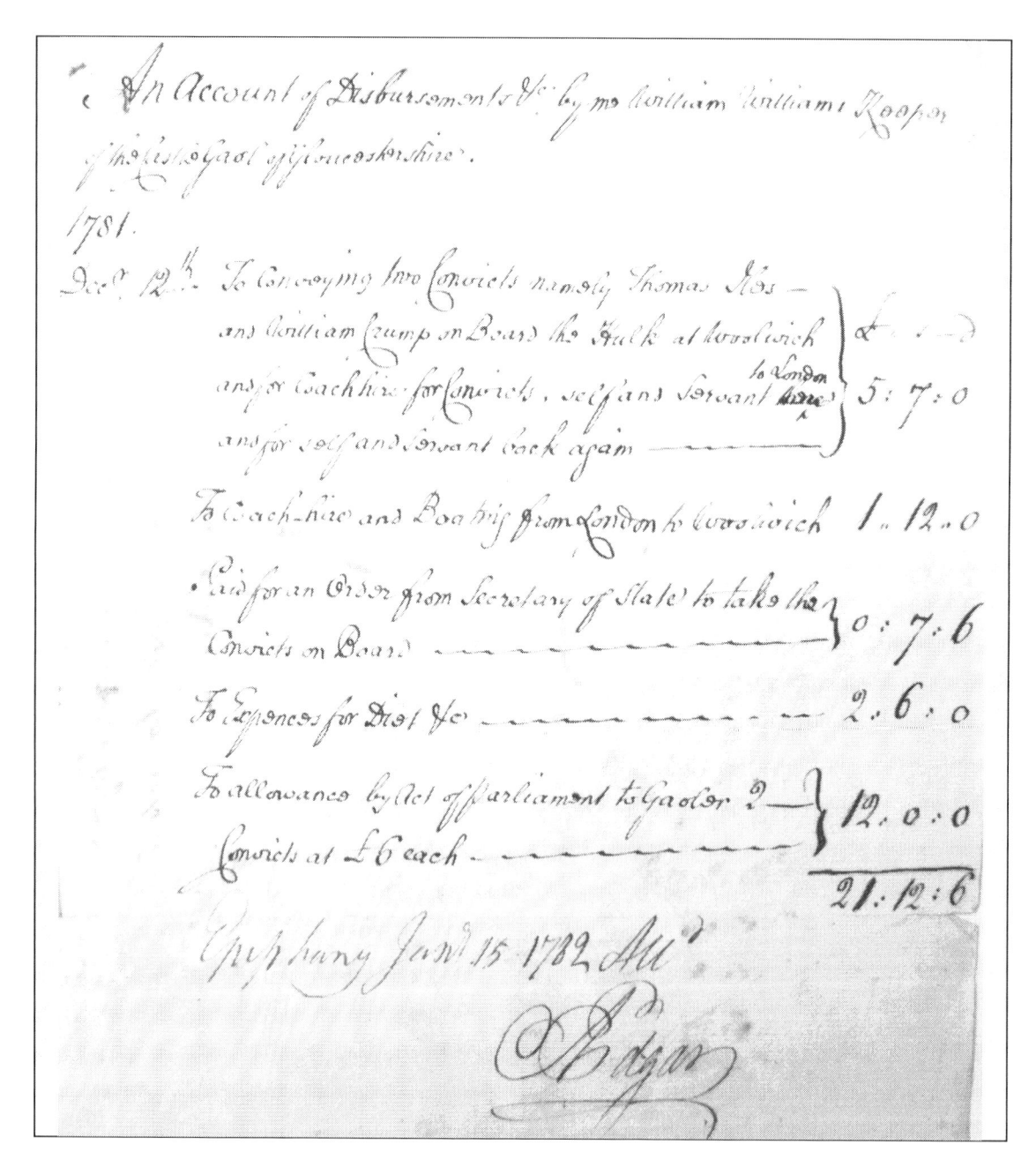

Expenses paid by the Keeper of Gloucester Gaol to transport Thomas Iles and William Crump to a hulk at Woolwich in 1782.
G.A. Ref: Q/CB/1

Over the next 80 years, over 150,000 prisoners were transported from these shores. Few records remain of the prisoners transported in the early years but an alphabetical list is given in Peter Wilson Coldham's book *The Complete Book of Emigrants in Bondage, 1615 – 1775*.

12. Gaols and Houses of Correction

For those transported from Gloucestershire, basic details of prisoners sent to Australia have been recorded in *Transportees from Gloucestershire to Australia, 1783-1842* edited by Irene Wyatt. The latter gives the name, age, address, occupation, sentence, means of transport and source of information for each prisoner. Occasionally, other details are added. One example informs us that:

> Giles Coates, aged 50, a clock and watch maker of Chedworth, was sentenced to transportation for life at the lent assizes in March 1834. He was transported on the ship 'George the Third' leaving on 12 December 1834. Sadly, Giles did not reach Australia as he was drowned when the ship was wrecked as it arrived at Hobart, Tasmania.

The names of those who were to be transported would be given in the newspaper report of the sentences handed out at the Assizes. Arrangements would be made to take them to their destination and those who were given the task of ensuring that they reached the penal settlement gave a bond to the justices that 'death and casualties of the sea excepted' they would transport them safely.

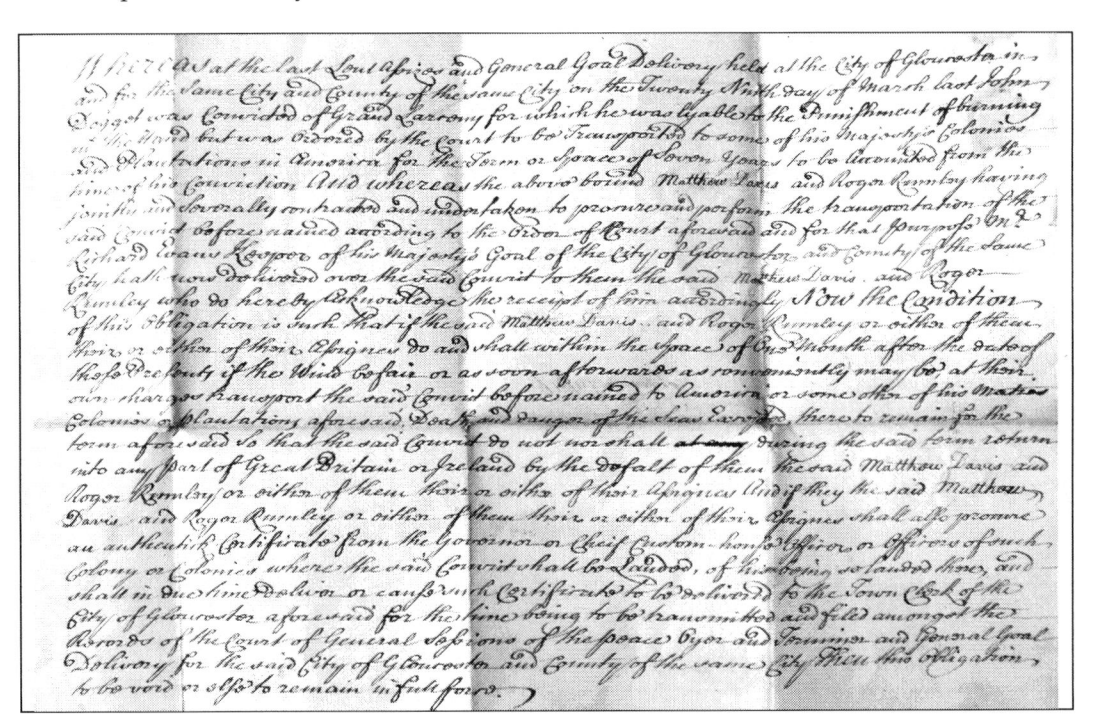

Part of a transportation bond of 1740 requiring Benjamin Heming and Samuel Heath to pay £200 if they fail to deliver to America convicts Ann Ellis, James Carry, Katherine Lewis, Henry Curtice, Kinard Harmer, William Davison, William Oland and Richard Kirby. Their original punishment of 'Burning in the hand' was commuted to 14 years for Ann and 7 years for the others.
G.A. Ref: GBR/G3/CB/1

Executions

Before 1792, those prisoners condemned to execution were taken in a cart to Over, just outside the city, where they were hanged on the gallows in a ceremony open to the public. Eighteen people are known to have been hanged at Over in the five years from 1786 until 1791, for crimes such as murder, rape, sheep stealing, housebreaking and burglary. After 1792, the condemned prisoners were hanged in public, 'over the drop' in Gloucester Gaol. This continued until 1872 when all executions were carried out in private inside the gaol.

The first prisoner to be hanged in the gaol itself was Charles Rackford, a 29 year old man from London who was convicted of highway robbery, along with John Hughes, a 19 year old Irishman. They were both executed on 14th April 1792.

A total of 140 hangings took place in Gloucester and Over between 1786 and 1939, nine of whom were women. The youngest was John Baker, aged 16, who was hanged for burglary in 1821, the oldest, John Evans, executed for a similar offence in 1793. All those executed at the gaol, were buried in the prison grounds. A list of those executed with some information on their crimes can be found in *The Murderers of Gloucestershire* by Bryan White.

The lodge at Gloucester Gaol where, until 1872, the front doors were opened to allow the public to witness the executions.

12. Gaols and Houses of Correction

[COPY.]

Gloucestershire, \
TO WIT.

An Inquisition indented taken for our Sovereign Lady the Queen at the County Prison in the North Hamlet near the City but in the County of Gloucester, on the Twelfth day of January, in the year of our Lord One thousand eight hundred and seventy four, pursuant to the directions of "The Capital Punishment Amendment Act, 1868," before Edward Walker Coren, Gentleman, one of the Coroners of our said Lady the Queen, for the said County, on view of the body of EDWIN BAILEY, now here lying dead at the said Prison known as the County Prison of and for the County of Gloucester, at Gloucester, within the Jurisdiction of the said Coroner, upon the oaths of the undersigned Jurors, twelve good and lawful Men of the said County, duly chosen, and who being then and there duly sworn and charged to enquire for our said Lady the Queen, when, where, how, and by what means the said EDWIN BAILEY came to his death, do upon their Oaths say, that the said EDWIN BAILEY was a Prisoner in the said Prison, indicted and convicted at the last Session of Gaol Delivery held for the said County for the wilful murder of SARAH JENKINS, and sentenced to death for the said offence, and that Judgment of Death was duly executed and carried into effect upon the said offender, EDWIN BAILEY for the said offence pursuant to the said sentence on the day and year aforesaid, within the walls of the said Prison, in which the said offender was confined at the time of execution. And the Jurors aforesaid upon their Oaths aforesaid, do further say that this Inquest is now here held on view of the body of the said offender by the Coroner of the Jurisdiction to which the said Prison belongs, within twenty-four hours after the execution of the said offender. And that the body of the said offender, EDWIN BAILEY now here lying dead, is the identical body of the said offender, who was so convicted and executed for the offence aforesaid. And that the said offender at the time of his death was a male person of the age of thirty-two years or thereabouts.

In Witness whereof as well the said Coroner as the Jurors aforesaid, have to this Inquisition set their hands and seals on the day and in the year and at the place first above written.

EDWARD WALKER COREN, L.S., Coroner.

JOHN WARD,	(L.S.)	GEORGE HENRY DAVIS,	(L.S.)
EDMD. D. WORSLEY,	(L.S.)	THOMAS HIRST,	(L.S.)
DANIEL TAYLOR,	(L.S.)	DONALD KNIGHT,	(L.S.)
ALBERT WILMOT,	(L.S.)	JOHN BYRNS,	(L.S.)
JOHN WYLES RIPPON,	(L.S.)	HENRY VAUGHAN,	(L.S.)
WILLIAM DORRELL,	(L.S.)	DANIEL JONES,	(L.S.)

The Coroner's Report on the body of Edwin Bailey, executed for the murder of Sarah Jenkins by poison. He was one of three prisoners executed at Gloucester Gaol on 12th January 1874.
G.A. Ref: D771/A/26

Law Enforcement

The sections on crime and punishment would not be complete without some mention of law enforcement in Gloucestershire. The early method of maintaining law and order was the existence of the parish constable or beadle but, as the population grew, and people moved to live in towns and cities, this became inadequate.

With the coming of the Industrial Revolution, life for the ordinary labourer became increasingly difficult and riots occurred throughout the county, such as the bread riots and Swing riots. The individual constables could not cope with this and, when necessary, the militia had to be called out to control the crowds.

Gradually, the number of officials dedicated to maintaining law and order in the county grew and small police forces were started in the larger towns. Eventually, in 1839, the County Police Act was passed in Parliament empowering local justices to appoint paid police forces. Later that same year, the first Chief Constable of Gloucestershire was appointed. Over 200 police officers were enrolled and allocated to different locations where they began their task of keeping order.

Gloucestershire Archives holds a vast range of documents relating to the Gloucestershire police (entering the word 'police' into the online catalogue gives over 1300 hits) covering such aspects as personnel records and photographs, police duties both criminal and civil, as well as documents relating to the general administrative and financial tasks of the organisation and the police stations and housing that went with the job. Many of the personnel records are still covered by the 100 year disclosure rule but some are available to be read. One such document (G.A. Ref: Q/Y/1/1) contains names and details of Gloucestershire Rural Constabulary for the period from 1839 to 1919.

Item	Details
Warrant Number	853
Date of Joining Force	11 Nov 1845
Names	Thomas Gwilliam
Age	23
Height	5ft 8½in
Trade	Labourer
County	Gloucester
Parish	St. Briavels
By whom recommended	Edward Machen, Esq., J.P. Coleford
Rank and Promotions	I.C. Const. 1 July 1848; Sergeant 1 July 1867.
Character	Very Good
Cause of Removal	Superannuated 1 Nov 1876.

Many of our ancestors were poor and, as a result, committed crimes, some petty and others more serious, to get more money, food or property to ease their living conditions. Their actions and resulting punishments make fascinating reading. A study of their crimes and subsequent punishments enhances our understanding of the lives of our ancestors.

Discover Gloucestershire Ancestors
Volume Two

Family history research is addictive! Once you start researching your ancestors, you are drawn into their world and want to find out more and more; where they came from, what they did to earn their living, what property they owned, what part they played in parish life, and generally what was life like for them. At every turn, you learn more about our history from a very personal point of view and discover more about Gloucestershire in the past.

To date, I have merely begun to discover the treasures in the archives. There are so many documents to help with family history research that my book has necessarily been split into two volumes. The next volume is already a work-in-progress! The following topics still have to be covered:

- The Parish Chest
- Education Records
- Military Service
- Workhouse Records
- Hospitals and Asylums
- Bankruptcy
- Taxation
- Apprenticeships
- Occupations and trades
- Immigration and Emigration
- Maps and Plans
- Deeds
- Newspapers
- Population lists
- Street and Trade Directories
- Business records
- Electoral registers
- Borough records
- Transport
- Manors and estates

I begin to wonder if there may even be a Volume 3 …..

Elizabeth Jack, 2012.

Bibliography

Austin, Roland, *Catalogue of the Gloucestershire Collection*, 1928.

Barratt, Nick, *Nick Barratt's Guide to Your Ancestors' Lives*, Pen & Sword Family History, 2010, ISBN: 978 1 84884 056 0.

Chapman, Colin R., *Ecclesiastical Courts, Officials and Records*, Lochin Publishing, 1997, ISBN: 1 873686 15 3.

Chapman, Colin R., *Marriage Laws, Rites, Records and Customs*, Lochin Publishing, 1997, ISBN: 1 873686 02 1.

Faraday, Michael A., *A Calendar of Probate and Administrative Acts in the Consistory Court of the Bishops of Hereford, 1407-1550*.

Fosbrooke, Thomas Dudley, *An Original History of the City of Gloucester*, Alan Sutton, 1976, ISBN: 0 904387 07 0.

Fowler, Simon, *Workhouse*, The National Archives, 2007, ISBN: 978 1 905615 03 2.

Frith, Brian, ed., *Historical, Monumental & Genealogical Collections, relative to the County of Gloucester, printed from the Original Papers of the late Ralph Bigland, Esq., Garter Principal King of Arms*, Bristol and Gloucestershire Archaeological Society, 1989 - 1995, ISBNs: 0 900197 28 5, 0 900197 30 7, 0 900197 34 X, 0 900197 40 4.

Frith, Brian, ed., *Marriage Allegations in the Diocese of Gloucester, 1637 - 1680*, Bristol and Gloucestershire Archaeological Society, 1954.

Frith, Brian, ed., *Marriage Allegations in the Diocese of Gloucester, 1681 - 1700*, Bristol and Gloucestershire Archaeological Society, 1970.

Fry, E. A., ed., *A Calendar of Wills and Administrations Registered in the Consistory Court of the Bishop of Worcester: 1451-1600*, Worcester Historical Society.

Gibson, J. S. W., *Quarter Sessions Records*, Federation of Family History Societies, 2007.

Gibson, Jeremy & Rogers, Colin, *Coroners' Records in England and Wales*, Federation of Family History Societies, 2009.

Gibson, Jeremy & Churchill, Elsie, *Probate Jurisdictions: Where to look for Wills*, Federation of Family History Societies, 2002, ISBN: 1 86006 152 4.

Grannum, Karen & Taylor, Nigel, *Wills and Probate Records*, The National Archives, 2009, ISBN: 978 1 905615 41 4.

Gray, I. E. & Gaydon, A. T., *Gloucestershire Quarter Sessions Archives 1660 – 1889 and Other Official Records*, Gloucestershire County Council, 1958.

Gray, Irvine & Ralph, Elizabeth, ed., *Guide to the Parish Records of Bristol and Gloucester*, Bristol and Gloucestershire Archaeological Society, 1963.

Herber, Mark, *Ancestral Trails*, Sutton Publishing, 2000, ISBN: 0 750924 84 5.

Hey, David, ed., *The Oxford Companion to Local and Family History*, Oxford University Press, 1998.

Higgs, Edward, *A Clearer Sense of the Census*, HMSO, 1996, ISBN: 0 114402 57 4.

Hollis, Denzil & Ralph, Elizabeth, ed., *Marriage Bonds for the Diocese of Bristol, 1637-1700*, Bristol and Gloucestershire Archaeological Society, 1952.

Howard, John, *The State of the Prisons*, J M Dent & Sons Ltd., re-printed 1929.

Hoyle, R. W., *The Military Survey of Gloucestershire, 1522*, Bristol & Gloucestershire Archaeological Society, 1993, ISBN: 0 900197 36 6.

Jack, Elizabeth, *Victorian Prisoners in Gloucester Gaol*, The History Press, 2009, ISBN: 978 0 752451 29 9.

Kear, Averil, *Bermuda Dick*, Lightmoor Press, 2002, ISBN: 1 899889 08 6.

Kirby, Isabel M., ed., *A Catalogue of the Records of the Bishop and Archdeacons*, Gloucestershire County Council, 1968.

Kirby, Isabel M., ed., *A Catalogue of the Records of the Dean and Chapter*, Gloucestershire County Council, 1967.

Matthews, A. G., Calamy Revised, Clarendon, 1934.

McLaughlin, Eve, *The Poor are Always with Us*, Varneys Press, 1994.

McLaughlin, Eve, *Nonconformist Ancestors*, Varneys Press, 1995

McLaughlin, Eve, *Illegitimacy*, Varneys Press, 1989.

Priestley, Philip, *Victorian Prison Lives,* Pimlico, 1999, ISBN: 0 712665 87 0.

Raymond, Stuart, *Words from Wills and Other Probate Records,* Federation of Family History Societies, 2004, ISBN: 1 899667 37 3.

Richards, M. E., and Smith, David J. H., *Gloucestershire Family History*, Gloucestershire County Council, 1993.

Scott, Miriam, *Prerogative Court of Canterbury, Wills and Other Probate Records*, PRO Publications, 1997, ISBN: 1 873162 23 5.

Smith, John, *Men & Armour for Gloucestershire in 1608*, Alan Sutton, 1980, ISBN: 0 904387 49 6.

Tate, W. E., *The Parish Chest*, Phillimore, 1983.

Thomas, Harry, *The History of the Gloucestershire Constabulary, 1839 – 1985,* Alan Sutton Publishing, 1987, ISBN: 0 951291 30 0.

VCH, *Victoria History of the County of Gloucester* volumes 2 - 12, 1972 – 2010, in progress.

Waller, Jill, ed., *A Chronology of Crime and Conflict in Cheltenham*, Cheltenham Local History Society, 2004.

Waller, Jill, ed., *A Chronology of Nonconformity and Dissent in Cheltenham,* Cheltenham Local History Society, 2007.

White, Bryan, *The Murderers of Gloucestershire,* 1985.

Whiting, J. R. S., *A House of Correction,* Alan Sutton Publishing Ltd, 1979, ISBN: 0 904387 27 5.

Whiting, J. R. S., *Prison Reform in Gloucestershire 1776 – 1820,* Unwin Brothers Ltd, 1975, ISBN: 0 850332 08 7.

Wyatt, Irene, ed., *A Calendar of Summary Convictions at Petty Sessions, 1781 – 1837* The Bristol and Gloucestershire Archaeological Society, 2008, ISBN: 978 0 900197 71 0.

Wyatt, Irene, ed., *Transportees from Gloucestershire to Australia 1783 - 1842*, Bristol & Gloucestershire Archaeological Society, 1988, ISBN: 0 900197 26 9.

Index

Place names are shown in **bold**. Surnames are shown in CAPITALS.

Abenhall 93, 203
Ablington 143
Abson 20
accident 180, 186
accounts 218
Act Books 112
Act of Supremacy 80
Act of Uniformity 80
Acton Turville 20
Adlestrop 52
Admington 19
adm(inistrati)ons 119
administrators 176
adoption 129, 196
adultery 151
affidavit 62
affiliation order 133
age at burial 62
age of marriage 61
Alderley 11
Alderton 11, 93
ALDINGTON 187
ALDRIDGE 41
Aldsworth 9, 93, 116, 143
alehouses 194, 209
allegation 141
ALLEN 178
Almondsbury 20, 167
Alstone 10
ALTON 223
Alveston 11, 20
Alvington 19, 84
Amberley 11
Andoversford 93
ANDREW(E)S 41, 150, 178
annulment 154
ANSTEY 211
ANTILL 211
Apperley 95
apprentices 3, 194
approved premises 26
Archdeaconry Courts 108
ARCHERLY 202
Arlingham 40, 52
Arnos Vale 167
Ashchurch 93
Ashelworth 211

Ashton under Hill 10, 19, 202
assizes 185, 210
Aston Blank 12
Aston Somerville 19
Aston sub Edge 19, 52
asylums 34, 209
Aust 20, 41
Avening 85, 90, 93
Avenis 41
Avon 9, 167, 195
Awre 52, 86, 90
Aylburton 19
AYLIFF 143
bachelor 28, 61
Badgeworth 54, 110
Badminton 20
Bagendon 148
BAILEY 211, 235
BAINES 196
BAKER 178, 192, 213, 234
BALL 191
BALLINGER 191
BALSTON 202
banns 54, 140
baptism 52, 58, 98
Baptists 83, 86, 100
BARBER 109
BARKER 178
BARNETT 182
Barnsley 9, 116, 143, 208
Barnwood 66, 94, 204
BARTLETT 211
BARTON 127
Barton Regis 7, 19
base born 131
bastard(y) 131, 194
BATHURST 201
Batsford 19
BAYLISS 223
beadle 236
BEALE 156
BECKETT 211
Beckford 10, 93
BEESLEY 137
beneficiaries 176
Bentham 109

Berkeley 7, 20, 85, 90, 94, 181, 195, 216
Berkshire 19
BERRY 177
Berry Hill 102
Beverston 109
Bible Christians 92
bibles 3
Bibury 9, 14, 86, 93, 116, 143, 199
Bishop's Cleeve 116
bigamy 155
BIGLAND 169
Bilson Mine 187
Bingham 12
birth certificate 25, 127
birth index 22
births 18, 20, 53
BISHOP 41, 211
Bishop of Gloucester 109
Bishop's Cleeve 9, 116
Bishop's court 82, 85, 108
Bishop's transcripts 62
Bishops Cleeve . 93, 143, 167, 191
Bisley 7, 41, 59, 86, 90, 93, 134, 136, 202
Bitton 10, 19, 20, 211
Blaisdon 19
Blakeney 163
Bledington 63, 93
Bledisloe 7
BLINKHORNE 157
Blockley 52, 86, 167
boats 34
Boddington 9, 116
bond 119, 141
Boothall 201
borough 7, 11, 123
Borough English 107
BOSTINE 203
Botloe 7
boundaries 18
Bourton on the Hill ... 11, 19, 182
Bourton on the Water 11, 86, 93, 163

240

Index

BOWER 204
Boyd's Marriage Index 68
BRADFORD 201
Bradley 7
Bradley Stoke 20
BRAY 201
Bredon's Norton 66
BRIDGEMAN 143
BRIDGES 189
Brightwell's Barrow 7
Brimscombe 167
Brinkworth 85
Brislington 167
Bristol...19, 30, 85, 90, 94, 98, 115, 124, 148, 163
Bristol City 146
Bristol Deanery 146
Bristol Diocese 146
Bristol Mercury 184
Bristol Record Office..12, 115
BRITTON 211
Broadwell 52
BROCK 201
Brockthrop 211
Brockweir 95
Bromsberrow 93
BROWN............................. 109
BROWNJOHN.................. 178
Brownshill 185
BUBB................................... 204
Buckland 52
BUCKNALL...................... 211
BURCHILL........................ 211
Burford 221
BURFORD 221
burial 52, 62, 161
burial boards 160
burial grounds 62, 84, 163
buried in wool 62
business records, ... 3
Bussage 41
BUTLER............................. 177
calendar 57
Calvinistic Methodist . 90, 92
Cam..................85, 90, 93, 94
CAMELL 150
Campden 195
canals 210
Canford 167
CARRIER 205
CARRY 233
CARTER......40, 185, 205, 211

Cathedral 5, 170
Catholics 194
cemetery 164
certificate...........3, 21, 57, 141
Chaceley 10, 52, 93
Chalford . 11, 41, 85, 163, 185
CHAMBERLAYNE..........178
CHANDLER.....................223
chapelry.............................64
CHAPLIN 205
Charfield 11, 20, 186
charity records 123
Charlton Kings 52, 86, 93, 167
Chedworth 90, 163, 233
Cheltenham.7, 11, 12, 19, 23, 30, 86, 88, 90, 91, 93, 94, 95, 96, 98, 99, 100, 108, 109, 118, 126, 163, 167, 172, 195, 196, 198, 211
Chepstow 19
Chief Constable................236
CHILD...............................222
Childswickham.............10, 19
China Engine Pit 188
Chipping Campden...11, 19, 86, 167
Chipping Norton 102
Chipping Sodbury......19, 86
cholera..............................167
Church of Christ 83, 88
Church of England 61, 80, 86
church rolls 85
Churcham..........................93
Churchdown................93, 94
CHURCHILL.....................211
churchwarden 127, 151
churchyard.......................161
Cinderford.12, 22, 86, 93, 94, 96, 157, 167
circuit..................................94
Cirencester ..7, 11, 12, 19, 30, 85, 86, 87, 90, 93, 94, 99, 101, 102, 163, 194, 195, 203, 204, 216, 217
civic cemeteries 84
civil partnership......20, 25, 28
civil registration...............137
Civil War.................53, 63, 82
clandestine marriages
     ....82,148, 150
CLAPHAM 143

CLAPPEN..........................143
Cleeve 7
Clerk of the Peace 201, 210
CLIFFORD.......................132
Clifford Chambers 10, 19
Clifton..................19, 98, 201
CLISSOLD 136, 211
Clopton.......................19, 93
Coaley 85
coalmining.......................187
Coalpit Heath 20
COATES............................233
Coberley 52
COCKES 201
codicil 105
Codrington......................86
COLCHESTER 201, 211
Cold Ashton................12, 20
Cold Aston 12
COLDHAM 232
CO(A)LE 143, 201, 204
Coleford .. 11, 19, 64, 90, 102, 167, 195
COLLETT 178, 211
Coln Rogers 93
Coln St Aldwyn 93
Commonwealth . 53, 108, 140
Commonwealth War Graves
     Commission 163
complaints 201
Congregational83, 89, 90, 96, 100
consecrated ground.164, 189
Consistory Court 108, 111, 134, 151, 154
constable 201, 236
CONSTABLE 203
convictions...............195, 218
COOK................................219
copy will 117
CORAM 129
CORNISH.........................150
coroner 176, 180, 210
Coroner's papers 126
Corse 9, 93, 116
cost of will 118
Cotswolds........5, 19, 181, 195
Countess of Huntingdon's
     Connexion 83, 90
county boundary 32
County Gaol 230, 234
Court for Divorce 154

241

Court of Chancery 106	Dissenters 80	**Fairford** 14, 86, 90, 93, 133, 195, 199
Court of Civil Commission 109	dissenting meeting houses 170	**Falfield** 20
Court of Kings Bench 180	divorce 153, 155	family collections 123
Court of Probate 109	DIXSON 150	FARADAY 111
Cow Honeybourne 19	**Dodington** 11, 20	**Faringdon** 19
Cowley 33	DOE 211	**Farmington** 93
COXWELL 143	**Donnington** 11	FAULKES 42
CRADOCK 203	DORMER 156	felo de se 189
craftsmen 194	**Dorsington** 10, 19, 63	Fertilisation and Embryology Act 25
Cranham 90	**Dowdeswell** 9, 116	FETTIPLACE 201
creditors 176	DOWDESWELL 201	**Filton** 20, 102, 167
Cremation 169	DOWLE 201	**Fleet Prison** 150
CRIPPS 143	**Down Hatherley** 65	FLETCHER 47
Cromhall 20, 201	**Doynton** 20, 211	FLOOKE 178
Cross Hands 195	Dr Williams' Library 82	folio 33
cross-roads 189	Dr. Barnardo's Homes 129	**Forest of Dean** .. 5, 14, 19, 30, 94, 123, 181, 187, 195
crown courts 210	DREW 177	Forest of Dean website 68
CROWSER 150	DRIVER 143, 205	**Forthampton** 9, 116
Crowthorne 7	Duchy of Lancaster 7	FOSBROOKE 170
CRUMP 232	**Dudstone** 7	foundling 127
curriculum vitae 3	Dursley19, 68, 85, 94, 96, 131, 134, 163, 167, 195	Foundling Hospital 129
CURTICE 233	DUTTON 201	**Frampton Cotterell** 11, 20, 90, 205
Cutsdean 10, 86	**Dymock** 52, 64, 86	**Frampton Mansell** 11
DANIEL 177	**Dyrham** 20	**Frampton on Severn** ... 11, 90
DASTON 178, 201	**East Dean** 93, 94	FRANKIS 197
Data Protection 23	**Eastington** 11, 93, 94, 211	FREAME 201
Dates 99	**Eastleach Martin** 52, 93	Free Church 101
DAVI(E)S48, 58,185, 202, 203	**Eastleach Turville** 93	FREEMAN 114, 201
DAVISON 233	**Ebley** 90	freeminer 187
DAY 186	**Ebrington** 19	French Protestants 102
Daylesford 10	electoral registers 210	**Frenchay** 20, 99
Deaneries 9	ELKINGTON 137	**Frocester** 170
death certificate . 28, 161, 184	ELLERY 205	FRY 115
death duties 176	ELLIS 233	funeral report 175
Death Duty Registers 176	ELS 223	GAISFORD 185
death index 23	**English Bicknor** 19	gallows 191
death notice 175, 176	enumerators 32, 33	gaols 227
deaths 18, 20	ESSEX 143, 221	GARD(I)NER 134, 135, 182
debtors 176, 226	estate papers 123	GARNE 143
Deerhurst 7, 9, 93, 95, 116, 143	ESTCOURT 201	Gavelkind 106
diaries 3	evangelical 90	General Register Office20, 21
Didbrook 64, 93	EVANS 143, 223, 234	*Gentleman's Magazine* 176
DIMMERY 150	**Evenlode** 10	GEORGE 115
diocese 7	**Evesham** 19	George Whitefield 90
Diocese of Bristol 53	examination 131	GFHS Baptism Index 67
Diocese of Gloucester ... 9, 53	examination certificates 3	GFHS Burial Index 67
Diocese of Worcester 53	execution 191, 216, 234	GFHS Marriage Index 67
Dirham 211	executors 176	GIBBS 185
disputed wills 112	Faculty Office Allegations 146	
dissenters 208		

242

Index

Gloucester ...5, 11, 14, 19, 63, 64, 85, 86, 88, 90, 91, 92, 93, 94, 96, 97, 98, 99, 112, 124, 127, 163, 167, 180, 195, 199, 201, 205, 209, 216, 223, 224, 225, 227
Gloucester Cathedral...... 173
Gloucester Cemetery 167
Gloucester Gaol 189, 191, 210
Gloucester Probate Registry 117
Gloucester St Aldate 63
Gloucester St Mary de Crypt 33, 170, 171
Gloucester St Mary de Grace 33, 63
Gloucester St Mary de Lode 64
Gloucester St Owen 63
Gloucestershire Archives. 12
Gloucestershire Collection 12
GLOVER 143
GOLDING......................... 41
GOODMAN..................... 109
Gordon Riots 98
Gotherington 90
GOUGH 170
Grand Jury 201
Great Badminton........ 42, 52
Great Barrington 93
Great Rissington 52, 93
Great Shurdington......... 114
Greenbank..................... 167
GREENE........................... 201
Gregorian Calendar 57
GREGORY 204
GREY 182
GRIME............................. 202
GRO Birth Indexes 128
Grumbald's Ash 7
Guardians of the Poor 127
GUBBINS 185
guilds............................... 194
GUNN 178
GUNTER............................ 43
GUY 178, 191
GWILLIAM.............221, 236
GWINNETT...24, 34, 65, 110, 112, 114, 118, 120, 121, 122, 123, 171, 172, 175, 177, 178, 191, 196, 206, 228

Gyde Home 129
HALE............................... 223
HALL......................204, 205
HALY 222
Hampnett 148
HAMPSON...................... 201
Hanham (Abbots) 19, 20, 202
HARDING...............143, 203
Hardwicke..................... 230
Hardwicke's Marriage Act 54, 82, 90, 99
HARMER......................... 233
Harnhill 203
HARRIS........................... 185
HARTLAND 150
Hartpury 11, 93
HARVEY......................... 223
HATHERALL.................. 143
HAWKER 143
Hawkesbury 20, 43, 86
Hawling 93
HAYWARD 43, 178, 205
headstone...................99, 169
HEANE 203
Hearth Tax 7
HEATH 233
HEAVEN 41
HEMING......................... 233
Hempsted 148
Henbury 7, 167
HENLEY 201
Hereford 111
Herefordshire 19
Hewelsfield....................19
HEWER 143
HEWES........................... 202
HICKES............................. 58
HICKS 201
Hidcote Bartrim.............19
highways...................194, 209
HIGNELL......................... 143
HILES 50
Hill 20, 64
HILL 48
HILLMAN 204
Hinton.....................20, 211
Hinton on the Green ..10, 19
HOBBES 178
Hockaday Abstracts 85
HODGES..................178, 203
Holborn 124
HOLBROW..................... 228

Honeybourne 10
Hopehill 40
HOPKINS 202
HORNSEY 133
Horsley 44, 86, 93, 94, 134, 170, 194, 195, 218
Horton............................ 20
HORTON......................... 201
hospital 34, 184
House of Correction 194, 210, 216
HOW 205
HOWARD 216
HOWELL 131
Howland's Burial Ground 160
HUDSON........................ 150
HUGGINS 185
HUGHES 205, 234
Huguenots...................... 102
HULANDS 203
HULLS 178
HUMPHREYS 112
Hundred 7, 195
Hundred of St. Briavel 187
HUNT 202
Huntley......................53, 75
HYETT 201
Icomb 10, 93
ILES 232
illegitimacy 126, 130, 200
Ilmington 19
imprisonment................. 216
inclosures....................... 210
incumbent................53, 108
Independent 83, 89, 100
Independent Methodists...92
indexes 64
Indictment books............ 201
inquest...............176, 180, 184
Inquisitiones Post Mortem 177
interment 164
International Genealogical Index 64, 162
Internet........................... 66
Interregnum 53, 63
inventory 119, 121
IRELAND 143
Iron Acton 20
irregular marriage 82, 148
IVINE 143

243

JACKSON 143	**Leonard Stanley** 93, 94	**Marston Sicca** 10, 19
JAKES 205	letters of administration 104, 106	MARTYN 201
JENKINS 187, 202, 235		MASTER(S) 201, 202
JENNINGS 156	LEWELLIN 202	MATTHEWS 185
Jewish 62, 83, 91	LEWIS 150, 233	**May Hill** 14
Jews 61, 82	licence 54, 85, 194	**Mayshill** 167
JOHNSON 150, 178	**Little Barrington** 93	McGREGOR 115
JONES 41, 112, 185, 197	**Little Sodbury** 20	medals 3
journals 3	**Little Washbourne** 10	medical records 3, 5
Julian Calendar 57	**Littledean** ..90, 163, 203, 218, 219	meeting houses 85
jurors 185		membership lists 85
jury 177, 180, 194	**Littleworth** 11, 148	memorial cards 173
Justice of the Peace 7, 194	London Gazette 176	memorial plaques 169
KEAR 188	LONG 143	memorial sites 84
KEBLE 143	**Long Marston** 10	MEREDITH 187
KEENE 143, 201	**Long Newnton** 10	Methodist 83, 92
Kemble 167	Longborough 64	Methodists New Connexion 92
Kemerton 45, 93	LONGDEN 114	
KEMP 114	Longhope 93	**Mickleton** 19
Keynsham 19	Longney 205	MIFFLIN 204
Kiftsgate 7	Longtree 7	military service 3
Kilcott 43	**Lower Lemington** 19	Militia Lists 7
KILMASTER 203	**Lower Swell** 93	MILLETT 205
KILMINSTER 229	LUCAS 114	MILLS 143
KING 123, 143	LUTON 185	**Minchinhampton** .85, 90, 93, 94
King's Barton 7	Lydbrook 86, 93, 94	
Kings Stanley 85, 86, 93	Lydney ...19, 93, 94, 122, 123, 167, 195	**Minety** 7
Kingswood 10, 11, 19, 20, 85, 90, 95, 167, 187, 230		**Minsterworth** 53, 93, 94
	LYSONS 170	**Miserden** 93
Kingswood Reformatory 230	MABBUT 201	**Miserdine** 211
KINSELLA 155	MACE 178	**Mitcheldean** . 90, 93, 163, 203
KIRBY 233	MACHEN 236	**Monmouth** 19, 93, 94
LAMB 219	magistrate 194	**Monmouthshire** 19
Lancaut 10, 19	maiden name 23	monumental inscriptions .85, 171
land tax 7, 210	maintenance orders 134	
LANE 41, 156, 203	MAIOR 205	Moravian 83, 95
LANG 115	MAISEY 108	**Moreton** 202
Langley 7	**Maiseyhampton** 86	**Moreton in Marsh** 19, 83, 90, 94, 167, 195
Lassington 148	**Mangotsfield** .19, 20, 94, 167, 187	
Latin 54		MORGAN 187, 202
Latter Day Saints 64	MANN 203	MORLEY 198
law enforcement 236	MANNING(E) 203, 204	MORRIS 170
Lawford's Gate 160, 194, 195, 216, 218, 219	manor 7	MORTIMER 202
	marital status 61	MOULDER 143
LAWRENCE 221	marriage 18, 52, 54, 98	Müller Orphanage 129
Lea 64	marriage brokers 148	murder 180
Lea Bailey 19	marriage certificate 26	**Nailsworth** 86, 90, 94, 99, 195
Lechlade 10, 19	marriage index 22	National Burial Index 163
Ledbury 11	marriage licence 140, 141	National Probate Calendars 117
legal impediment 140	marriage settlement 150	
legal separation 154	marriage-mongers 148	**Naunton** 46, 52
Leigh, The 9, 93, 116	**Marshfield** 20, 90, 167	Navy 134

NELME............................ 201
Nettleton Bottom............. 33
NEWELL........................ 211
Newent.....14, 19, 90, 94, 167, 195, 202
NEWINGTON................. 178
Newington Bagpath..53, 148
Newland19, 53, 64, 86, 90, 94
NEWMAN.................185, 204
Newnham......90, 94, 194, 195
newspaper.155, 175, 185, 213
NEWTON.................178, 223
NICHOLLS....................... 223
nonconformist .26, 61, 62, 80, 194, 208
nonconformist burial ground......................... 161
nonconformist registers . 162
Non-Parochial Registers Act 82
NORRIS............................ 199
North Cerney 203
North Cotswold............... 30
North Nibley.............. 85, 90
North Tidworth.............. 143
Northavon 102
Northleach.11, 14, 19, 90, 94, 167, 195
Norton 94
nuncupative will 104, 107
Nympsfield 204
Oakridge......................41, 163
oaths................................. 194
oaths of allegiance........... 206
obituaries..................175, 176
Oddington.................94, 148
OFFER 185
O'HARE............................ 84
OLAND 233
Oldbury 11
Oldbury on Severn ... 11, 20, 52, 53
Oldbury on the Hill......... 11
Oldland 19, 20
OLIFFE 203
Olveston 11, 20
online database............... 111
order a certificate 21
Order Book. 204
order of precedence 119
orphans...................127, 129
OSBOURNE 208

outsize wills.....................111
Over................................191
overseas wills 110
overseers of the poor.........32
Overseers of the Poor.......32, 131, 134
Owlpen............................85
Oxenhall...........................53
Oxford Circuit.................210
Oxford Methodist circuit ..94
PACE........................201, 205
Painswick..54, 64, 85, 86, 90, 94, 99, 167, 189, 204, 211, 228
PAISH..............................143
Pallot's Marriage Index.....68
Papist..............80, 83, 84, 207
parchment registers...........62
parental consent................61
parish..................................7
parish chest.....................123
parish clerks 32
parish magazines 176
Parkend............................86
PARRETT.........................178
PARSONS........................202
Patchway 20
PAUL........................218, 226
Pauntley.......................52, 94
pauper graves..................164
paupers 57
PAYNE............................201
PEACOCK 149
Pebworth....................10, 19
Peculiar Courts................108
peculiar wills 116
peculiars......................9, 143
PEETERS.........................204
PEGLER 178
penal settlements 231
penance...................135, 136
PENFIELD.......................178
PERRINE.........................202
Personal Name Index........85
Petty Jury 201
Petty Sessions 130, 194
Phillimore's Marriage Index 67
PHIPPS..............................83
photographs 3
photography....................229
piece.................................33

pillory..............................216
Pilning..............................20
Pinkney............................85
Pinnock cum Hyde............64
Pitchcombe.......................90
plan.................................172
police 209, 210236
poll books 210
POOLE.............143, 201, 205
Poole Keynes.....................10
poor law..........................194
Popish Recusants Act........80
PORTER...........................143
post mortem 185
postcards............................3
posthumous.....................131
Postlip.............................102
Poulton 10
POWELL..........................202
Prerogative Court of Canterbury (PCC) 109
Prerogative Court of York (PCY)..........................109
Prerogative Courts 108
Presbyterian ...83, 89, 96, 100
presentment.....................201
Prestbury..................94, 204
Preston 11
Preston on Stour 11, 19
PRICE..............................126
Pridend.............................40
PRIGGE...........................205
Primitive Methodists.........92
Primogeniture 106
Principal Probate Registry 117
Principal Registry of the Family Division 117
prison 5, 34, 184
prison hulks.....................231
prisoners 211, 228
privacy.............................64
probate............................104
probate accounts.............119
Probate Act of 1857..........117
probate clause 112, 117
probation records 210
PROCTOR 84
pronunciation.....................5
Protestant.........................82
Protestant Methodists 92
Protestation Oath............206

public house 184
Pucklechurch......... 7, 20, 187
purchased graves 164
PURLEWENT 170
putative father 130
Quakers 61, 82, 83, 99, 137
Quarter Sessions 85, 130, 134, 180, 184, 194
Quedgeley 94
Quinton 11, 19
RACKFORD..................... 234
Randwick 94
Rangeworthy 20
Rapsgate 7
REASON 150
recognizance 201, 206
Recorder 194
recusant 80
Red Lodge Reformatory. 230
Redmarley (D'Abitot). 11, 94
REEVES 143
reformatory 216, 230
regimental magazines 176
Register Office 90
registered will 117
Registers 53
registrar 18, 61
regular marriage 149
Religion Act 80
removal 194
reputed father 59, 200
RICH 205
RICHARDS 131
RICHBILL 203
RICKETTS 207
RIDDELL 211
RIDDIFORD 192
RIDER 204
Ridgeway Park 167
riots 236
Rising Sun Engine Pit 188
ROBERT 178
ROBERTS 178
ROBINS 201
Rockhampton 20, 204
Rodborough 85, 90
RODMAN 205
Rodmarton 94
Roe's Marriage Index 67
ROGERS 109
Rogers Tillstone 185
Roman Catholic diocese ... 98

Roman Catholics ... 61. 62, 80, 82, 83, 98, 206
Ross 19
Royal Infirmary 231
Ruardean .. 19, 52, 90, 94, 203
Rudford 94
RUTTER 201
Saddlewood 43
SADLER 47
Saintbury 19
SALE 205
Salem Free Church 102
Salperton 11
Sandhurst 52, 94, 177
SANDY 202
Sapperton 11, 167
Saul 53
schedule 33
school reports 3
sentences 211
serviceman 163, 173
SESSIONS 143
settlement 194
Severn Beach 20
Severn Vale 5
Severnside 14
Sezincote 64
sham parson 149
SHARP 40
SHAYLOR 178
Sheepscombe 64
Shenington 11, 64
SHEPPARD 201
Sherborne 94
Sherston 85
Shipston on Stour 19
Shipton Moyne 202
Shipton Oliffe 94
Shipton Sollars 64
SHIPWAY 228
Shirehampton 167
Shorncote 11
Shurdington 61, 110, 206
SHURMER 143
SIMS 40
singlewoman 131
Siston 19, 20
SKIPP 223
SLATTER 48
Slaughters, The 7, 195
Slimbridge 64, 85, 86, 90, 197
SMITH 109, 143, 192

SNOWE 204
Snowshill 53
Society of Friends .. 82, 83, 85, 99, 100, 137
Sodbury 19, 20, 195
solicitors' deposits 123
Somerford Keynes 11
SOSBE 157
South Bristol 167
South Cerney 132, 205
South Gloucestershire 9, 12, 20, 30, 66, 115
South Hamlet 148
Southport 21, 23
special licence 141
Speech House Hill 188
spinster 28, 61, 105
Spoonbed 228
spurious 131
St Briavels 7, 19, 90, 216, 217
STAITE 143
STALKS 134, 135
stamp duty 57
Stanton 11
Staunton 11, 19, 94
Staverton 9, 52, 94, 116
Steanbridge 41
STEEL 184
STEPHENS 50, 201
stillbirths 126
Stinchcombe 85
STINCHCOM(E) 43, 58
stocks 216
Stockwell 33
Stoke Archer 178
Stoke Gifford 20
Stoke Orchard 9, 116, 178
Stonehouse 11, 90, 94
Stow on the Wold 12, 14, 19, 86, 94, 102, 167
STRANGE 143
Stratford upon Avon 19
Stratton 48, 167
Stroud .. 12, 14, 19, 20, 23, 30, 50, 58, 60, 85, 86, 89, 90, 94, 101, 102, 167, 181, 191, 195, 202, 203, 211
suicide 180, 189
surgeon 182
Sutton under Brailes 11
SWAYNE 204
Swinehead 7

Index

SYMONDS 201
TARLING 196
TARVER 192
tax assessments 210
taxation 194
TAYLOR 137, 170
TAYLOR, Henry Y. J. 91
Taynton 52
testator 105
Tetbury 19, 85, 86, 90, 94, 195, 205
Tewkesbury 7, 11, 12, 14, 19, 86, 90, 94, 96, 99, 132, 143, 167, 180, 195, 209, 216, 217, 223
THOMAS 110
Thornbury ... 7, 19, 20, 58, 90, 167, 194, 195
Througham 41
THURSTON 205
Tibaldstone 7
Tibberton 94
Tidenham 10, 11, 19
TIMPANY 143
TINGLE 187
Tirley 9, 94, 116
Toddington 94
Todenham 10, 11, 19
Toleration Act 82
Tormarton 20
Tortworth 20
TOWN(E)SEND 202, 203, 221
TOWNLEY 221
transportation ... 155, 216, 231
transportation bond 233
treadwheel 223
Treasury returns 227
Tresham 43
TRESSELL 143
TRINDER 143
True Bill 201
TUCK 134
Turkdean 94
TURNER 143
turnpike trusts 210
TYLER 205
Tytherington 20
Uley 85, 86, 90, 109
unconsecrated ground 99
Undenominational 83, 101
undertaker 174

Unitarian 83, 100
Unitarian Relief Act 100
United Brethren 95
United Reformed Church 89, 90, 96
Upleadon 52
Upper Slaughter 52, 62, 94
Upton St Leonards 52, 94
Vaccination 196
variants 21
Vicar General's Marriage Allegations 146
Victoria County History 7, 13
victuallers 209
VINER 196
vital records 3
Vital Records Index 66
VIZARD 134
WAINE 143, 150
WALKLEY 44, 219
war memorials 84
WARNER 203
Warwickshire 19
WATHEN 201
WATT 201
WEARE 185
WEBB 143
Welford 11, 19
WELLES 58
Wesleyan Methodists 92
WEST 44
West Dean 19, 86, 94
Westbury 7
Westbury on Severn .. 11, 19, 52, 90, 94
Westbury on Trym 94
Westbury upon Trym 11
Westcote 94
Westerleigh 20, 167, 187
Westminster 7
Weston sub Edge 19
Weston upon Avon 10, 11, 19
Westonbirt 85
Wheatenhurst 19, 52
WHEELER 143, 150
WHITE 149, 234
WHITEHEAD 143
Whitminster 52, 94, 195
WHITMORE 195
Whitstone 7

Whittington 11, 52
Wick 20
Wickwar 20, 90, 126, 167
Widford 11
widow 61, 105
widower 61
WILKINS 58, 137
will 104
Willersley 19
WILLET 201
WILLIAMS 109, 123, 133, 150, 185
WIL(L)SON 143, 150
WILSE 170
WILTON 194
Wiltshire 99
Winchcombe ... 11, 19, 52, 90, 94, 102, 167, 195, 211, 216, 218
WINDOW 44
Windrush 94
WINNIATT 229
Winson 9, 11, 116, 143
Winterbourne 20, 90, 96
Withington 9, 11, 94, 116, 143
witnesses 61, 177
WITTS 222
WOOD 204
WOODARD 12
Woodchester 86, 202
WOODHOUSE 223
Woodmancote 90
Woolaston 19, 94, 202
Woolstone 53
Worcester 111
Worcestershire 19
WORK(E)MAN 177, 203
workhouse 34, 41, 126, 184
Wormington 178
Wotton under Edge ... 85, 86, 90, 96, 167, 195
WRAGGE 198
WYATT 233
Yate 20
YEARP 47
York 124
York Probate Sub-Registry 118
Yorkley 86

247